WRITINGS FOR YOUNG CHILDREN

WRITINGS FOR YOUNG CHILDREN

LEO TOLSTOY

Translated and edited by Michael R. Katz

With an Introduction by Linda Torresin

Illustrated by Jake Scott

BOSTON

2025

Library of Congress Cataloging-in-Publication Data

Names: Tolstoy, Leo, graf, 1828–1910 author | Katz, Michael R. translator |
    Torresin, Linda writer of introduction | Scott, Jake (Illustrator) illustrator
Title: Leo Tolstoy's writings for young children / translated and edited by Michael R. Katz ;
    with an introduction by Linda Torresin ; illustrated by Jake Scott.
Description: Boston : Cherry Orchard Books, 2025. | Includes bibliographical references.
Identifiers: LCCN 2025018540 (print) | LCCN 2025018541 (ebook) | ISBN 9798887198316
    hardback | ISBN 9798887198323 paperback | ISBN 9798887198330 adobe pdf |
    ISBN 9798887198347 epub
Subjects: LCSH: Tolstoy, Leo, graf, 1828-1910–Translations into English
Classification: LCC PG3366.A13 K36 2025 (print) | LCC PG3366.A13 (ebook) | DDC
    891.78/309–dc23/eng/20250415
LC record available at https://lccn.loc.gov/2025018540
LC ebook record available at https://lccn.loc.gov/2025018541

Cover design by Ivan Grave
Illustrations by Jake Scott
Book design by Lapiz Digital Services

Published by Cherry Orchard Books, an imprint of Academic Studies Press
1007 Chestnut St.
Newton, MA 02464, USA
press@academicstudiespress.com
www.academicstudiespress.com

Contents

"Not only a Writer, but also an Educator:

Leo Tolstoy, Children, and Pedagogical Stories"

Linda Torresin

University of Padua, Italy

Since the 1960s, academics have become increasingly interested in Leo Tolstoy the educator and educational theorist, focusing especially on the links between his aesthetics and children's literature.[1] This is no accident: Tolstoy frequently wrote about pedagogy and often ranked his work on the subject above his literary achievements. Indeed, pedagogical and cognitive processes are often at the center of his fiction. For example, the pseudo-autobiographical trilogy consisting of *Childhood*, *Boyhood*, and *Youth*,[2] which marks the beginning of Tolstoy's literary career, is about the physical and spiritual upbringing of a typical nineteenth-century Russian child named Kolya. In short, children were very dear to Tolstoy: with their naiveté, vitality, spontaneity, and creativity, they represented the human ideal, which school—he believed—had the task of protecting.

Tolstoy's educational project went through several phases. Of particular relevance to our discussion is the first—1849–51 and 1859–63. This period, which covers his best-known activities as an educator, was characterized by the opening and management of the Yasnaya Polyana School, a free school for

---

1 See, among others, Bernaz (2017); Berthoff (1978); Cohen (1981); Crosby (1904); Gejdoš (2021); Goncharov (1962); Hapenciuc (2021); Lushchevska (2014); Moulin (2008, 2023); Moulin-Stożek (2022); Murphy (1992); Read (1995); Roberts (2017); Roberts and Saeverot (2018); Robertson (2016); Torresin (2016); Vinitsky (2015).
2 *Detstvo, Otrochestvo, i Yunost'* (1852–57).

peasant children that the young Tolstoy established on his family's estate, not far from Tula in Russia.

The school emphasized self-directed learning and self-discipline in child development. Pupils—local village boys and girls aged seven to thirteen—were not required to attend lessons; they could come and go as they pleased, and there was no homework. Abandoning traditional top-down educational methods, lessons were designed to encourage interaction between teachers and students. Tolstoy and the other staff at Yasnaya Polyana worked hard to foster their pupils' creative instincts and personalities by placing them in an unrestricted environment and giving them the freedom to realize their independence. To meet the needs of students, educators, and parents, then, learning curricula were complex, broad in scope, and flexible. Tolstoy's pedagogy was founded on a humanistic view of education and respect for the child's individuality.[3]

In addition to becoming a teacher, Tolstoy published an educational journal entitled *Yasnaya Polyana* that was devoted to both theoretical and practical issues. Unfortunately, Tolstoy's work at the school did not endure. Yasnaya Polyana was shut down in 1863 due to the repressive nature of the tsarist monarchy. However, Tolstoy's pedagogical activities continued. Along with his most celebrated novels, Tolstoy wrote letters and essays about topics related to education until the end of his life. In fact, as we will see, his philosophical and ethical ideas were firmly based on the child.

***

Tolstoy's educational theories consisted of three fundamental and interrelated principles.[4] The first principle stressed the importance of education as a basic human right that should be accessible to all. Tolstoy's view in his article "On Popular Education"[5] that "[t]he need of education lies in every man; the people love and seek education, as they love and seek air for breathing" (1967, 5) arose from his observations (mostly negative), made while traveling abroad, of the educational methods used in Western European schools.

Tolstoy's commitment to universal and accessible education, as well as its humanization and democratization, underpinned the second principle of his pedagogy. The writer's progressive view was that capitalist science and

---

3   See, among others, Baudouin (1921); Blaisdell (2000, 1–23); Crosby (1904); Duane (1968); Egorov (1994); Hans (1963, 86–100); Moulin (2011, 29–47); Murphy (1992, 45–63); Simmons (1949, 218–37).

4   See also Bunnell (1955); Calam (1963); Goncharov (1962); Hans (1963); Mossman (1993); Moulin (2011, 67–136); Murphy (1992, 82–122); Zweers (1970).

5   "O narodnom obrazovanii" (1874).

technology should not solely benefit the governing aristocracy, but rather the demands of Russian society as a whole. Education should serve the common people's everyday life. To put it another way, "instead of drill and mechanical training in reading, writing and arithmetic," in Goncharov's words (1962, 59), Tolstoy "set education the task of promoting the organic growth of the child and of giving even the peasant child the opportunity to arrive independently at an understanding of the most important problems of life."

It is worth mentioning that during Tolstoy's pedagogical practice in the second half of the nineteenth century, most Russian peasants were still illiterate,[6] further separating them from the upper classes of Russian society. For this reason, Tolstoy's insistence on universality, common access to education, and its democratic dimension struck a chord with the concerns of the Russian peasant class at the time.

The third principle of Tolstoy's pedagogical thought, which was also implemented at the Yasnaya Polyana School, was the notion of free and voluntary education. Tolstoy thought knowledge was difficult to impose on children. It had to be generated spontaneously by pupils' own interests, attitudes, passions, and feelings, without the intervention of teachers or authorities. As Moulin (2011, 2–3) puts it:

> He [Tolstoy] saw the freedom of pupils as an essential condition for genuine education to take place. Otherwise how could a teacher know that what they taught was neither harmful for the student, nor pointless? For Tolstoy, true education could not be a form of induction into a preconceived conception of life, or for instrumental ends. Rather it should be a humanistic enterprise, based on each child's individual motivation and an educator's desire for them to become "equal" in knowledge with their teacher.

To fully grasp Tolstoy's stance, it is essential to understand the distinction between the Russian concepts of *vospitaniye* and *obrazovaniye*. Tolstoy clarified the difference between these two terms in "Upbringing and Education."[7] In this article, whereas *vospitaniye* (upbringing) is associated with compulsory training, *obrazovaniye* (education) is closer to the idea of *Bildung*, which can be translated as "culture." In other words, the writer—from an educational standpoint sides

---

6   For more details, see Mironov (1991, 234–35) and Reitblat (2020, 173).
7   "Vospitaniye i obrazovaniye" (1862).

with *obrazovaniye* against *vospitaniye*, which, due to its forced and constricting nature, is incapable of leading to full child development. Instead, such a task is carried out by *obrazovaniye*, because this term refers to voluntary and natural education in all of its various aspects, as well as the overall formation of tomorrow's adults, which includes each side of their personality and their intellectual, spiritual, ethical, and artistic development (Tolstoy 1967, 105–51).[8]

Tolstoy's essay "Should the Peasant Children Learn to Write from Us, or Should We Learn from the Peasant Children?"[9] makes a clear contrast between *vospitaniye* and *obrazovaniye*:

> In bringing up, educating, developing, or in any way you please, influencing the child, we ought to have and unconsciously do have, one aim in view—to attain the greatest harmony possible in the sense of truth, beauty, and goodness. If time did not run, if the child did not live with every side of himself, we should be able quietly to attain this harmony by supplementing there, where there seems to be a lack, and by reducing where, there seems to be a superfluity. But the child lives; every side of his existence strives after development, trying to outstrip every other side, and, for the most part, we mistake the progress of these sides of his being for the aim, and cooperate in this development only, instead of aiding the harmony of the development. In this lies the eternal mistake of all pedagogical theories. (Tolstoy 1967, 220)

Tolstoy criticizes educators of his time for their lack of understanding of children's psychological lives and for treating them merely as a conglomeration of psychic functions, rather than individuals.

"As if it were not enough," remarked Tolstoy, "that the soul of the individual was split, like a compound substance, into memory, intellect, feeling, and so on, they know how many specific exercises are needed for each element . . . . They had everything figured out in advance; ready-made, unalterable patterns were provided for all aspects of the development of human nature" (quoted in Goncharov 1962, 48).

Unlike those educators, Tolstoy saw in the young child a "real" growing self that the teacher needed to know and comprehend in order to nurture. His

---

8 See also Goncharov (1962, 53–54).
9 "Komu u kogo uchit'sya pisat', krestyanskim rebyatam u nas, ili nam u krestyanskikh rebyat?" (1862).

theories recalled the humanistic approach to pedagogy, but were also rooted in his original educational perspectives.

***

Tolstoy modeled his teaching on the humanistic approaches of Democritus, Socrates, Confucius, Hegel, Kant, and others, all of whom considered learning as a second birth for the soul. Tolstoy argued that this kind of pedagogy had a unique role in awakening a child's spiritual essence. This tradition was discussed in Russia during the nineteenth and twentieth centuries by intellectuals such as Ushinsky, Fyodorov, Solovyov, Florensky, Vernadsky, Dostoevsky, and others. They deliberated on educational challenges and came to the conclusion that education should primarily develop the metaphysical, immaterial element of an individual's identity, the so-called "interior man" (*vnutrenny chelovek*).

Tolstoy praised humanistic pedagogy for focusing its educational views on children's spiritual growth. This attention to the spiritual dimension coincided with the author's deepest convictions, which would ultimately flow into the synthesis of his philosophical and religious elaborations described in *The Pathway of Life*,[10] where the writer declares: "It is well to remember frequently that our true life is not the outward physical life which we live here on earth, before our eyes, but that alongside of this life there is within us another life, an inner and spiritual life which has no beginning and no ending" (Tolstoy 2016, 476–47).

Along with humanistic pedagogy, Tolstoy based his educational theory on the philosophy of Kant and Rousseau, as well as on the pedagogy of Pestalozzi and Froebel. It is intriguing to compare their methods of thinking. As evidenced by his writings, Tolstoy conceived individual self-education and self-improvement as the essential goal in life. "To make himself better, to improve himself by labor," he points out, "is the principal task of a man's life" (Tolstoy 2016, 464–45). The philosophy of Kant seemed to best justify such an orientation. In fact, in Kant's lecture notes "On Pedagogics" (1803), the philosopher states: "Man's duty is to improve himself; to cultivate his mind; and, when he finds himself going astray, to bring the moral law to bear upon himself" (Kant 2003, 11).

Tolstoy drew on Kant's ideas about education and morality. As is well known, the philosopher emphasized the importance of moral rectitude, also called "moral training," as it would enable individuals to choose "none but good ends" (Kant 2003, 20). "Providence has willed," argues Kant, "that man shall bring forth for himself the good that lies hidden in his nature, and has spoken, as it were, thus to man: 'Go forth into the world! I have equipped you with every

---

10 *Put' zhizni* (1910).

tendency towards the good. Your part—let it be to develop those tendencies'" (Kant 2003, 11). Tolstoy, like Kant, thought that educational practices should aim to improve children's "moral character" by channeling their inherent tendencies toward righteousness. "Among all the sciences man must know," he affirmed, "the main one is the science about how to live, doing the least evil possible and the most good possible" (Tolstoy 1984, 148).[11]

Kant and Tolstoy believed that education would benefit humanity as a whole. The Russian author had treasured and internalized Kant's renowned phrase from the lecture "On Pedagogics": "Children ought to be educated, not for the present, but for a possibly improved condition of man in the future; that is, in a manner, which is adapted to the *idea of humanity* and the whole destiny of man" (Tolstoy 1984, 14).

In addition to Kant's ethical vision, Tolstoy's own conception of pedagogy owed much to Rousseau, and specifically to his idea of the innate goodness of a child. Tolstoy read Rousseau at the age of fifteen (Gusev 1927, 136). However, the Genevan's influence on him lasted throughout Tolstoy's life and was reflected in his pedagogical studies. The defense of children's natural goodness was the Rousseauian principle most relevant to Tolstoy's educational outlook. He states in the essay "Should the Peasant Children Learn to Write from Us" that "'Man is born perfect' is a great word articulated by Rousseau, and this word will remain firm and true, like a rock" (Tolstoy 1967, 221).

Rousseau was convinced that man was born "free and good," but at the same time society might (and *would*) undermine this initial condition:

> Coming from the hand of the Author of all things, everything is good; in the hands of man, everything degenerates. Man obliges one soil to nourish the productions of another, one tree to bear the fruits of another; he mingles and confounds climates, elements, seasons; he mutilates his dog, his horse, his slave. He overturns everything, disfigures everything; he loves deformity, monsters; he desires that nothing should be as nature made it, not even man himself. To please him, man must be broken in like a horse; man must be adapted to man's own fashion, like a tree in his garden. (Rousseau 1889, 11)

The goal of teaching was to protect man's inherent goodness and freedom. For this purpose, Rousseau encouraged the all-round development of each pupil,

---

11 Here and henceforth, translations from Tolstoy's letters are mine.

which should support and improve a child's intellectual and physical potentialities, or, in Tolstoyan terms, "every side of his existence" (Tolstoy 1967, 220). As Rousseau writes: "Give him constant physical exercise; make his body sound and robust, that you may make him wise and reasonable. Let him be at work doing something; let him run, shout, be always in motion; let him be a man in vigor, and he will the sooner become one in reason" (Rousseau 1889, 87).

Tolstoy agreed with Rousseau, identifying proper education as a means of safeguarding a child's self-perfection. As a result, educators were faced with a difficult responsibility, well expressed in the Swiss thinker's warning: "Remember that, before you venture undertaking to form a man, you must have made yourself a man; you must find in yourself the example you ought to offer him" (Rousseau 1889, 59). In short, both Rousseau and Tolstoy held that teachers, besides their own honesty and morality, should be equipped with sensitivity and tact. To use a Tolstoyan metaphor, they had to be good sculptors to ensure a normal, progressive expansion of learners' abilities and knowledge without disrupting their fundamental harmony (Tolstoy 1967, 221–22).

In addition to Kant and Rousseau, Tolstoy's educational proposals drew upon the conception of the child and their development advanced by Pestalozzi and Froebel. It should be observed that, although Tolstoy's *Diaries* strongly criticize Pestalozzi's and Froebel's views on teaching, the impact they had on his pedagogy cannot be ignored. In particular, with regard to Pestalozzi, Tolstoy shares the idea of a child's harmonious development. Pestalozzi (1827, 7) notes: "A child is a being endowed with all the faculties of human nature, but none of them is developed: *a bud not yet opened* [the pedagogue's italics]. When the bud opens, every one of the leaves unfolds: not one remains behind. Such must be the process of education." Such an understanding of education is consistent with the Russian's humanistic pedagogy. In this respect, Pestalozzi's view of education as the development of a child's inner resources, combined with an acknowledgment of the spiritual nature of learning experiences, resonated with all the Tolstoyan educational cornerstones.

According to Pestalozzi, a good education should not favor one aspect of a child's personality over another, but rather stimulate and develop all of his physical ("arms"), intellectual ("intellect"), and moral-emotional ("heart") capabilities. He proposes that "The faculties of man must be so cultivated that no one shall predominate at the expense of another, but each be excited to the true standard of activity; *and this standard is the spiritual nature of man*" (1827, 18; the pedagogue's italics).

In Pestalozzi's opinion, nature serves as a model for the child's gradual and cohesive development:

> The mechanism of Nature as a whole is great and simple. Man! imitate it. Imitate this action of great Nature, who out of the seed of the largest tree produces a scarcely perceptible shoot; then, just as imperceptibly, daily and hourly by gradual stages, unfolds first the beginnings of the stem, then the bough, then the branch, then the extreme twig on which hangs the perishable leaf. (1898, 321)

Tolstoy could not help but support such an organic view of schooling. He was especially committed to Pestalozzi's idea of the relationship between education and the observation of reality, expressed in the motto: "Sense-impression of Nature is the only true foundation of human instruction, because it is the only true foundation of human knowledge" (Pestalozzi 1898, 316). This maxim, which belongs to Pestalozzi's *Method* (1828), is put into practice by Gertrude, the loving wife and mother in the Swiss pedagogue's novel *Leonard and Gertrude* (1781), who educates her children to "an accurate and intelligent observation of common objects and the forces of nature" (Pestalozzi 1889, 131).

Pestalozzi advocated a pragmatic vision of education, maintaining that "the ultimate end of education is not perfection in the accomplishments of the school, but fitness for life" (Pestalozzi 1827, 85). Likewise, Tolstoy urged the importance of a "nonscholastic" education that brought pupils closer to nature and prepared them for real life. In fact, as the writer asserts in "On Popular Education," "Every instruction ought to be only an answer to the question posed by life, whereas school not only does not call forth questions, but does not even answer those that are called forth by life" (1967, 15).

Drawing on Pestalozzi's pedagogical theories in his major work *The Education of Man* (1826), Froebel developed an educational practice which characterized children as "all-sided self-developing beings" (Froebel 1885, 5). Froebel, like Pestalozzi, thought of pedagogy in Romantic terms and contended that education was key to bringing man to consciousness of his divine nature: "The divine in man, his nature, therefore, is to be and must be developed to consciousness by education; and man must be raised to free, conscious living in accordance with the divine, thus to free representation of the divine which acts within him" (Froebel 1885, 3).

Tolstoy met with Julius Froebel, the German educator's nephew, in Kissingen in 1860 and discussed his uncle's pedagogy (Murphy 1992, 55). Though the Russian writer did not like Froebel's educational games for children, he embraced and shared his approach to education as the "representation of the divine" and as a full, free, and spontaneous development of pupils' potentialities, free of any constraints, since—in the pedagogist's words—"all active, dictatorial, invariable, and forcibly interfering education and instruction must necessarily have a disturbing, checking, and destructive effect upon the action of the divine" (Froebel 1885, 5). Tolstoy showed his closeness to Froebel by writing, in *The Pathway of Life*, that "[t]he greatest joy a man may know is the joy of realizing the existence within himself of a free, rational, loving and therefore happy being, in other words the consciousness of God within" (Tolstoy 2016, 62).

The Froebelian idea of the spontaneity of the educational process could only be fully embraced by Tolstoy who, as we know, was opposed to all violence in education and, indeed, made the principle of free and voluntary education (*obrazovaniye*) one of the founding principles of his pedagogical convictions.

Tolstoy and Froebel believed that educators had equal responsibilities in children's upbringing, whether good or bad. Froebel writes: "It is certainly a very deep truth... that it is mostly the man, often the educator, who first makes the child and the body bad" (Froebel 1885, 76). For Froebel and Tolstoy, the teachers' work is a true vocation; as Froebel remarks, educators "must perceive and contemplate the divine in the human, and evince the nature of man in God, and strive to represent both in one another in life" (Froebel 1885, 10).

In his article "On Methods of Teaching Literacy,"[12] the analysis of different methods for teaching reading leads Tolstoy to express these considerations:

> The best teacher will be he who has at the tip of his tongue the explanation of what it is that is bothering the pupil. These explanations give the teacher the knowledge of the greatest possible number of methods, the ability of inventing new methods, and, above all, not a blind adherence to one method, but the conviction that all methods are one-sided, and that the best method would be the one which would answer best to all the possible difficulties incurred by a pupil, that is, not a method, but an art and talent. (Tolstoy 1967, 58)

In conclusion, I wish to summarize the main components of Tolstoy's pedagogy derived from Kant, Rousseau, Pestalozzi, and Froebel. The author borrowed from his sources, made them his own, and adapted them to work with his personal educational views: 1) early childhood is central to an individual's maturation and entry into adulthood; and 2) global education is essential and teachers have a duty to preserve children's self-perfection and spiritual autonomy.

---

12 "O metodakh obucheniya gramote" (1862).

Tolstoy's educational thought was applied in the *ABC Book* and *Russian Books for Reading*, which will be discussed below.

***

The *ABC Book* (*Azbuka*) was the result of Tolstoy's fourteen years of teaching and studying during the 1850s and 1860s (Nikolayeva 2010). It was first drafted in 1868, completed between 1871 and 1872, and published in November 1872. A revised version was published in 1875 under the title *New ABC Book* (*Novaya azbuka*), and the Ministry of Education even adopted it for Russian public schools (Babayev 1989; Putilova 2006; Zaydenshnur 1974).

The *ABC Book* was a highly important project for Tolstoy, and he dedicated a great deal of time and effort to it. In a letter dated March 16, 1872, he confesses to a fellow poet: "My *ABC Book* gives me no peace and time for any other occupation . . . . What will come out of it I don't know; but I have put my whole soul into it" (Tolstoy 1936–57, 61:277). The author had lofty goals for his primer, hoping that it would teach reading to entire generations of aristocratic and peasant children. He even confided to his great-aunt Alexandra Tolstaya on January 12, 1872 that "After having completed the *ABC Book*, I can die in peace" (Tolstoy 1936–57, 61:269).

In its first version, the *ABC Book* presented itself as a complex of four books that included everything the author thought would be useful to a nineteenth-century Russian school-aged child as part of their education: a) the alphabet and fundamentals of grammar; b) readings for elementary literacy instruction; c) religious content; and d) scientific concepts. "The aim of the book," Tolstoy wrote to the minister of education, Dmitry Tolstoy, in 1872, "is to guide Russian pupils of all ages and classes in the learning of reading, writing, grammar, Slavonic language, and arithmetic" (1936–57, 61:338).

To guide children's educational processes and spiritual growth, Tolstoy divided each book of his *ABC Book* into three (Books II, III, and IV) or four sections (Book I), with the goal of providing students with a primary, gradual, multifaceted education that covered various areas of knowledge and was appropriate to age and ability.

Thus, the first section of Book I covered the Russian alphabet, syllabification principles, word formation, and pronunciation. The initial phase was to teach students how to recognize, read, and write the single letter connected with an image—"s" for "sugar," say. Teachers would then use a "syllabic-acoustic method" to introduce children to reading syllables and short sentences, and next move on to simple texts; the texts would slowly get more complicated as children developed mentally.

The second section of Book I aimed to focus the child's attention on fables and tales, which Tolstoy believed facilitated grammar rule revision and encouraged oral output by teaching students how to tell a story. The third section introduced youngsters to religious texts written in Slavonic, such as the Bible and the *Lives of the Saints*. Finally, the fourth section discussed fundamental computational algebra. Tolstoy ended Book I with some general advice for teachers.

Book II no longer included a section on the Russian alphabet. It was taken that children had already mastered literacy and grammar, and that all they needed was practice to improve their written, oral, and reasoning skills. As a result, Books II, III, and IV had the same structure: the first section was devoted to fables, tales, and short stories; the second contained religious and ethical writings; and the third was on arithmetic. Furthermore, each book came with a guide for teachers on how to use each section of the *ABC Book*.

The *ABC Book* was later reworked by Tolstoy into a new version completed in 1875, which took the name *New ABC Book*. In this volume, most of the texts were separated from the *ABC Book* proper and collected into four *Russian Books for Reading* (*Russkiye knigi dlya chteniya*), edited and considerably enriched with new material (for example, twelve new short stories were added).

***

It is evident from what we have said above that Tolstoy's *ABC Book* encompassed a whole pedagogy. The author's concern was to provide educational material for the intellectual and spiritual growth of Russian children. Specifically, in his *ABC Book*, Tolstoy created a pedagogic theory and practice that was built on three key assumptions, serving his educational views in general.

Firstly, Tolstoy attributed great importance to children's overall education. Embracing Pestalozzi's and Froebel's belief that education should maximize a young student's potential, Tolstoy reinterpreted in encyclopedic terms the canonical bipolar composition of *bukvar'* (primer), which included both a technical and a practical part (McEneaney 1997): the *ABC Book* was intended to be a sort of primary and essential key to the world for future generations of Russian children and teenagers. Traditional educational concepts were combined with religious content and moral teachings (Egorov 1994). According to the Tolstoyan distinction between *vospitaniye* and *obrazovaniye*, the child was supplied with an all-around *obrazovaniye* rather than the customary, partial, and forced *vospitaniye*. Didactic goals were met by avoiding abstract concepts in reading materials: they were, instead, always based on reality and children's experiences. "Self-knowledge ... is the centre from which all human instruction must start," Pestalozzi stated (1898, 334), and Tolstoy agreed wholeheartedly.

Furthermore, the *ABC Book*'s learning materials were provided in a progressive order, intended to correspond to children's natural cognitive development, in keeping with another Pestalozzi's motto: "Learn to make the simple perfect before going on to the complex" (1898, 319).

Secondly, Tolstoy defended the relevance of a suitable teaching method. As previously seen, Book I of the *ABC Book* offered instructions and suggestions for teachers. Tolstoy had no doubt that teachers played an important part in children's lives. However, in his "General Remarks for the Teacher" ("Obshchiye zamechaniya dlya uchitelya"), he urged instructors to reconsider their role as educators, placing students at the center of the educational process. According to Tolstoy, teachers enjoy their jobs and students, so they create the best learning conditions for them: educators conduct their lessons in a concise, understandable, and captivating manner, remove all possible sources of anxiety and fear, and, last but not least, readily listen to learners' personal needs (Tolstoy 1936–57, 22:180–85). These positions anticipate the most recent pedagogical ideas.

Thirdly, the *ABC Book* was grounded on the idea of the morality of art. Reading materials were endowed with ethical value, then. Tolstoy's *ABC Book* fully supported the author's defense of children's *obrazovaniye*, which encompasses cognitive skills as well as impressions, emotions, and religious feelings. As we know, in his educational practice Tolstoy viewed childhood development as a heuristic and spontaneous process. Nonetheless, whereas Tolstoy's pedagogy was based on the educational systems of Kant, Rousseau, Pestalozzi, Froebel, and others, his teaching tactics were simultaneously very "Tolstoyan." In fact, Tolstoy thought that children's harmonious development should include creative and artistic pursuits. As a result, the primary innovation of the *ABC Book* was its introduction of a moral dimension to children's reading. Like Rousseau and Kant, the novelist strongly promoted the moral nature of education. He believed that art, especially literature, with a moral component, should be at the heart of education. With this in mind, each volume of the *ABC Book* contained a large number of fables, proverbs, and short stories. By arousing children's emotions, curiosity, and imagination, these writings were intended to improve their literacy—both oral and written—and transmit moral and religious messages to pupils.

In essence, the *ABC Book* and the *New ABC Book*'s reading materials, and particularly Tolstoy's fables and short stories, later published separately in the *Russian Books for Reading*, demonstrate that Tolstoy understood how to teach children. They reflected the writer's conviction that education should prioritize the development of thought, pique the student's personal interest, and combine reality and information. The "real child" was Tolstoy's object of analysis and interlocutor in these stories, rather than an "abstract child." All of these factors made the readings from the *ABC Book,* the *New ABC Book,* and the *Russian Books for Reading* an ideal setting for Tolstoy's educational research.

***

The essay "What Is Art?"[13] presents Tolstoy's belief that art must serve a moral purpose: to help people on their journey to the good. Tolstoy's "aesthetic of austerity" stemmed from his devotion to didactic art. *A Calendar of Wisdom*[14] compares true art to the faithful wife, who requires no decoration, whereas false art is compared to an overly adorned harlot. In his works, Tolstoy endorses the idea that art should be sober and beautiful, but not frivolous or vain (Murphy 1992, 123–58). This perspective on art was previously revealed in the short stories in the *ABC Book,* which were intended to supplement a lack of reading options for youngsters.

The reading materials, which were later collected in the *Russian Books for Reading,* range from translations and adaptations of Aesop's fables and Greek classical writers to Russian, Indian, Arabian, American, French, German, and Turkish folk tales, as well as Tolstoy's original writings.

The key to Tolstoy's reading materials resides in the blending of didactic tasks aimed at educating learners about ethical ideals, with a realistic background taken from the peasant child's actual life and experiences (Lehman 1984, 69–70; Simmons 1949, 330–31). Tolstoy labored hard to develop the style of his short stories. In his unfinished 1862 essay "On the Language of Popular Books" ("O yazyke narodnykh knizhek"), in which the writer addressed the issue of language in children's literature and provided guidelines for authors, he emphasizes how, in books for children, style should be understandable, clear, synthetic, and especially "good," by avoiding highly colored popular expressions and foreign words, and the content should not be "empty" (Tolstoy 1936–57, 8:427–31). Thus, when writing his fables and tales, Tolstoy chose to communicate complex concepts to youngsters in a simple manner. Stories were influenced by the overall design of the *ABC Book,* which was supposed to be "fine, short, simple, and, above all, clear" (Tolstoy 1936–57, 61:283); they provided masterful examples of stylistic clarity, simplicity, and brevity. The fact that the stories were written in common people's Russian not only intrigued students (who had only recently begun spelling out words and enjoying funny proverbs and riddles) to become

---

13 *Chto takoye iskusstvo?* (1897–98).
14 *Krug chteniya* (1906–8).

acquainted with literary language (Zaydenshnur 1974, 30–35), but also fostered children's emotional involvement. All of this encouraged Tolstoy's young readers to take an active role in their education. Certainly, the short stories in the *ABC Book*, the *New ABC Book*, and the *Russian Books for Reading* appealed to children, since their protagonists were none other than children themselves, making them the real protagonists of their own educational journey.

Tolstoy's observations on pupils' upbringing are both uncommon and fascinating. The Russian author frequently maintained that school education, which generated the "school state of mind" that was so detrimental to a child's health and peace, should be replaced by "life education." Therefore, Tolstoy denied instructors or anyone else the right to train youngsters. As he states in "Should the Peasant Children Learn to Write from Us":

> It is impossible and absurd to teach and educate a child, for the simple reason that the child stands nearer than I do, than any grown-up man does, to that ideal of harmony, truth, beauty, and goodness, to which I, in my pride, wish to raise him. The consciousness of this ideal is more powerful in him than in me. All he needs of me is the material, in order to fill out harmoniously and on all sides. (Tolstoy 1967, 222)

In Tolstoy's opinion, teachers could only serve as "knowledge intermediaries"; real answers lay in the hands and hearts of the students. In other words, he believed education came from within, from the child himself. Within this context, the fables, tales, and short stories in the *ABC Book*, *New ABC Book*, and *Russian Books for Reading* are vivid evidence of the prominent role that children were called upon to play in nineteenth-century Russian society. By going through a process of self-education under the noninvasive guidance of their teachers, students could become aware of the qualities and virtues that were already within them, transforming them into dependable, kind, and generous adults. In this sense, schoolboys and girls were Russia's new "moralizers," since they served as the best role models for their peers.

***

In Tolstoy's *ABC Book*, *New ABC Book*, and *Russian Books for Reading*, the short stories feature children as both protagonists and narrators. This implies that the Russian author's young readers were expected to identify with the young heroes of the stories, who spoke a childish language similar to their own. It is no surprise: as we know, Tolstoy held that children ought to educate themselves.

Therefore, stories conveyed moral and religious teachings through children's own words, feelings, and experiences. This was a radically new approach to the learning process.

Tolstoy's stories were designed to pique children's interest, wonder, and imagination. In this way, learning met reality, because his stories for children combined simplicity and intelligibility of style and content with captivating strength and effectiveness, school and life, thus leading to *obrazovaniye*. And the "sense of happiness" felt by children when reading the *ABC Book* (Babayev 1989) demonstrated that Tolstoy's passion for teaching and students had had an impact.

Readings from the *ABC Book*, the *New ABC Book*, and the *Russian Books for Reading* which took place in a peasant milieu best demonstrate Tolstoy's pedagogy. Peasant stories and tales frequently evoke children's emotions, desires, and concerns by representing the whole breadth of their spiritual universe. Most of the stories' narrators and main characters are children themselves. Even content, language, and style are based on the perspective of the youngest readers. The following stories, translated by Michael Katz for the present edition, are representative: "How Auntie Learned to Sew" ("Kak tyotushka rasskazyvala o tom, kak ona vyuchilas' shit'"), "How the Boy Endured a Thunderstorm in a Forest" ("Kak mal'chik rasskazyval pro to, kak ego v lesu zastala groza"), "How the Little Boy Stopped Being Afraid of Blind Beggars" ("Kak mal'chik rasskazyval o tom, kak on perestal boyat'sya slepykh nishchikh"), and "The Boy's Story of How They Didn't Take Him into Town" ("Kak mal'chik rasskazyval pro to, kak ego ne vzyali v gorod").

Tolstoy borrowed diction from his Yasnaya Polyana pupils for the first three stories, while Vasya Morozov, a student of Tolstoy's, wrote "The Boy's Story of How They Didn't Take Him into Town" (together with "A Soldier's Wife's Way of Life") in the 1860s. Tolstoy later updated and adapted the language of these stories to match the *ABC Book*'s instructive moral purposes, but he kept the original storyline as envisioned by the children (Gusev 1963, 68–69). The writings given here as examples of Tolstoy's pedagogical contents and style were included in the first *Russian Book for Reading*.

All of these stories serve an ethical purpose, and feature children themselves. Tolstoy's young readers are educated by their own morality, which the author, like Socrates, extracts from them, introducing a new way of viewing learning practice.

Among the short stories and tales that look to children for inspiration, is "How Auntie Learned to Sew," which talks about a six-year-old girl's difficult apprenticeship. The story is told in the girl's own words, now that she is a woman with a young daughter.

When I was six years old, I kept asking my mother to let me sew. She said,

"You're still young; you'll merely prick your fingers." But I kept pestering her.

My mother took a piece of red cloth from her trunk and gave it to me; then she threaded a needle with red thread and showed me how to hold it. I began to sew, but couldn't make even stitches; one stitch came out large, and another wound up at the very edge of the rag and tore through it. Then I pricked my finger and tried not to cry, but my mother asked me, "What's wrong?" I couldn't restrain myself and burst into tears. Then my mother told me to go out and play.

When I went to bed, I kept dreaming of stitches: I kept thinking about how I could learn to sew quickly, and it seemed so hard that I thought I'd never learn. But now I'm all grown up and I don't recall how I learned to sew, and when I teach my own little girl to sew, I'm surprised when she can't hold the needle properly.

The subject, like the other stories we are going to look at, is based on Tolstoy's pupils' schoolwork, which Tolstoy later adapted. In effect, "How Auntie Learned to Sew" resembles a school composition. Despite the fact that the narrator is supposed to be an adult woman, the language used is extremely simple and childlike, with a high prevalence of parataxis, direct speech, an abundance of subjective and objective personal pronouns, a basic, clear vocabulary, and frequent repetition of connecting words: these are all stylistic elements frequently employed in children's communication and literature.

Furthermore, the story's content reflects the way children think. The protagonist, most likely a woman of humble origins, tells us about an apparently inconsequential childhood experience that served as a form of initiation for her as a little girl: her sewing apprenticeship. The emphasis on minor details (for example, she recalls how she pricked her finger and began screaming, prompting her mother to tell her to go play) evokes the spontaneous fluency and naiveté of the youngest in their speech.

Tolstoy replicates the world of children and their sensitivity in order to provide his young readers with a life lesson and a role model which comes from children themselves. The six-year-old girl in this tale experiences numerous challenges before learning to sew, but she perseveres, and as she grows older, she teaches her own daughter what she has learned. For this reason, the protagonist of Tolstoy's short story may potentially be regarded as a positive model of determination and purposeful behavior for Russian girls at the time. Children needed nothing extraordinary for their education: they already had all that was necessary to grow up as themselves. "How Auntie Learned to Sew" shows how Tolstoy put into practice the ideas of Froebel and Pestalozzi, by building his pedagogy on the principle of the autonomy and self-perfection of children.

While the narrator of "How Auntie Learned to Sew" is an adult woman, the narrator of "How the Boy Endured a Thunderstorm in a Forest" is an adult man who recounts his childhood experiences. He recalls, in particular, what happened when he was a child and was alone in the woods gathering mushrooms when a big storm hit.

> Once when I was little, they sent me into the forest to pick mushrooms. I got to the forest, picked the mushrooms, and was about to return home. Suddenly it became dark, it started raining and thundering. I was frightened and sat down under a large oak tree. Such bright lightning flashed that it hurt my eyes, and I had to shut them. Just above my head something cracked and began to thunder; then something hit me on my head. I fell down and lay there until it stopped raining. When I came to, water was dripping from all the trees, birds were singing, and the sun was shining. The large oak had toppled and there was smoke coming from the stump. All around me were scattered chips of the old oak tree. My clothing was soaked and was sticking to my body; there was a bump on my head and it was a little painful. I found my cap, picked up the mushrooms, and ran home. No one was there; I got a piece of bread and climbed onto the stove. When I awoke, I saw from the stove that the mushrooms had been cooked, placed on the table, and that people were getting ready to eat them.
>
> I cried, "Why are you eating without me?"
> They replied, "Why are you sleeping? Come quickly and eat."

Like the preceding work, the storyteller and protagonist are one and the same individual at two different stages of his life: as an adult and as a youngster. However, the story is always told from the perspective of the child. In fact, the "I" who speaks, utilizes the Russian language in a childlike manner. For example, in the original version the narrator uses diminutive forms of nouns and adverbs, which is a feature of children's speech.

Aside from the language, the story's theme revolves around childhood feelings and emotions. The (mis)adventure of the small hero, who harvests mushrooms in the woods for his family until he is abruptly caught in a storm, is presented in an impressionistic manner, reflecting the startled child's observations. The sky, which is rapidly darkening; the rain, which is pelting down; the rumbling thunder and flickering lightning: these images and sounds allow us to see and hear the storm through the young boy's own sensitivity and dread.

A seemingly innocuous event appears to the inexperienced child as a terrible calamity, a threat to his life; a crescendo of inchoative verbs emphasizes the boy's mounting panic and apprehension ("it became dark," "it started raining and thundering," "something cracked and began to thunder," etc.), culminating in his eventual collapse under a large oak. Nonetheless, the boy remains a role model for children, similar to the little girl in "How Auntie Learned to Sew." The two protagonists demonstrate what growing up entails—its big and small events, its joy and fear: a fascinating mystery to be discovered on one's own, which relies on one's own strength and determination to go on, live, and learn.

"How the Little Boy Stopped Being Afraid of Blind Beggars" celebrates, instead, the triumph of pity over fear. Like the previously examined stories about children's initiation into life, this tale depicts a child's maturation, as his reaction to blind beggars evolves from an unjustified, puerile fear to a wise Christian compassion.

> When I was young, they used to frighten me with blind beggars, and I was afraid of them. Once I came home and two blind beggars were sitting on the porch. I didn't know what to do; I was afraid to run back and afraid to walk past them; I thought that they might snatch me. Suddenly one of them (he had eyes that were as white as snow), stood up, took me by the hand, and said:
>
> "Young lad! How about giving me some alms?"
>
> I tore myself away from him and ran to my mother. She sent me back out with some money and some bread.
>
> The beggars were delighted with the bread; they crossed themselves and ate. Then the beggar with the white eyes said:
>
> "Your bread is tasty—may God save you.
>
> And he took me by the hand again and touched it.
>
> I began to feel sorry for him and from then on I stopped being afraid of blind beggars.

The story is told from the point of view of the protagonist, a little boy. We can easily verify this by paying attention to the subjective childlike perspective of the first-person narrator, who relates the facts as a child would; for example, his use of intense color comparisons (one of the two beggars is said to have "eyes as white as snow") can be traced back to children's speech.

"How the Little Boy Stopped Being Afraid of Blind Beggars" exemplifies, once again, how a child's world is filled with insecurity and fear, as well as the desire to conquer them, grow up, and become an adult. According to Tolstoy, this will happen as a result of the child's own efforts, rather than anyone else's. The writer strongly believed in children's self-education and self-moralization. We know that the little boy in the tale is extremely afraid of blind beggars. However, after meeting two of them in the doorway, and giving them some bread and money, he comes to a surprising realization: he is no longer terrified of them; rather, he feels a tremendous sense of sympathy for their plight. As a result, a negative feeling unexpectedly transforms into a positive one, and passivity and panic give way to activity and engagement in the life of others.

Although it is the youngster's mother who sends him to the beggars with a handout, the spiritual growth occurs within the boy himself, via the discovery of charity and Christian compassion. The little hero serves as an example of the value of good moral behavior and morality itself, which springs from within children's hearts.

The short narrative "The Boy's Story of How They Didn't Take Him into Town," adapted from a story by Vasya Morozov, focuses on another Christian characteristic: patience. As in the previous stories, Tolstoy analyzes a peasant child's life episodically through the child's own narration in order to provide moral guidance to his readers.

The rural child-narrator of the story wishes, in vain, that his father would take him to town. The youngster becomes depressed; but when his father arrives back home, he cheers up, especially after eating the white bread (*kalach*) that his parent bought for him in town:

> My father was about to go into town and I said to him: "Papa, take me with you."
>
> But he said, "You'll freeze to death there; why go?"
>
> I turned away, started crying, and went into the storeroom. I cried and cried and then fell asleep. I dreamt that there was a small path leading from our village to a chapel, and I saw—Papa was walking along this path. I caught up with him, and we went into town together. I was walking and saw a stove burning in front of us. I said: "Papa, is that the town?"
>
> And he said, "Yes, it is."

Then we reached the stove, and I saw that sweet rolls were baking.

I said: "Buy me a little sweet roll."

He bought one and gave it to me. Then I awoke, stood up, put on my shoes, took my mittens, and went outside. Some boys were ice-skating and sledding. I began to sled with them and did so until I nearly froze. Just when I went inside and climbed up on the stove, I heard my papa return from town. I rejoiced and asked, "Papa, did you buy me a little sweet roll?"

He said, "I did," and he gave it to me.

I jumped down from the stove onto a bench and began dancing with joy.

To the peasant youngster in this story, the town represents the magical realm of *kalachi*, the special kind of white bread that he enjoys. So, when his father decides to travel to town alone, concerned that the son may get cold, the youngster nearly loses hope. In Tolstoy's vision, his attitude is somewhat natural, but it is not ethically correct. The boy does not appear to realize that patience is the most important virtue for a Christian. Only at the end of the story, when the father returns and brings him the *kalach* he has long desired, does the boy recognize this.

Tolstoy's story aims to help children empathize with the protagonist and consider the morality or immorality of their own actions. The little boy in the story teaches them that being naughty is pointless; instead, children need to be patient and, by doing so, they will almost certainly obtain what they wanted. Tolstoy's character tell younger readers to embrace their lives as they are rather than expect more. Thus, the story serves as a Tolstoyan lesson in Christian endurance and the ability to be pleased with a little. Such insight is derived (once again) from a child's own voice and experience.

In essence—as in the other stories—"The Boy's Story of How They Didn't Take Him into Town" can be interpreted as a true representation of what life has in store for every one of us. Many of Tolstoy's young readers, particularly those from the lower classes, may have identified in these readings their own biographies—full of joy, sadness, and unexpected events.

***

Tolstoy attempted to bridge the gap between the world of peasants and Russian literary tradition. His anthologies of basic school materials—the *ABC Book*, the *New ABC Book*, and *Russian Books for Reading*—embodied this approach while also exerting a high pedagogical impact on the Russian educational system. Tolstoy's methods of teaching children how to read reconciled various nondogmatic educational perspectives by emphasizing pupils' individuality and uniqueness, the importance of free, self-directed learning, moral and religious formation, and educators' ethical responsibilities, many of which show similarities with the pedagogical thought of Kant, Rousseau, Pestalozzi, Froebel, Ushinsky, and others.

Tolstoy's readings merit a special position in modern education, however, since they promoted the holistic development of learners, which the author thought began with children themselves. Tolstoy believed this synthesis of information, spontaneous sensations, and creative potential aided pupils' difficult journey to adulthood by establishing children as the foundation of ethics and aesthetics.

Works Cited

Babayev, E. G. 1989. "Bol'shaya azbuka, ili oshchushcheniye shchastya" [The Big *ABC Book*, or the Feeling of Happiness]. In *Knizhnyye sokrovishcha mira: iz fondov Gos. bibl. SSSR im. V. I. Lenina*, edited by E. G. Babayev, 94–109. Moscow: Knizhnaya palata.

Baudouin, C. 1921. *Tolstoï éducateur* [Tolstoy as Educator]. Neuchâtel: Éditions Delachaux et Niestlé S. A.

Bernaz, O. 2017. "Anthropologie et pédagogie chez Tolstoï et Vygotski" [Anthropology and Pedagogy in Tolstoy and Vygotsky]. *Revue philosophique de la France et de l'étranger* 3: 325–40. https://doi.org/10.3917/rphi.173.0325.

Berthoff, A. E. 1978. "Tolstoy, Vygotsky, and the Making of Meaning." *College Composition and Communication* 29 (3): 249–55. https://doi.org/10.2307/356939.

Blaisdell, B., ed. 2000. *Tolstoy as Teacher: Leo Tolstoy's Writings on Education*. New York: Teachers and Writers Collaborative.

Bunnell, W. S. 1955. "Tolstoy and Freedom: An Examination of the Implications of His Educational Ideals." *Research Studies* 11: 32–51.

Calam, J. 1963. "Tolstoy on Education." *Saturday Review of Literature* 51: 80.

Cohen, A. 1981. "The Educational Philosophy of Tolstoy." *Oxford Review of Education* 7 (3): 241–51. https://www.jstor.org/stable/1050157.

Crosby, E. H. 1904. *Tolstoy as a Schoolmaster*. Chicago, IL: Hammersmark.

Duane, M. 1968. "Tolstoy at School." *New Society* 7: 81–93.

Egorov, S. F. 1994. "Léon Tolstoï (1828–1910)" [Leo Tolstoy (1828–1910)]. *Perspectives: revue trimestrielle d'éducation comparée* 24 (3–4): 677–90.

Froebel, F. 1885. *The Education of Man*. Translated by J. Jarvis. New York: A. Lovell & Company.

Gejdoš, M. 2021. "Pedagogical Views of Leo Nikolayevich Tolstoy." *International Journal of New Economics and Social Sciences* 14 (2): 35–41. https://doi.org/10.5281/zenodo.5971810.

Goncharov, N. K. 1962. "The Pedagogical Ideas and Practice of L. N. Tolstoy." *Sovetskaya pedagogika* 3: 47–59. https://doi.org/10.2753/RSS1061-1428040147.

Gusev, N. N. 1927. *Tolstoy v molodosti* [Tolstoy in His Youth]. Moscow: Izdatel'stvo Tolstovskogo muzeya.

———. 1963. *Lev Nikolayevich Tolstoy: Materialy k biografii s 1870 po 1881 god* [Leo Nikolayevich Tolstoy: Materials for Biography from 1870 to 1881]. Moscow: Izdatel'stvo Akademii Nauk SSSR.

Hans, N. 1963. *The Russian Tradition in Education*. London: Routledge.

Hapenciuc, A. 2021. "Lev Nikolayevich Tolstoy—The Pedagogy of Freedom." *International Journal of Social and Educational Innovation* 8 (15): 31–37. https://journals.aseiacademic.org/index.php/ijsei/article/view/178.

Kant, I. 2003. *On Education*. Translated by A. Churton. Mineola, NY: Dover Publications.

Lehman, K. 1984. "Tolstoy's Fables: Tools for a Vision." *Children's Literature Association Quarterly* 9 (2): 68–70.

Lushchevska, O. 2014. "Reasoning as a Pedagogical Tool: Tolstoy's Real Happening Stories for Children." *Children's Literature in Education* 45: 60–73. https://doi.org/10.1007/s10583-013-9206-7.

McEneaney, J. E. 1997. "Teaching Them to Read Russian: Four Hundred Years of the Russian *Bukvar*." *Reading Teacher* 51 (3): 210–26.

Mironov, B. N. 1991. "The Development of Literacy in Russia and the USSR from the Tenth to the Twentieth Centuries." *History of Education Quarterly* 31 (2): 229–52. https://www.jstor.org/stable/368437.

Mossman, E. 1993. "Tolstoi and Peasant Learning in the Era of the Great Reforms." In *School and Society in Tsarist and Soviet Russia*, edited by B. Eklof, 36–69. London: Palgrave Macmillan. https://doi.org/10.1007/978-1-349-22817-1_3.

Moulin, D. 2008. "Leo Tolstoy the Spiritual Educator." *International Journal of Children's Spirituality* 13 (4): 345–53. https://doi. org/10.1080/13644360802439490.

———. 2011. *Leo Tolstoy.* London: Continuum.

———. 2023. "Tolstoy on the Injustice of the Philosophy of Education." *Journal of Philosophy of Education* 57 (3): 643–60. https://doi.org/10.1093/ jopedu/qhad042.

Moulin-Stożek, D. 2022. "Peasant Schools and Education." In *Tolstoy in Context*, edited by A. A. Berman, 136–43. Cambridge: Cambridge University Press. https://doi.org/10.1017/9781108782876.022.

Murphy, D. 1992. *Tolstoy and Education.* Dublin: Irish Academic Press.

Nikolayeva, E. V. 2010. "Iz predystorii raboty L. N. Tolstogo nad 'Azbukoy'" [From the Prehistory of L. N. Tolstoy's Work on the *ABC Book*]. *Vestnik Moskovskogo gosudarstvennogo gumanitarnogo universiteta im. M. A. Sholokhova.* Filologicheskiye nauki 3: 30–50.

Pestalozzi, J. H. 1827. *Letters on Early Education; Addressed to J. P. Greaves, Esq.* London: Sherwood, Gilbert and Piper.

———. 1889. *Leonard and Gertrude.* Translated by E. Channing. Boston, MA: D. C. Heath and Co.

———. 1898. *How Gertrude Teaches Her Children.* Translated by L. E. Holland and F. C. Turner. Syracuse, NY: C. W. Bardeen.

Putilova, E. 2006. "Lev Tolstoy i ego 'Azbuka'" [Leo Tolstoy and his *ABC Book*]. *Detsky sad so vsekh storon* 23: 8–11.

Read, J. B. 1995. *The Educational Principles and Methods of Tolstoy's Pedagogy of Freedom at Yasnaya Polyana (1859–1862).* Ithaca, NY: Cornell University Press.

Reitblat, A. 2020. "The Reading Audience of the Second Half of the Nineteenth Century." In *Reading Russia: A History of Reading in Modern Russia*, edited by D. Rebecchini and R. Vassena, 2: 171–209. Milan: Ledizioni.

Roberts, P. 2017. "Tolstoy, Education, and the Meaning of Life." *Encyclopedia of Educational Philosophy and Theory*: 1–5. https://doi. org/10.1007/978-981-287-532-7_557-1.

Roberts, P., and H. Saeverot. 2018. *Education and the Limits of Reason: Reading Dostoevsky, Tolstoy and Nabokov.* London: Routledge.

Robertson, G. 2016. "Alternative Approaches to Education: Tolstoy's Thinking on Teaching and Learning and Its Relevance for Today." *Research in Teacher Education* 6 (1): 12–17. https://doi.org/10.15123/PUB.5092.

Rousseau, J.-J. 1889. *Émile; Or, Concerning Education; Extracts.* Translated by E. Worthington. Boston, MA: D. C. Heath and Company.

Simmons, E. J. 1949. *Leo Tolstoy.* London: John Lehmann.

Tolstoy, L. N. 1936–57. Vols. 8 (*Pedagogicheskiye stat'i 1860–1863*), 22 (*Azbuka [1871–1872]*), and 61 (*Pis'ma 1863–1872*) of *Polnoye sobraniye sochineny* [Complete Works], edited by V. G. Chertkov et al. Moscow: Khudozhestvennaya literatura.

———. 1967. *On Education.* Translated by L. Wiener. Chicago, IL: The University of Chicago Press.

———. 1984. *Pis'ma 1882–1899.* Vol. 19 of *Sobraniye sochineny v 22 tomakh* [Collected Works, 22 vols.], edited by M. B. Khrapchenko et al. Moscow: Khudozhestvennaya literatura.

———. 2016. *The Pathway of Life: Teaching Love and Wisdom.* Translated by A. J. Wolfe. Hollister: YogeBooks.

Torresin, L. 2016. "Tolstoy's *ABC Book*: A New Approach to Child Development." *International Journal of Russian Studies* 5 (2). https://www.ijors.net/issue5_2_2016/articles/torresin.html.

Vinitsky, I. 2015. "Tolstoy's Lessons: Pedagogy as Salvation." In *Before They Were Titans: Essays on the Early Works of Dostoevsky and Tolstoy*, edited by E. C. Allen, 299–316. Boston, MA: Academic Studies Press. https://doi.org/10.1515/9781618116833-014.

Zaydenshnur, E. E. 1974. "'Azbuka' Tolstogo i mnogonatsional'naya detskaya literatura v SSSR" [Tolstoy's *ABC Book* and Multinational Children's Literature in the USSR]. In *Yasnopolyansky sbornik 1974: Stat'i . Materialy. Publikatsii*, 27–42. Tula: Priokskoye knizhnoye izdatel'stvo.

Zweers, A. F. 1970. "Tolstoy on Education." *Canadian Slavonic Studies* 4: 347–48.

Translator's Preface

Michael R. Katz

Middlebury College, VT

This translation is based on the materials included in volumes 21 and 22 of the *Polnoe sobranie sochinenii* [Complete collected works] of L. N. Tolstoy published by the State Publishing House for Literature, Moscow, 1957.

The *Novaya azbuka* [New ABC Book] and the *Russkie knigi dlya chteniya* [Russian Books for Reading] were first published in 1874–75. The *New ABC Book* is a revision of his first edition published in 1872.

The language of the stories included presented few difficulties, since they were written for children. Occasionally agricultural terms had to be searched in the seventeen-volume Academy of Sciences dictionary. By and large, Tolstoy trimmed his complex literary style to bare bones since he was writing "for the people."

Acknowledgements

I wish to express my deepest gratitude to Professor Emeritus Stephen Donadio of Middlebury College for first suggesting this project and supporting my interest in undertaking it; to Lecturer Emerita Alexandra Baker for her devoted assistance in the preparation of this manuscript; to Linda Torresin of the University of Padua, Italy, for agreeing to write the excellent introduction to this volume; and to my former Bread Loaf student Jake Scott for his original and clever illustrations.

THE NEW ABC BOOK: SELECTED WRITINGS

The Load (A Fable)

After the French had retreated from Moscow, two peasants came to search for treasure. One was clever, the other, stupid.

They came together to the burnt part of the city, and found some scorched wool. They said, "That will come in handy at home."

They gathered up as much as they could carry and started for home.

Along the way they saw some cloth lying in the street. The clever peasant threw down the wool he was carrying, grabbed as much cloth as he could carry, and loaded it on his shoulders. The stupid one said:

"Why throw away the wool? It is nicely tied up and securely attached." But he didn't take any of the cloth.

They continued on further and saw some finished clothes that had been thrown away lying in the street. The clever peasant unloaded the cloth, picked up the clothes, and loaded them on his shoulders. The stupid one said:

"Why should I throw away the wool? It is nicely tied up and securely fastened on my shoulders."

They continued on their way, and saw some silver plates scattered about. The clever peasant threw down the clothes, and gathered up as many of the silver plates as he could, and started off with them; but the stupid one didn't throw away his wool, because it was nicely tied up and securely attached.

Going still further, they saw some gold lying on the road. The clever peasant threw down his silver plates and picked up the gold; but the stupid one said:

"What's the good of throwing away the wool? It is nicely tied up and securely fastened to my shoulders."

And they went home. On their way it started raining, and the wool became so water-soaked that the stupid man had to throw it all away, and thus came home empty-handed; but the clever peasant brought home the gold and became rich.

The Big Oven (A Fable)

Once a man had a large house, and in the house stood a big stove; but this man's family was small, consisting only of his wife and himself.

When winter came, the man tried to keep his stove hot; and in one month he burnt all his firewood. He had nothing to feed the fire, and it was very cold.

Then the man began to break up his fences, and use the wood for fuel. When he had burnt all his fences and the house, now without any protection against the wind, they became colder than ever, and still around (the house) had no firewood.

Then the man began to pick apart the ceiling in order to use it for heating.

It got even colder in the house—but there was no more wood.

A neighbor noticed that he was tearing down his ceiling, and said to him: "What's wrong with you, neighbor, have you lost your mind? You're pulling down your ceiling in the middle of winter. You and your wife will freeze to death!"

But the man replied:

"No, brother; you see, I'm pulling down my ceiling to have something to heat my stove with. We have such a strange stove: the more I heat it, the colder we get!"

The neighbor laughed, and said:

"Well, then, after you've burnt up your ceiling, you'll be tearing down your house. You won't have anywhere to live; only the stove will be left, and even that will be cold!"

"Well, that's my misfortune," said the man. "All my neighbors have enough firewood for the whole winter, but I've already burnt my fences and the ceiling of my house, and I have nothing left."

The neighbor replied:

"All you need is to have your stove rebuilt"

But the man said:

"I know you're envious of my house and my stove because they're bigger than yours, so you advise me not to tear down my house."

And he turned a deaf ear to his neighbor's advice, burnt up his ceiling, burnt his whole house, and then had to go live with strangers.

The Find (A True Story)

An old woman lived with her granddaughter in a village. They were very poor and had nothing to eat. It was Easter time. People were rejoicing. Everyone brought some food to break the fast. Only the old woman didn't have anything to offer. They wept and begged God to help them. The old woman recalled that in bygone days, during the French occupation, peasants had buried their money in the earth. So the old woman said to her granddaughter:

"Take a shovel and go to the old settlement; pray to God, then dig in the soil; maybe God will send us something."

The granddaughter wondered how one could find a treasure.

"Well, I will do as my grandmother orders."

She took a shovel and left the house. She dug a hole and thought to herself: "I've dug enough. I'll go home." As she was about to raise her shovel, she heard it strike something. She bent over to look and saw a large strongbox. She shook it and something jingled. She tossed down her shovel, ran to her grandmother, and shouted:

"Grandma! I've found a treasure!"

They opened the strongbox and it was full of silver coins, paper rubles, and kopecks. Grandmother and her granddaughter bought supplies for the holiday to break their fast; they also bought a cow, and gave thanks to God, that He had heard their prayer.

The Little Girl and the Robbers (A Fairy Tale)

A little girl was guarding a cow in a field. Some robbers came and carried her off. They brought her to their house in the forest and ordered her to cook, clean, and sew. The little girl lived with the robbers, worked for them, but didn't know how to escape. Whenever the robbers left, they would lock up the little girl.

One day all the robbers went out and left the little girl alone. She brought in some straw, fashioned a doll out of it, dressed the doll in her own clothes, and sat it next to the window. Then she smeared herself with honey, rolled in some feathers, and began to look like a scary bird. She jumped out of the window and took off.

Just as she got to the road, she saw the robbers coming toward her from the other direction. The robbers didn't recognize her and asked, "Scarecrow, what's our little girl doing?" The little girl replied:

"She's washing, cooking, sewing, and waiting for the robbers by the window." Then she took off running as fast as she could.

The robbers came home and saw that someone was sitting by the window. They greeted her and said, "Hello, little girl; open up for us." They saw that the little girl didn't move and remained silent. Then they broke down the door and planned to kill the little girl—but they saw that it wasn't the little girl at all, just a doll made of straw. The robbers threw it aside, and exclaimed:

"That little girl fooled us!"

And the little girl got to the river, washed herself clean, and went back home.

The Nut Branch (A Fairy Tale)

There once lived a wealthy merchant, and he had three daughters. He was planning to go on a trip to purchase some goods and asked his daughters:

"What should I bring you?"

The eldest daughter asked for some beads. The second daughter asked for a ring, and the youngest said, "I don't need anything. If you think of me, bring me a branch of a nut tree."

The merchant left on his trip, finished his business, and bought some beads for his eldest daughter and a ring for his second daughter. He was already on his way back through a large forest, when he remembered that his youngest daughter hadn't asked for anything, only a branch from a nut tree. He climbed down from the cart and went to fetch one. All of a sudden he saw that the branch wasn't all that plain, but that there were golden nuts hanging from it. The merchant thought: here's a gift for my clever, youngest daughter; he bent the branch and broke it off. Suddenly, a bear appeared out of nowhere: he grabbed the merchant by the arm and said:

"How dare you break off my branch? Now I shall eat you up."

The merchant got frightened and said: "I wouldn't have taken the branch, but my youngest daughter asked for one."

So the bear said: "Go home, but remember: whoever greets you first when you get home, you'll have to give to me."

The merchant agreed and promised, and the bear released him. The merchant continued his journey and arrived home.

As soon as he had driven into his courtyard, his favorite, the youngest child, came running to meet him. The merchant remembered what he had promised the bear, namely, that whomever he met first he must give to him, and he was struck with fear.

The merchant related everything that had happened and said that he was obligated to give his youngest daughter to the bear. Everyone began to weep. The mother said: "Don't cry; I know what to do. When the bear comes for our daughter, we'll dress up the shepherd's daughter and give her to him instead."

One day they were all seated at home and saw a carriage entering their court-yard. They looked and saw a bear getting out of the carriage. He came up to the merchant and said: "Give me your daughter." The merchant didn't know what to say. But the mother had the sense to dress up the shepherd's daughter and bring her to the bear. The bear helped her into the carriage and set off. As they drove away, the bear began growling and was just about to eat the shepherd's daughter. Then she admitted that she was really the shepherd's daughter, not the merchant's child.

The bear returned to the merchant and said: "You deceived me. Give me your own daughter." They all wept, dressed their daughter, said their farewells, and gave her to the bear. The bear put her in the carriage and off he went. They drove for a very long time: they entered a large forest and stopped. The bear climbed out of the carriage and said: "Here's my house; follow me."

The bear climbed into his den and the young girl followed him. Then the bear opened a large door, led the girl into a dark cellar, and said: "Follow me." The young girl shuddered from fear and thought that her end had come; still, she followed the bear. Suddenly something began to rumble like thunder, it became light, and the girl saw that she was not in a cellar, but in a luxurious palace: it was bright; music was playing, and well-dressed people were greeting and welcoming her; next to her stood a handsome young prince. The prince approached her and said: "I'm not a bear, but a prince, and I want to marry you."

Then they sent for her father and mother, invited guests, and held a wedding. They lived happily ever after and always kept the branch of the nut tree.

The Little Bird (A True Story)

It was Seryozha's name day and he received many different gifts: tops, hobby horses, and pictures. But Seryozha's uncle gave him a gift that he prized above all the rest; it was a trap for catching birds.

The trap was constructed in such a way that a board was fitted on the frame and closed upon the top. One had to scatter some seeds on the board, and then put it out in the yard. A little bird would fly down, hop on the board, it would give way, and the trap would shut with a clap.

Seryozha was delighted, and he ran into the house to show his mother the trap. His mother said:

"It's not a good plaything. What will you do with the birds? Why do you want to torture them?"

"I'm going to put them in cages," Seryozha said. "They'll sing, and I'll feed them."

He got some seeds, scattered them on the board, and set the trap in the garden. Then he stood by and waited for the birds to fly down. But the birds were afraid of him and wouldn't come anywhere near the net. Seryozha went in to have dinner, and left the trap.

After dinner he went out to look at it. The cage had shut, and in it a little bird was struggling in the net.

Seryozha was delighted and carried the bird into the house.

"Mother, look, I've caught a bird!" he cried. "I think it's a nightingale; how its heart is beating!"

His mother said it was a pine siskin. "Be careful! Don't hurt it; it's better to let it go."

"No," he said. "I'm going to give it something to eat and drink."

Seryozha put the bird in a cage, and for two days he fed it seeds and water and cleaned its cage. But on the third day he forgot all about it, and didn't change the water.

So his mother said, "See, you've forgotten about your bird. You should let it go."

"No, I won't forget. I'll give it some water right away and will clean its cage."

Seryozha reached his hand into the cage and began to clean it, but the little bird was frightened and fluttered its wings. After Seryozha had cleaned the cage, he went to get some water. His mother saw that he had forgotten to shut the cage door, and she called him back.

"Seryozha, shut the cage, or else your bird will fly out and hurt itself."

She had hardly spoken the words when the bird found the door of the cage, was delighted, spread its wings, and flew around the room toward the window. But it didn't see the glass, bumped into it, and fell on the windowsill. Seryozha came running in, picked up the bird, and put it back in the cage. The bird was still alive, but it lay on its breast, its wings spread wide, breathing heavily. Seryozha looked and looked at it, and began to cry.

"Mother, what am I to do now?" he asked.

"You can do nothing now," she replied.

Seryozha sat by the cage all day. He did nothing but look at the bird. And all the time the bird lay on its breast, breathing hard and fast.

When Seryozha went to bed, the bird was still alive. Seryozha couldn't fall asleep for a long time; every time he shut his eyes, he seemed to see the bird lying there, breathing heavily.

In the morning when Seryozha went to the cage, he saw the bird lying on its back, its legs folded in, and all stiff.

Since then Seryozha never caught any birds again.

The Three Bears

Once a little girl left her house and went into the forest. She got lost there and began looking for a way to get home. But she didn't find it; instead she came to a little hut in the forest.

The door was open: she looked in, saw that no one was home, and she went in. Three bears lived in this little house. One was the father and his name was Mikhail Ivanych. He was big and shaggy. The other one was the mama bear. She was smaller and her name was Nastasya Petrovna. The third one was a little bear cub named Mishutka. No one was home; the bears had gone for a walk in the forest.

There were two rooms in the hut: a dining room and a bedroom. The little girl entered the dining room and saw three bowls with soup on the table. The first bowl, very large, was Mikhail Ivanych's. The second, a smaller one, was Nastasya Petrovna's. And the third, a blue bowl, was Mishutka's. A spoon lay next to each bowl: a big one, a middle-sized one, and a little one.

The little girl picked up the biggest spoon and tasted the soup in the biggest bowl; then she took the middle-sized spoon and tasted the soup in the middle-sized bowl; then she picked up the little spoon and ate some soup from the blue bowl, and she liked Mishutka's bowl of soup best of all.

The girl wanted to sit down and saw three chairs next to the table: a great big one belonging to Mikhail Ivanych, the next one, smaller, to Nastasya Petrovna, and the smaller third one with a blue pillow, to Mishutka. She climbed onto the biggest chair and fell off; then she sat down on the middle-sized chair and it felt uncomfortable; then she sat on the small chair and began laughing, because it felt just right. She put Mishutka's blue bowl of soup on her lap and began to eat. She finished all the soup and began rocking in the chair.

But the little chair broke and the girl fell to the floor. She stood up, picked up the chair, and went into the other room. In there stood three beds: a great big one, belonging to Mikhail Ivanych; a medium-sized bed, Nastasya Petrovna's; and the third one, very small, belonging to Mishenka. She lay down on the biggest one, but it was too big; she lay down on the middle-sized bed, but it was too high; and she lay down in the little bed, and it was just right and she fell fast asleep.

Meanwhile, the three bears came home hungry and wanted to have their dinner. The big bear picked up his spoon, looked at his soup, and roared in a ferocious voice: "Who has been eating from my bowl?"

Nastasya Petrovna looked at her bowl and growled, but not as loud, "Who's been eating from my bowl?"

And Mishutka saw his empty bowl and squeaked in his high voice: "Who's been eating from my bowl and finished all my soup?"

Mikhailo Ivanych took a look at his chair and roared in a terrible voice: "Who's been sitting in my chair and moved it from its usual place?"

Nastasya Petrovna glanced at her chair and growled, but not so loud, "Who's been sitting in my chair and moved it from its usual place?"

Mishutka looked at the pieces of his little chair and squeaked, "Who's been sitting in my chair and broken it?"

The bears went into the other room. "Who's been lying on my bed and crumpled it?" roared Mikhailo Ivanych in a terrible voice. "Who's been lying on my bed and crumpled it?" growled Nastasya Petrovna, not as loud. And Mishenka placed a bench next to his bed, climbed on it, wanting to lie down on his bed, and he whined, "Who's been lying on my bed?" And all of a sudden he saw the little girl and squealed, as if someone was stabbing him: "Here she is! Grab her! Hold her! There she is; right there. Hey! Grab her!" He wanted to bite her. The little girl opened her eyes, saw the three bears, and rushed to the window. The window was open and she jumped out and ran away. And the bears couldn't catch up with her.

Uncle Semyon Told Us What Happened to Him in the Forest

Once during winter I went into the forest to get some wood; I cut down three trees, lopped off the branches, and trimmed them. I looked around and saw that it was already getting late: time to go home. The weather was bad: there was a snowstorm. I thought that night would soon fall and I wouldn't be able to find the road. I kept driving my horse, but couldn't find the way out. The forest was thick. I thought, my fur coat was in bad shape: I'll freeze. I kept driving, but there was no road, and now it was dark. I was about to unharness the sleigh and lay down to sleep under it. Then I heard some sleigh bells jingling not far away. I headed toward the sound and saw a troika with three light brown horses, their manes woven with ribbons, their bells shining, and two young fellows seated in it.

"Greetings, brothers!"

"Greetings, peasant!'

"Where's the road, brothers?"

"We're on it."

I rode towards them and looked. What a miracle: the road was smooth and not covered by snow.

"Follow us," they said, and spurred on their horses.

My little mare was weak and couldn't keep up.

I began to shout: "Wait, brothers!"

They stopped and began laughing.

"Sit up here with us," they said. "Your horse will be better off without a load."

"Thanks," I said.

I climbed up into their sleigh. It was a nice one, lined with rugs. I'd only just mounted it, when they whistled:

"Come on, my darlings!" The light-brown horses raced ahead so fast that snow rose up in a column. I looked and what luck! It became bright, the road was smooth as ice, and we were moving so fast that it took my breath away. My face was being lashed by branches. I was beginning to get frightened. I looked ahead: there was a very, very steep hill, and before it, a precipice. The horses were rushing right for the precipice. I got frightened and shouted:

"Good heavens! Slow down! You'll kill us all!"

But the men only laughed and whistled.

I saw that all was lost. We were heading for the precipice. I looked and saw a branch hanging down just over my head. "Well," I thought, "let them perish alone."

I stood up and grabbed hold of the branch and hung on. As soon as I did, I shouted, "Hold on!"

And I also heard some women calling:

"Uncle Semyon, what's the matter?"

"Hey, women, you women! Light the fire."

"Something's wrong with Uncle Semyon," they yelled.

They lit a fire.

I came to. I was in my own hut, clinging to my sleeping-bench, screaming at the top of my lungs.

Everything I had seen had been a dream.

The Cow (A True Story)

The widow Marya and her six children lived with her mother. They were very poor. But they bought a brown cow with their last rubles so there would be milk for the children. The older children fed Buryonushka in the field and gave her slops at home. Once the mother was away and the older boy Misha climbed up on the shelf to get some bread, knocked over a glass, and broke it. Misha was afraid that his mother would scold him, so he collected the large pieces of glass from the floor, carried them into the courtyard, and buried them in the manure pile; then he picked up the shards of glass and tossed them into the washtub. The mother missed the glass and began asking about it, but Misha didn't say a word; and so the matter rested.

The next day the mother went to give Buryonushka the slops from the washtub, and saw that the cow was sick and wouldn't eat her food. They tried to treat her, and called in an old midwife. She said that the cow wouldn't live long, and should be slaughtered for her meat. They summoned a peasant and he set about slaughtering the cow. The children heard Buryonushka lowing in the courtyard. They gathered on the stove-bench and began to cry. After they'd slaughtered Buryonushka, they removed her skin, cut her into pieces, and there, in her throat, they found some pieces of glass.

And so they figured out that she'd died because she'd swallowed some glass in the slops. When Misha found this out, he began to weep bitter tears, and confessed to his mother that he'd broken a glass. His mother didn't say anything, but she also started crying. She said: "We slaughtered our Buryonushka and have no money left to replace her. How will the children survive without milk? Misha began crying even louder and wouldn't come down from the stove-bench, when everyone else was eating jellied cow's head. He dreamt every day how Uncle Vasily was carrying the dead cow's head home by the horns, with her red neck and her eyes wide open.

From then on the children had no more milk. They drank milk only on holidays, when Marya would beg her neighbor for a mug of milk.

It so happened that the lady of that estate needed a nanny for her child. The grandmother said to her daughter:

"Let me go. I'll become her nanny, and perhaps God will help you manage alone with your children. Meanwhile, God willing, I can earn enough money in a year to buy us a cow."

That's what they did. The grandmother went off to work for the lady of the estate. Life got even harder for Marya and the children. The children lived a whole year without milk: they ate nothing but *kisel*[1] and bread soaked in *kvass*,[2] and they became thin and pale.

A year passed; grandmother came home and brought twenty rubles. "Well, daughter!" she said. "Now we can buy a cow."

Marya was delighted, as were all the children. Marya and her mother got ready to go to the market to buy a cow. They asked a neighbor to stay with the children and they asked another neighbor, Uncle Zakhar, to go with them and help them choose a cow. They said a prayer and went off to town.

The children went out into the street to see if they could see a cow coming. They began discussing what color she might be: brown or black. They began talking about how they would feed her. They waited and waited all day. They even walked out a verst to meet the cow; it started to get dark so they turned back.

All of a sudden, they saw a cart coming along the road, and in it sat their grandmother, and next to the rear wheel, a multicolored cow was tied up by the horns, and their mother was walking behind the cow, urging her on with a stick.

The children came running out and began examining the cow; they brought along bread and grass and tried to feed her. The mother went into the hut, changed her clothes, and came back outside with a towel and a milk pail. She sat down next to the cow and wiped the cow's udders. The Lord be praised! She started milking the cow and the children all stood around watching her and listening to the milk stream into the pail from under their mother's hands. After the mother had filled the pail half-full, she carried it down to the cellar, and poured some milk into the mug so the children could have milk for their supper.

---

1 A simple dish, belonging to the group of cold-solidified desserts, although it can be served warm.
2 A fermented cereal-based low-alcohol beverage with a slightly cloudy appearance, light-brown color, and sweet-sour taste.

Filippok (A True Story)

There was a little boy whose name was Filipp. One day all the other children were going off to school. Fillip picked up his cap and also wanted to go with them. But his mother said to him, "Where are you off to?"

"To school," he replied.

"You're still too little: you can't go," she said and left him home.

The other children went off to school. Father had already gone to work in the forest, and mother went off to her daily job. Fillipok was left at home along with his grandmother, who was on the stove-bench. He became bored at home; his grandmother fell asleep and he began looking for his cap. He couldn't find his own, so he took his father's old cap, and he went off to school.

School was at the edge of the village, near the church. When Fillipp was walking through his own neighborhood, dogs didn't bother him: they recognized him. But when he reached other courtyards, Zhuchka[3] jumped out of a yard and began to bark; and then a large dog named Volchok followed. Fillipok took off running and the dogs chased him. He started to yell, stumbled, and fell. A peasant heard him, came out, chased away the dogs, and said, "Where are you going, you little rascal, all alone?"

Fillipok didn't reply, pulled up the flaps of his coat, and started to run. He arrived at the school. No one was on the porch, but he could hear the children's voices coming from inside. Now Fillipok was feeling frightened: "What if the teacher chases me away?" He began wondering what he should do. If he went back, the dogs might bite him. And if he entered the school, he'd be afraid of the teacher.

A peasant woman carrying a pail walked past the school and said, "Everyone's inside studying. Why are you standing out here alone?"

So Fillipp entered the school. He took off his cap in the entryway and opened the door. The schoolroom was full of children. They were all talking at once; the teacher was wearing a red scarf and walked up and down among them.

"What do you want?" he shouted at Fillipok.

Fillipok clutched his cap and made no reply.

"Who are you?"

Fillipp said nothing.

"Are you mute?"

Fillipok was so frightened he couldn't speak.

"Well then, if you're not going to say anything, go home."

---

3   A typical Russian name for a black dog.

Fillipok would have been glad to say something, but his throat was parched with fear. He looked at the teacher and burst into tears.

Then the teacher began to feel sorry for him. He stroked his head and asked the other children who this little fellow was.

"It's Fillipok, Kostyushka's brother; he's been wanting to come to school for a long time, but his mother wouldn't let him come; he must have snuck out on his own."

"Well, sit down on the bench next to your brother. I'll ask your mother to let you come to school, too."

The teacher began to teach Fillipok the letters, but he knew them already and could even read a bit.

"Well, then, spell your name."

Fillipok recited: "*Khe-e-khi-le-i-li, peok, pok.*" Everyone laughed.

"Well done," said the teacher. "So who taught you to read?"

Fillipok grew braver and said, "Kostyushka. I'm clever and I learned quickly. I'm very smart!"

The teacher began laughing and said:

"Do you know your prayers?"

Fillipok replied, "I do," and he began reciting the "Hail, Mary." But he mispronounced every word.

The teacher interrupted him and said, "You shouldn't boast. First learn a few things."

And from that day on, Fillipok began to attend school with the other children.

THE FIRST RUSSIAN BOOK FOR READING

The Ant and the Dove (A Fable)

An ant went down to the brook to have a drink of water. A wave knocked him over and he almost drowned. A dove was flying by with a twig in her beak; she saw the ant drowning and tossed the twig into the water. The ant climbed onto the twig and was saved. Then a hunter threw a net over the pigeon and was about to pull it tight. The ant crawled up to the hunter and bit his foot; the hunter cried out and dropped the net. The dove took wing and flew away.

The Blind Man and the Deaf Man (A True Story)[1]

A blind man and a deaf man went into a field to pick some peas. The deaf man said to the blind man: "You listen and tell me; I'll look and tell you."

They entered the field of peas and sat down.

The blind man felt the peas and said: "Are they in pods?"

And the deaf man said: "Where is it knocking?"

---

1   This story is based on clever wordplay and makes little sense in English translation.

The blind man stumbled over the boundary marker and fell down.

The deaf man asked, "What's the matter?"

The blind man said, "It's a boundary marker!"

The deaf man said: "Should we run?" and he started running.

The blind man followed him.

The Turtle and the Eagle

A turtle was asking an eagle to teach her to fly. The eagle advised against it because she was ill-suited for it. But the turtle kept insisting. The eagle took her into its talons, flew up, and let her go: she fell onto some rocks and was smashed to smithereens.

The Foundling (A True Story)

A poor woman had a daughter named Masha. One morning Masha went to fetch some water and saw that something was lying next to the door wrapped in rags. Masha put down her buckets and unwrapped the rags. When she touched the rags, there came the sound of a cry from under them: "Wah, wah, wah!" Masha bent down and saw that it was a tiny, reddish baby. It was shouting loudly, "Wah, wah!"

Masha picked it up, brought it home, and began feeding it some milk.

Her mother said: "What did you bring home?"

"A little child; I found it next to our door."

Her mother said, "We're poor as it is; how can we feed a little baby? I'll go see the head of the school and tell him to take it."

Masha began to cry and said: "Mama, it won't eat very much; let it stay. Look at its little red hands and its wrinkled fingers."

Her mother took a look and felt sorry for the baby. She let it stay. Masha fed and swaddled the child, and sang it lullabies when it went to bed.

The Head and Tail of the Snake (A Fable)

A snake's tail quarreled with the snake's head about which one of them should lead the way.

The head said, "You can't go first: you don't have any eyes or ears."

The tail replied: "On the other hand, I'm strong; I make you move; if I wrap myself around a tree, you won't be able to budge from that spot."

The head said: "Let's part ways!"

So the tail separated from the head and crawled forward. But as soon as it crawled away from the head, it fell into a crevice and fell to the bottom.

The Rock (A True Story)

A poor man went to see a rich man to beg for alms. The rich man didn't give him anything and said, "Get out!" But the poor man wouldn't leave.

Then the rich man got angry, picked up a rock, and threw it at the poor man.

The poor man picked up the rock, put it onto his bosom and said: "I shall carry this rock around until I'm forced to throw it at him."

And that time came. The rich man did some bad thing: they took away everything he had and were taking him off to prison.

As they were taking him to prison, the poor man walked up to him; he took the rock off his bosom and raised his arm to throw it; then he reconsidered. He threw the rock on the ground and said:

"I held onto this rock for so long for no good reason; when the man was rich and strong, I was afraid of him; but now I pity him."

Eskimos (Description)

There is on earth a land where summer lasts only three months, and it's winter for the rest of the year. Days are so short during the winter that the sun scarcely rises before it sets again. For three months during the middle of winter the sun doesn't rise at all and it's completely dark. People live on this land: they're called Eskimos. These people speak their own language; they don't understand other languages and never leave their own land. Eskimos aren't very tall, but they have very large heads. Their bodies aren't white, but brown, and their hair is black and wiry. They have slim noses, broad cheekbones, and small eyes. Eskimos live in houses made of snow. This is how they build them: they chop blocks from the snow, and build a house with them the way one builds a stove. Instead of windows, they place blocks of ice in the walls, and instead of doors, they carve a long tunnel under the snow and crawl into their house through this tunnel.

When winter arrives, their houses are buried in snow and this makes them warmer. The Eskimos eat reindeer, wolves, and polar bears. They catch fish in the sea using sticks with hooks on one end and nets. They kill wild beasts with spears and bows. Eskimos eat their meat raw like wild animals. They don't have any flax or hemp to make shirts and rope; there's also no wool to make cloth; they fashion rope from the sinew of animals, and clothes—from animal skins.

They put two skins together, with the fur on the outside, piercing the hides with fish bones and sewing them together with tendons. In this way they also make shirts, trousers, and boots. They have no iron. They fashion spears and arrows from bones. Most of all, they love to eat the fat of wild beasts and fish. Men and women dress alike. But women wear boots with wide tops. They insert their young children in these wide openings and carry them around in that way.

In the midst of winter the Eskimos have three months of darkness. But in the summer the sun hardly sets, and they have no nights whatsoever.

The Polecat (A Fable)

A polecat went to a blacksmith's shop and began licking the iron filings. His tongue began to bleed, but the polecat was pleased; he kept on licking—he thought that the blood came from the filings, and he ruined his whole tongue.

How Auntie Learned to Sew (A Tale)

When I was six years old, I kept asking my mother to let me sew. She said, "You're still young; you'll merely prick your fingers." But I kept pestering her.

My mother took a piece of red cloth from her trunk and gave it to me; then she threaded a needle with red thread and showed me how to hold it. I began to sew, but couldn't make even stitches; one stitch came out large, and another wound up at the very edge of the rag and tore through it. Then I pricked my finger and tried not to cry, but my mother asked me, "What's wrong?" I couldn't restrain myself and burst into tears. Then my mother told me to go out and play.

When I went to bed, I kept dreaming of stitches: I kept thinking about how I could learn to sew quickly, and it seemed so hard that I thought I'd never learn. But now I'm all grown up and I don't recall how I learned to sew, and when I teach my own little girl to sew, I'm surprised when she can't hold the needle properly.

Thin Threads (A Fable)

A man ordered some fine thread from a spinner. A spinner spun some fine thread for him, but the man said: "This thread isn't any good. I need the finest thread."

The spinner said: "If this isn't fine enough, here are some others," and she pointed to an empty space. He said that he couldn't see them.

The spinner said, "You don't see them because they're so fine; I can't see them either."

The fool was delighted and ordered some more thread just like that one, and he even paid her money for both.

Strength from Speed (A True Story)

Once a railroad car was traveling very fast along a railroad track. And right on that railway, at an intersection, stood a horse with a heavy load. A peasant was trying to drive the horse across the rails, but the horse couldn't move the cart because a rear wheel had fallen off. The conductor shouted to the train driver: "Stop," but the engine driver didn't listen to him. He realized that the peasant couldn't move the horse and cart away, nor could he turn around, and it was impossible to stop the train so quickly.

The driver didn't even try to stop, drove the engine, and hurtled toward the cart at full speed. The peasant ran away from the cart, and the engine tossed the cart and the horse from the road like a splinter of wood; the engine didn't even feel the crash, but raced on ahead. Then the driver said to the conductor, "This way we killed only one horse and destroyed one cart, but if I'd listened to you, we would've been killed, and would've crushed all the passengers. At full speed we threw the cart off the rails, but didn't feel the jolt; but at slow speed, we would have been derailed."

The Lion and the Mouse (A Fable)

A lion was asleep. A mouse ran across his body. He woke up and caught the mouse. The mouse begged to be released; it said, "If you spare me, I'll do you a favor someday."

The lion started laughing when the mouse said it would do him a favor, and he released it.

Then some hunters caught the lion and tied him to a tree with a rope. The mouse heard the lion's roar, came running, gnawed though the rope, and said: "Do you remember that you laughed and thought I could never do you a favor? Well, now you see—some good can come even from a mouse."

The Fire Dogs (A True Story)

It often happens in towns that in the case of a fire, children are left inside houses and it's impossible to rescue them because they're hiding from fear and remain silent, and it's impossible to locate them because of all the smoke. As a result, in London dogs are taught to do this. The dogs live with firemen; when a house starts burning, the firemen send in the dogs to rescue children. Such a fire dog in London managed to rescue twelve children; his name was Bob.

Once a house was on fire. When the firemen arrived at

the house, a woman came running out. She was crying and said that her two-year-old little girl had been left inside the house. The firemen sent in Bob. The dog ran up the stairs and disappeared in the smoke. Five minutes later he came running out and in his teeth he was holding a little girl wrapped in a shirt. The mother rushed to her daughter and wept with joy that she was alive. The firemen petted the dog and examined him to see if he was burned; but Bob was straining to go back into the house again. The firemen thought there was someone else alive inside and let him return. The dog ran into the house and soon came back out carrying something in his teeth. When the crowd looked to see what he was carrying, they burst out laughing: he was carrying a large doll.

The Monkey
(A Fable)

A man went into the forest, chopped down a tree, and began sawing it up into pieces. He lifted the end of the tree onto a stump, sat astride on it, and began sawing. Then he drove a wedge into the split that he'd made, and continued sawing. He sawed it through, removed the wedge, and drove it in further down.

A monkey was sitting up in a tree watching him. When the man lay down to sleep, the monkey sat astride the tree and wanted see if he could do the same thing; but when he removed the wedge, the tree shrank back and caught his tail. He began to struggle and yell. The man woke up, gave the monkey a good beating, and tied him up with a rope.

The Boy's Story of How They Didn't
Take Him into Town

My father was about to go into town and I said to him: "Papa, take me with you."

But he said, "You'll freeze to death; why go?"

I turned away, started crying, and went into the storeroom. I cried and cried and then fell asleep. I dreamt that there was a small path leading from our village to a chapel, and I saw—Papa walking along this path. I caught up with him, and we went into town together. I was walking and saw a stove burning in front of us. I said: "Papa, is that the town?"

And he said, "Yes, it is."

Then we reached the stove, and I saw that sweet rolls were baking.

I said: "Buy me a little sweet roll."

He bought one and gave it to me. Then I awoke, stood up, put on my shoes, took my mittens, and went outside. Some boys were ice-skating and sledding. I began to sled with them and did so until I nearly froze. Just when I went inside and climbed up on the stove, I heard my papa return from town. I rejoiced and asked, "Papa, did you buy me a little sweet roll?"

He said, "I did," and he gave it to me.

I jumped down from the stove onto a bench and began dancing with joy.

The Liar (A Fable)

A boy was guarding the sheep, pretended he saw a wolf, and began shouting: "Help! A wolf! A wolf!"

The peasants came running and saw that it wasn't true.

The boy did this two or three times; then it happened that a wolf really did show up. The boy started to shout: "Come here, hurry up, there's a wolf!"

The peasants thought he was fooling them once again, and paid him no attention.

The wolf saw that there was nothing to fear; he killed the whole flock easily.

How a House Was Once Repaired in the City of Paris (A True Story)

In a large house in Paris the walls began to separate. People began to pull them back together without breaking the roof. One man devised a plan. He installed iron lugs on both sides of the walls: then he made an iron band, which was just short of being able to reach from lug to lug. Then he bent hooks at the ends, so that the hooks would go into the lugs. Then he heated the ends in a fire: the band stretched and reached from hook to hook. Then he fastened the hooks onto the lugs and left it like that. When the band began to cool, it shrank and pulled the walls back together.

The Donkey and the Horse (A Fable)

A man owned a donkey and a horse. They were walking along the road. The donkey said to the horse, "It's hard for me to pull the whole load. Take at least a little bit from me." The horse didn't listen. The donkey collapsed from exhaustion and died. Then the man took the entire load off the donkey and placed it on the horse, as well as the donkey's hide. The horse complained: "Oh, woe is me! Poor, unfortunate me! I didn't want to help the donkey even a little, and now I have to carry everything, including even his hide."

How the Boy Endured a Thunderstorm in a Forest (A True Story)

Once when I was little, they sent me into the forest to pick mushrooms. I got to the forest, picked the mushrooms, and was about to return home. Suddenly it became dark, it started raining and thundering. I was frightened and sat down under a large oak tree. Such bright lightning flashed that it hurt my eyes, and I had to shut them. Just above my head something cracked and began to thunder; then something hit me on my head. I fell down and lay there until it stopped raining. When I came to, water was dripping from all the trees, birds were singing, and the sun was shining. The large oak had toppled and there was smoke coming from the stump. All around me were scattered chips of the old oak tree. My clothing was soaked and was sticking to my body; there was a bump on my head and it was a little painful. I found my cap, picked up the mushrooms, and ran home. No one was there; I got a piece of bread and climbed onto the stove. When I awoke, I saw from the stove that the mushrooms had been cooked, placed on the table, and that people were getting ready to eat.

I cried, "Why are you eating without me?"

They replied, "Why are you sleeping? Come quickly and eat."

The Jackdaw and the Doves (A Fable)

A jackdaw saw that some doves were being fed well. So she painted herself white and flew into the dovecote. The doves thought at first that she was also a dove and let her in. But the jackdaw forgot and cried as jackdaws do. Then the doves began pecking at her and drove her away. The jackdaw flew back to her own kind, but they got frightened of her because now she was white, and the jackdaws also drove her away.

The Peasant and the Cucumbers (A Fable)

Once a peasant went to a garden to steal some cucumbers. He crept up to the cucumbers and thought: "I'll carry away a bag of cucumbers, which I'll sell; and with the money, I'll buy a hen.

"The hen will lay eggs, hatch them, and raise a lot of chicks. I'll feed the chicks and sell them; then I'll buy a young sow, and she'll bear a lot of piglets.

"I'll sell the piglets and buy a mare; the mare will give birth to some foals. I'll raise the foals, and sell them.

"I'll buy a house and start a garden. In the garden I'll sow some cucumbers. I won't let them be stolen, but will keep a sharp eye on them. I'll hire watchmen and station them in the cucumber patch; then I myself will come upon them unexpectedly, and shout: 'Hey, you, keep a watch out!'"

The peasant fell into such musing, that he forgot he was in someone's garden, and he shouted as brashly as he could. The watchmen heard him, rushed out, and gave the peasant a sound beating.

The Peasant Woman and the Hen

A hen laid one egg every day. The owner thought that if she gave the hen more feed, the hen would lay two eggs. And that's what she did. But the hen got so fat that she stopped laying altogether.

The Old Grandfather and His Little Grandson

A grandfather grew very old. His legs wouldn't carry him, his eyes couldn't see, his ears couldn't hear, and he had no teeth left. When he ate, the food would drop out of his mouth. His son and daughter-in-law stopped allowing him to sit at their table and gave him food to eat while he was sitting behind the stove. Once they brought him his food in a bowl. He wanted to move it closer, but dropped it and the bowl broke. His daughter-in-law began to scold him for breaking everything in their house, dropping their dishes, and she said she'd give him a wooden tub to eat from. The old man merely sighed and said nothing in reply.

Once the man and his wife were sitting at home and they saw that their little son was sitting on the floor and playing with some wooden blocks—he was making something. His father asked him: "What's that you're making, Misha?"

Misha replied, "I'm making a wooden tub, Papa, so that when you and Mama get old, I will feed you from it."

The husband and wife looked at each other and began crying. They felt ashamed that they had so mistreated the old man; and from that time on, they seated him at their table and started to take good care of him.

Sharing the Inheritance (A Fable)

A father had two sons. He said to them: "When I die—divide everything in half." When the father died, the two sons couldn't divide everything without a quarrel. They went to their neighbor to ask him to act as judge.

The neighbor asked them: "How did your father order you to divide everything?"

They replied: "He told us to divide everything equally."

The neighbor said, "Then tear all the clothes in two, break all the dishes in two, and cut all the livestock in half."

The brothers obeyed the neighbor and they had nothing left at all.

Where Does the Water Flow from the Sea? (Discussion)

Water flows from springs, sources, and swamps into streams; from there it flows into rivulets, then into large rivers, and finally out to the seas. From other sides more rivers flow into the seas, ever since the world was created. Where does the water go from the sea? Why doesn't it overflow onto the land?

Water from the sea rises in fog; the fog rises higher and forms clouds. The clouds are driven by the wind and are carried around the earth. From these clouds water falls on the land. From the land, the water flows into swamps and rivulets. From the rivulets it flows into rivers and from there into the sea again. The seawater rises into clouds and the clouds are carried all over the earth....

The Lion, the Bear, and the Fox (A Fable)

A lion and a bear procured some meat and began to fight over it. The bear didn't want to yield, and the lion didn't either. They struggled for so long that they were both exhausted and lay down. A fox saw the meat lying between them, grabbed it, and ran away.

The Little Boy Told How He Found Queen Bees for His Grandfather (A Story)

My grandfather spent the summer living in an apiary.[2] When I used to visit him, he would give me some honey.

Once I went to the apiary and started walking among the hives. I wasn't afraid of bees, because my grandpa taught me how to walk quietly among the rows.

And the bees grew used to me and didn't sting me. In one hive I heard someone clucking. I went to the hut where my grandfather was and told him about it.

He came with me, listened, and said, "One swarm with its old queen has already flown away from this hive; now the young queens have hatched. They're the ones shouting. Tomorrow they'll fly out with another swarm."

I asked my grandfather what sort of queens they were. He replied:

"A queen bee is just like a tsar with his people: without her there can be no hive."

I kept asking: "What do they look like?"

He said: "Come tomorrow; God willing, there will be another queen flying away. I'll show you and give you some honey."

When I came to visit my grandfather the next day, two covered hives with bees were hanging in the entrance. Grandpa told me to put on a net, and he tied a kerchief around my neck; then he took one hive covered in bees, and carried it to the apiary. Bees were buzzing in it. I was afraid of them and tucked my hands into my trousers; but I wanted to see the queen, and I followed my grandpa. In the apiary Grandpa went up to an empty water trough, adjusted the cover to it, opened the hive and shook out the bees onto the cover. The bees started crawling on the cover, and Grandpa kept moving them with a little broom.

"There's the queen!" Grandfather pointed with the broom and I saw a long bee with little wings. She crawled past the other bees and disappeared. Then Grandpa took the net off me and went into his hut. Then he gave me a large piece of honey; after eating it, my cheeks and hands were smeared with honey. When I got home, my mother said:

"Once again your grandpa spoiled you by giving you some honey."

But I said: "He gave me honey because I found the hives with young queens; today he and I housed a swarm."

---

2 A place where bees are raised.

The Fire (A True Story)

At harvesttime the peasant men and women left for work. The only people remaining in the village were either very old or very young. A grandmother and her three grandchildren were left in one hut. The grandmother lit a fire in the stove and lay down to rest. Flies were settling on her and biting her. She covered her head with a towel and fell asleep. One of her granddaughters, Masha (three years old), opened the stove, raked some coals into a broken piece of pottery, and went into the vestibule. Some sheaves were lying there. The women had prepared these sheaves for fastening.[3] Masha brought in the coals, placed them under the sheaves, and began to blow. When the straw began to catch fire, she was delighted; she went into the hut, took her little brother Kiryushka by the hand (he was a year and a half old and he had just learned how to walk), and said: "Look, Kilyuska, look at the stove I lit." The sheaves had already caught fire and were crackling. When the entrance filled with smoke, Masha got frightened and went running back into the hut. Kiryushka tripped on the threshold, fell, hurt his nose, and began crying; Masha pulled him into the hut, and they both hid under the stove-bench. Their grandmother was fast asleep and heard nothing. The elder lad, Vanya (he was eight years old), was outside. When he saw smoke pouring out of the vestibule, he ran through the door, and into the hut through the smoke, and tried to wake his grandmother; but she was half-asleep and confused, and had forgotten about the children. She jumped up and ran through the courtyards to find help. Meanwhile, Masha was sitting under the bench in the hut and keeping quiet; only the little boy was howling because he'd hurt his nose. Vanya heard his cry, looked under the bench, and shouted to Masha, "Run, or you'll burn to death!" Masha ran into the entryway, but she couldn't get to the door because of the smoke and flames. She turned and went back. Then Vanya opened the window and told her to climb out. After she did, Vanya grabbed his little brother, and pulled him. But the little fellow was heavy and resisted, and Vanya couldn't do it. He was crying and pushing Vanya away. Vanya fell twice, as he was dragging his brother to the window; the door of the hut was already on fire. Vanya pushed the little boy's head through the window, and wanted to push him out; but the little boy (he was very scared), grabbed onto the window frame and wouldn't let go. Then Vanya shouted to Masha: "Pull him by the head!" Meanwhile, he pushed from behind. Finally they managed to drag him out through the window into the street and they themselves jumped out.

---

3   Straw braids to fasten the sheaves.

The Frog and the Lion (A Fable)

A lion heard a frog croaking loudly, and got frightened. He thought that a wild beast was making such a loud noise. He waited a little while and then he saw a frog hop out of the swamp. The lion squashed it with his paw and said: "In the future I won't get frightened unless I see everything clearly."

The Elephant (A True Story)

An Indian owned an elephant. He fed him poorly and forced him to work a great deal. Once the elephant got angry and stepped on its owner. The Indian died. His wife started weeping, brought her children to the elephant, and threw them under the elephant's feet. She said: "Elephant! You killed their father, now kill them, too!" The elephant looked at the children, picked up the eldest with his trunk, slowly lifted him up, and placed him on his neck. Then the elephant began to obey this boy and work for him.

The Monkey and the Peas (A Fable)

A monkey was carrying two handfuls of peas. One pea happened to fall out of his hand: the monkey wanted to pick up that pea. While doing so, he dropped twenty more peas. As he rushed to pick them up, he dropped the rest of them. Then he got angry, scattered all the peas, and ran away.

How the Little Boy Stopped Being Afraid of Blind Beggars (A Tale)

When I was young, they used to frighten me with blind beggars, and I was afraid of them. Once I came home and two blind beggars were sitting on the porch. I didn't know what to do; I was afraid to run back and afraid to walk past them; I thought that they might snatch me. Suddenly one of them (he had eyes that were as white as snow), stood up, took me by the hand, and said:

"Young lad! How about giving me some alms?"

I tore myself away from him and ran to my mother. She sent me back out with some money and some bread.

The beggars were delighted with the bread; they crossed themselves and ate. Then the beggar with the white eyes said:

"Your bread is tasty—may God save you."

And he took me by the hand again and touched it.

I began to feel sorry for him and from then on I stopped being afraid of blind beggars.

The Milk Cow (A Fable)

A man owned a cow: every day she gave him a pitcher of milk. The man invited some guests; in order to collect more milk for his guests, the man didn't milk his cow for ten days. He thought that on the tenth day the cow would give him ten pitchers of milk.

But all the milk spoiled inside the cow and she gave less milk than before.

The Chinese Empress Silhinchi (A True Story)

The Chinese emperor Ghuayonghchi had a beloved wife whose name was Silhinchi. The emperor wanted all his people to remember his beloved empress. He gave her a silkworm to look at and said:

"Learn what to do with this worm and how to maintain it; that way the Chinese people will never forget you."

Silhinchi began watching the silkworms and noticed that when they were still, they would be covered by a web. She unwound the web, spun it into threads, and made a silk kerchief.

Then she noticed that silkworms prefer to live on mulberry trees. She began gathering mulberry leaves and feeding them to the silkworms. She bred a lot of them and taught her people to raise them.

Five thousand years have passed since that time and the Chinese people still remember and celebrate the name of the great Chinese empress Silhinchi.

The Grasshopper and the Ants (A Fable)

One autumn the ants' grain got slightly wet: they were drying it out.

A hungry grasshopper came along and asked for some food.

The ants said: "Why didn't you gather forage during the summer?"

The grasshopper replied: "There was no time: I was singing songs."

The ants began laughing and said, "If you played during the summer, then you can dance during the winter."

The Mouse Girl (A Tale)

A man was walking alongside the river and saw that a raven was carrying a mouse. He threw a stone at the bird and the raven let go of the mouse: the mouse fell into the water. The man rescued it from the water and brought it home. He didn't have any children of his own and he said, "Ah! If only this mouse would turn into a little girl!" And the mouse did turn into a little girl.

When the girl grew up, the man asked her: "Whom do you want to marry?"

The girl said: "I want to marry the man who is the strongest one in the whole world."

The man went to the sun and said: "Sun! My little girl wants to marry the strongest one in the whole world. You are stronger than anyone else: marry my little girl."

The sun said, "I am not stronger than everyone: clouds cover me."

The man went to the clouds and said: "Clouds! You are stronger than anyone: marry my little girl."

The clouds replied, "No, we're not the strongest of all; the wind chases us away."

The man went to the wind and said, "Wind! You are stronger than anyone: marry my little girl."

The wind replied, "No, I'm not stronger than anyone. The mountains block me."

The man went to the mountains and said: "Mountains! Marry my little girl; you are stronger than anyone."

The mountains replied: "The rat is stronger than us: he gnaws us."

Then the man went to the rat and said: "Rat! You are stronger than anyone; marry my little girl." The rat agreed. The man returned to the girl and said:

"The rat is stronger than anyone: he gnaws the mountains, the mountains block the wind, the wind chases away the clouds, the clouds cover the sun, and the rat wants to marry you."

But the girl said: "Ah! What am I to do? How can I marry a rat? "

Then the man said: "Ah! If only my little girl would turn back into a mouse!"

And the girl turned back into a mouse, and the mouse married the rat.

The Hen and the Golden Eggs (A Fable)

A farmer had a hen that laid golden eggs. But he wanted more gold at once, so he killed the hen (he thought there was a lot of gold inside her); but inside she was just like any other hen.

Lipunyushka (A Tale)

There once lived an old man and an old woman. They didn't have any children. The old man went to plow in the field, and the old woman stayed home to make pancakes. The old woman made some pancakes and said:

"If we had a son, he would take some pancakes to his father; but now, with whom can I send them?"

Suddenly, a little son crawled out of some cotton and said: "Hello, Mother!"

The old woman said: "Where did you come from, son, and what's your name?"

And the son replied: "Mother, you unwound the cotton and put it in a row, and that's where I hatched. My name is Lipunyushka. Mother, let me take the pancakes to father."

The old woman said: "Will you be able to take them all the way, Lipunyushka?"

"I will, Mother. . . ."

The old woman tied the pancakes in a bundle and gave them to her little son. Lipunyushka took the bundle and ran into the field.

In the field he came across a hummock on the road. So he shouted: "Father, Father, carry me over this hummock! I brought you some pancakes."

The old man heard a voice from the field: someone was calling him. He went to meet his son, carried him over the hummock, and said: "Where are you from, Son?" And the boy said: "Father, I hatched in some cotton," and he served the pancakes to his father. The old man sat down to have his breakfast, and the boy said: "Let me, Father: I will plow."

And the old man said: "You don't have the strength to plow."

But Lipunyushka took up the plow and began to work. He plowed all by himself, and as he did, he sang songs.

A gentleman was driving past that field and saw the old man sitting there, having his breakfast, and his horse was plowing all alone. The master got out of his carriage and said to the old man: "How can it be, old man, that your horse is plowing alone?"

And the old man answered: "I have a boy plowing out there, and he's one also singing songs." The master came closer, heard the songs, and saw Lipunyushka.

And so the master said: "Old man! Sell me that boy."

And the old man said: "No, I can't sell him, That's the only one I have."

And Lipunyushka said to the old man: "Sell me, Father, and then I will run away from him."

And so the man sold the boy for one hundred rubles. The master handed over the money, took the boy, wrapped him in a handkerchief, and put him in his pocket. The master came home and said to his wife: "I brought you joy." And the wife said: "Show me what it is." The master took out his handkerchief from his pocket, unwrapped it, but there was nothing in it. Lipunyushka had run back to his father a long time ago.

The Wolf and the Old Woman (A Fable)

A hungry wolf was searching for prey. At the edge of the village he heard a little boy crying in a hut, and an old woman was saying:

"If you don't stop crying, I'll give you away to the wolf."

The wolf didn't go any further and began to wait to be given the little boy. Night fell—he was still waiting and then he heard the old woman warning the little boy again:

"Don't cry, child; I won't give you away to the wolf. If the wolf comes, we'll kill him."

The wolf thought: "Obviously here they're saying one thing, but doing another," and he left the village.

The Kitten (A True Story)

Once upon a time there was a brother and a sister—Vasya and Katya. And they had a cat. That spring the cat disappeared. The children looked for her everywhere, but couldn't find her. Once they were playing near the barn and heard something meowing in a faint voice above their heads. Vasya climbed up the ladder under the barn roof.

Katya waited below and kept asking? "Did you find it? Did you?"

But Vasya didn't answer her. Finally Vasya shouted, "I found her! Our cat. . . . And she has kittens; they're amazing; come up right now to see them."

Katya ran home, got some milk, and brought it back for the cat.

There were five little kittens. When they had grown a bit and were beginning to climb out of the corner where they were born, the children chose one of them, a gray one with white paws, and brought him home. Their mother gave away all the other kittens, and left that one for her children. They fed him, played with him, and even took him to bed to sleep with them.

One time the children went to play on the road and took the kitten along.

The wind was blowing straw across the road and the kitten was playing in it; the children were thrilled. Then they found some sorrel next to the road, went off to gather some, and forgot all about the kitten. Suddenly they heard someone shouting loudly, "Back, get back!" and they saw a hunter riding on a horse; ahead of him ran two dogs, which had seen the kitten and were about to grab him. The foolish kitten, instead of running away, sat down on the ground, arched his back, and stared at the dogs. Katya got scared of the dogs and screamed. She ran away from them. But Vasya ran as fast as he could towards the kitten; he got to him at the same time the dogs reached him. The dogs wanted to grab the kitten, but Vasya fell on the ground and covered the kitten with his body, shielding him from the dogs.

The hunter galloped up and drove off the dogs; then Vasya brought the kitten home and no longer took him out to the field to play.

The Learned Son (A Fable)

A son came home from town to see his father in the country. His father said: "Today we'll cut the hay; take a rake (*grabli*) and let's go together; you'll help me."

But the son didn't feel like working and said: "I've studied a great deal, and have forgotten all the peasant words; what is a rake (*grabli*)?"

As soon as he started crossing the courtyard, he stepped on a rake; it smacked him on the forehead. Then he remembered what a rake (*grabli*) was. He grabbed his forehead and said: "What fool left a rake (*grabli*) out here?"

How the Bukharans Learned to Raise Silkworms[4] (A True Story)

The Chinese alone knew how to raise silkworms and they didn't reveal this art to anyone, and sold their silks for a very high price.

The Bukharan tsar heard about this and he wanted to procure silkworms and learn this business. He asked the Chinese to give him some seeds, worms, and trees. They refused. Then the Bukharan tsar wanted to arrange a match with the

---

4 Bukharans were the residents of territory in Central Asia, now part of Uzbekistan and Tadjikstan.

daughter of the Chinese emperor, and ordered that his bride be told that he had everything in abundance in his kingdom, with the exception of one thing: silk brocades. So she should bring him some seeds of a mulberry tree secretly and some worms, because otherwise she would have nothing beautiful to wear.

The tsar's daughter gathered some seeds, worms, and trees, and placed them in her headdress.

When they began to examine her belongings at the border, in order to see if she was perhaps carrying something that was forbidden to take out of the country, no one dared to unwrap her headdress.

And the Bukharans sowed mulberry trees and grew silkworms, and the tsarevna taught them how to raise them.

The Peasant and the Horse (A Fable)

A peasant went into town in search of oats for his horse. Just after he left his village, his horse began to turn back toward home. The man struck his horse with his whip. The horse continued on its way and thought about the peasant: "Where is he, the fool, taking me? It would be better to go home."

They hadn't quite reached the town when the peasant saw that his horse was having a hard time because of the mud; he turned onto the cobblestone road, but the horse refused to go and turned away from it. The peasant hit it with his whip and yanked his horse: the horse began walking along the road and thought: "Why has he turned me onto this cobblestone road; I'll only damage my hooves. It's too hard under them."

The peasant reached the shop, bought some oats, and took off for home. When he got home, he gave his horse some oats. The horse started eating and thought: "People are so stupid! They love to show off their intelligence to us, but they're less intelligent than we are. What was he fussing about? He drove somewhere and made me go. No matter how much we traveled, we returned home. It would have been better if we'd stayed at home from to begin with; he would have sat on the stove-bench and I would have eaten some oats."

Auntie Told the Grandmother How the Robber Yemelka Pugachev Gave Her a Ten-Kopeck Piece (A True Story)

I was about eight years old and we were living in our little village in the province of Kazan. I remember how my father and mother began to worry and kept mentioning Pugachev.[5] Later I learned that it was then Pugachev-the-Robber had appeared. He called himself Tsar Peter III, gathered many robbers, hanged all the gentry, and liberated the peasants and all the serfs. They said that with his band of robbers, he was getting very close to where we lived. My father wanted to leave for Kazan, but was afraid to take us children along because the weather was cold and the roads were in bad condition. All this occurred in November and it was dangerous to travel. So my father planned to travel to Kazan alone, with only my mother; he planned to take some Cossacks from there and to return for his children.

They left and we remained behind with our nurse Anna Trofimovna. We all lived downstairs in one room. I recall that one evening we were sitting alone; our nanny was rocking my sister and walking around the room: my sister had a tummy ache, and I was playing with a doll. Parasha, our maid, and the sexton's wife were sitting at the table, drinking tea, and chatting—all about Pugachev. I was dressing the doll, and listening to everything, especially the horrors that the sexton's wife was relating.

"I remember," she said, "how Pugachev arrived at our neighbors' house some forty versts away and how he hanged the master on the gate and killed all his children."

"How did the villains kill them?" asked Parasha.

"Just so, my dear. Ignatych used to say, 'They would take them by the feet and smack them against the corner.'"

"Oh, stop telling these horror stories in front of the child!" said the nanny. "Go to bed, Katenka, it's already time."

I was about to go to bed, when suddenly we heard knocking at the gates, dogs barking, and voices shouting.

The sexton's wife and Parasha went to look and came running right back. "It's him, it's him!"

Nanny forgot that my sister had a tummy ache, tossed her onto her little bed, ran to the trunk, and fetched a shirt and a little peasant dress. She took everything off me, including my shoes, and dressed me in peasant clothes. She covered my head with a kerchief, and said:

"Listen: if they ask you, say that you're my granddaughter."

They had barely finished dressing me, when we heard the sound of boots stamping above. We could tell that many people had arrived. The sexton's wife came down to see us and Mikhailo-the-lackey.

---

5 Yemelyan Pugachev (1726–1775) was a Cossack, pretender to the Russian throne, and the leader of an unsuccessful peasant rebellion against Catherine II (1773–1775).

"He's here: he's come himself! He's ordered to slaughter some sheep. He's asking for wine and liqueur."

Anna Trofimovna said: "Give him everything he wants. Make sure you don't say that these are nobles' children. Say that the gentry have left. And as for her, say that she's my granddaughter."

We didn't sleep that whole night. Drunken Cossacks kept dropping in on us.

But Anna Trofimovna wasn't afraid of them. As soon as one of them came to us, she asked, "What do you need, my dear? We have nothing for you. There are only young children here, and I'm old."

And the Cossacks left her alone.

I fell asleep toward morning; when I awoke, I saw that in our room, there stood a Cossack in a green velvet coat, and Anna Trofimovna was bowing down low to him.

He was pointing to my sister and asking, "Who does she belong to?"

Anna Trofimovna replied: "She's my granddaughter, my daughter's child. My daughter departed with the gentry and left her here with me."

"And what about this girl?" He pointed at me.

"She's also my granddaughter, your majesty."

He gestured to me with his finger.

"Come over here, you clever girl." I got frightened.

Anna Trofimovna said: "Don't be afraid." I walked up to him.

He pinched my cheek and said, "What fair skin you have; you'll be a beauty." He took a handful of silver coins out of his pocket, picked out a ten-kopeck piece, and gave it to me.

"This is for you: remember your tsar," and he left.

They stayed as guests in our house for two days; they ate and drank everything, broke things, but didn't burn the house down, and then they left.

When my mother and father returned, they didn't know how to thank Anna Trofimovna; they offered her freedom from serfdom, but she didn't accept it, and lived with us until she was very old and died at our place. They jokingly called me Pugachev's bride. And as for the ten-kopeck piece that Pugachev gave me, I've kept it all this time: and when I look at it, I remember my childhood years and Anna Trofimovna's kindness.

The Vizier Abdul (A Fairy Tale)

The Persian tsar had an upright vizier named Abdul. Once he traveled through the town to see the tsar. The townspeople were planning to stage a revolt. As soon as they saw the vizier, they surrounded him, stopped his horse, and began threatening to kill him, if he didn't do what they wanted. One man was so bold that he grabbed hold of the vizier's beard and tugged it.

After they released the vizier, he made his way to the tsar and asked him to help the people and not to punish them for mistreating him.

The next morning a shopkeeper came to see the vizier. The vizier asked him what he wanted. The shopkeeper replied: "I came to disclose to you the name of the man who offended you yesterday. I know him—he's my neighbor and his name is Nagim; send for him and punish him."

The vizier let the shopkeeper go and sent for Nagim. Nagim guessed who'd betrayed him and went to see the vizier, and fell at his feet.

The vizier helped him up and said: "I didn't summon you to punish you; I did it only to tell you that you have a neighbor who is a very bad man. He betrayed you; keep an eye on him. Now, Godspeed."

How the Thief Betrayed Himself (A True Story)

One night a thief climbed into a merchant's attic. He picked out some fur coats and linens and wanted to escape with them, but he tripped over a fishing net, and made some noise. The merchant heard something above his head, woke his worker, took a candle, and together they made their way to the attic. The workman had woken up and said to the merchant, "Why look? There's nothing to see: there's no one here. Maybe it was the cat."

But the merchant went up to the attic anyway. As soon as the thief heard someone coming, he put the fur coats and linens back where they were before, and began to look for a place to hide. He saw a large pile of something. It was a pile of tobacco leaves. The thief dug into the tobacco, climbed into the middle of the bundle, and covered himself up. Then the thief heard two people entering the attic talking.

The merchant said: "I heard something heavy making a noise."

And the worker replied: "What could be making a noise: it was either the cat or a house spirit."

The merchant walked past the bundle of tobacco, didn't notice a thing, and said: "It must only have seemed so. There's no one here. Let's go."

The thief heard them leaving and thought: "Now I'll gather everything again and climb out the window." But it was then that the thief suddenly felt something was tickling his nose and he felt like sneezing. He covered his mouth with his hand, but it tickled even more: he couldn't keep from sneezing. The merchant and worker were already on their way out of the attic. They heard: someone in the corner sneezing. "Ah-choo, ah-choo, ah-choo!"

They turned around and caught the thief in the act.

The Burden (A Fable)

Two men were walking together along a road and each was carrying a burden. One man was carrying it without stopping along the way; the other man would stop, put down his burden, and sit down to rest for a little while. But each time that man had to lift the burden again and then load it onto his shoulders. The one who kept putting his burden down grew more exhausted than the one who was carrying his burden without stopping.

The Pit (A True Story)

One day a mother bought some plums to give to her children after dinner. The plums were lying on a plate. Vanya had never tasted plums and he kept smelling them. He decided that he would like the fruit. He really wanted to taste one. He kept walking around the plate of plums. As soon as no one else was in the room, he couldn't resist; he grabbed a big plum and ate it quickly. Before dinner, his mother counted the plums and saw that one was missing. She told her husband.

During dinner, the father asked: "Well, children, has any of you eaten a plum?" Each child answered in turn, "No." Vanya turned red like a lobster and also said, "No, I didn't eat it."

Then the father said, "One of you ate the plum and that's a bad thing; but that's not the worst. You see, plums have pits, and if you don't know how to eat a plum and swallow the pit, you will die the next day. That's what I'm afraid of."

Vanya turned pale and said: "I threw the pit out the window." Everyone started laughing and Vanya burst into tears.

Two Merchants (A Fable)

A poor merchant was setting off on a trip and took all his ironware to a wealthy merchant to watch over. When he returned home from his trip, he went to the rich merchant and asked for the return of his ironware.

The wealthy merchant had sold all of it; to excuse himself somehow, he said: "An accident occurred with your ironware."

"What happened?"

"I placed it in the grain barn. There are a lot of mice there. They gnawed through all the ironware. I myself saw how they were chewing on it. If you don't believe me—go take a look."

The poor merchant didn't try to argue. He said: "Well, what's there to see? I believe you. I know that mice always gnaw on iron. Farewell." And the poor merchant left.

On the street he saw a young boy playing—the son of the wealthy merchant. The poor merchant stroked the lad's head, picked him up, and took him home with him.

The next day the wealthy merchant met the poor merchant and shared his grief: his son had disappeared. He asked: "Have you seen him or heard from him?"

The poor merchant replied: "Yes, indeed. I saw him. Just as I was leaving your place yesterday, I saw: a hawk flew down to your son and carried him off."

The wealthy merchant got angry and said:

"Aren't you ashamed to make fun of me? Can it really be that a hawk could carry away a little boy?"

"No, I'm not laughing at you. What's so surprising that a hawk can carry away a little boy, when mice can devour a hundred poods of ironware.[6] Anything can happen."

Then the wealthy merchant understood and said: "Mice didn't devour your ironware; I sold it and will pay you twice what I got for it."

"If that's the case, then I can tell you that a hawk didn't carry off your son, and I'll give him back to you."

The Dog of San Gotthard (Description)

Two countries share a border: Switzerland and Italy. Between them stand the Alps. These mountains are so high that the snow never melts on them. On the road from Switzerland to Italy, it's necessary to cross these mountains. The road passes through the town of San Gotthard. On the very top of this mountain, along the road, stands a monastery where monks reside. These monks pray to

---

6   A Russian measure of weight, approximately thirty-six pounds.

God and welcome travelers stopping for a rest or a night's lodging. It's always overcast on San Gotthard: in summer there's fog and nothing can be seen. And in winter there are snowstorms that pile up to five arshins of snow.[7] Both those riding and walking often freeze in these snowstorms. The monks have dogs, which are trained to search for people in the snow.

Once a woman and her little baby were traveling along the road to Switzerland. A snowstorm blew in and the woman lost her way, sat down in the snow, and froze to death. The monks went out with their dogs and found the woman with her baby. They revived and reared the child. The woman was already dead, so they brought to the monastery and buried her in the cemetery.

The Peasant's Story of Why He Loves His Older Brother

I love my brother very much anyway, but most of all because he went into the army and became a soldier instead of me. This is how it happened: we began to cast lots. It fell to me: I had to enlist and become a soldier, and it was only one week after I'd married. I didn't want to leave my young wife.

My mother started to weep and said: "How can Petrushka go? He's so young."

There was nothing to be done; they started to get me ready. My wife sewed me some shirts, collected some money for me, and the next day I was to report to the headquarters in town. My mother was grieving—she wept, and I thought that I would have to go; my heart pounded, as though I were going to my death.

We gathered towards evening to have supper. No one felt very much like eating. My elder brother, Nikolai, lay on the stove-bench and kept silent. My young bride was wailing. My father sat there in anger. When my mother placed the kasha[8] on the table, no one moved. My mother began to call Nikolai to come down from the stove to have his supper. He got down, crossed himself, sat at the table and said: "Don't grieve, Mother, I'll go become a soldier instead of Petrushka; I'm older than he is. Maybe I won't be killed. I'll serve my term and then return home.[9] And you, Pyotr, take care of Father and Mother and don't treat my wife badly." I was pleased and my mother also stopped grieving; they began to prepare Nikolai to leave.

The next morning when I awoke and started thinking that my brother would go instead of me, I began to feel ill. "Don't go, Nikolai, it's my turn. I'll go." But

---

7 Russian measure of distance, a little less than a yard.
8 Cooked grain or groats.
9 A recruit served a term of twenty-five years.

he kept silent and made his preparations to leave. And so did I. We both went into town to the headquarters. He got in line and so did I. We were both good lads: we stood there and waited to see if they would reject us. My elder brother looked at me—smiled and said, "Enough, Pyotr; go home. Don't suffer for me. I'm going willingly." I started crying and went home. And now whenever I remember my brother, it seems I would give my life for him.

How I Killed a Rabbit for the First Time (A Landowner's Story)

I had an uncle named Ivan Andryeich. When I was thirteen years old he taught me how to fire a gun. He got a small rifle and let me fire it when we went for walks. And once I killed a jackdaw and another time I shot a magpie. But my father wasn't aware that I knew how to shoot. Once, in autumn, on my mother's name day, we were expecting my uncle to come to dinner, I sat by the window and looked in the direction he would come from, while my father was pacing around the room. Then I saw four gray horses and a carriage come from behind the grove; I shouted, "He's coming, he's coming!"

My father looked out the window and saw the carriage, took his cap, and went out onto the porch to meet him. I went running after him. My father greeted my uncle and said: "Climb out." But my uncle said: "No. Get your rifle and come with me. Over there, just beyond the grove, a gray hare is lying in the grasses. Take your rifle; let's go and get him." Father ordered that his fur coat and his rifle be brought to him; I ran upstairs to my own room to grab my fur hat and to bring my own rifle. When my father got in the carriage with my uncle, I hid on the rear footboard with my rifle, so no one would see me.

Right after we emerged from the grove, my uncle told the driver to stop; he stood up and said: "Look over there, at the gray spot at the boundary line. To the right there are some tall weeds, and to the left, about five paces away—do you see?" My father looked for a long time, but he didn't see anything. And from where I sat down below, there was nothing visible. Finally, my father saw it, and he and my uncle set off into the field. My father carried his loaded gun, and my uncle showed him where to look. I walked behind them with my rifle, but still couldn't see anything. Still I was glad they hadn't noticed me. We walked about 100 paces. My father paused, wanted to take aim, but my uncle stopped him. "No, it's still too far; wait, we'll get closer. He'll let us approach." Father obeyed, but as soon as they'd gone a little further, the hare jumped up; it was then that I saw him. He was large, almost white, only his back was silvery. He jumped, lifted one ear, and easily started hopping away from us. Father aimed—bang! The hare went running. Father fired from the other barrel. The hare continued running. I forgot all about my father and everything else. I aimed and fired—bang! I looked and couldn't believe my own eyes—the hare had turned over on its back, lay there, kicking one hind leg. My father and my uncle looked behind them. "Where did you come from? Well, what a lad!" From then on they gave me a gun and allowed me to hunt.

Tom Thumb (A Tale)

A poor man had seven children, each one smaller than the last. The smallest was so small that when he was born, he was no bigger than a thumb. Then he grew a little, but still he was just a little bit bigger than a thumb: as a result, people called him Tom Thumb. But, though he was small, he was very nimble and cunning.

His father and mother became poorer and poorer; they wound up so poor, that they had nothing to feed their children. They thought and thought and decided to take their children into the forest and leave them there, so they wouldn't be able to return home. When the father and mother were talking about this plan, Tom Thumb was awake and heard it all. The next morning Tom Thumb woke up before anyone else, ran to the river, and filled his pockets with white pebbles. When his father and mother led their children into the forest, Tom Thumb came last and kept taking white pebbles out of his pocket and dropping them along the road.

After the father and mother had led the children deep into the forest, they ducked behind a tree, and then ran away. The children began calling them; when they saw that no one was coming, they began to cry.

The only one who didn't cry was Tom Thumb. He said in his own thin voice, "Stop your crying; I'll lead you out of the forest." But his brothers were crying so loud that they didn't hear him. When they did hear him, he told them that he had dropped white pebbles along the way and would lead them out; they rejoiced and followed him. Tom Thumb proceeded from pebble to pebble and thus led them back home.

It so happened that on that same day that their mother and father had led the children into the forest, the father had received some money. The father and mother said: "Why did we take our children into the forest? They'll perish there. Now we have some money and can feed our children." Mother started to cry and said, "Ah, if only we had our children with us!" Tom Thumb heard her from outside the window and said, "Here they are!"

Mother was delighted, ran out to the porch, and then all the children, one after another, entered the house.

Now they could buy everything they needed and begin to live as before. They could live well, until the money ran out.

But the money ran out again, and the father and mother began to discuss what to do, and once again decided to lead their children into the forest and leave them there.

Tom Thumb heard their scheme, and as soon as it was morning, he planned to go back to the river secretly to collect more white pebbles. Just as he reached the door and tried to open it, he found that it was bolted shut; he wanted to move it, but no matter how much he tried, he couldn't reach the bolt.

It was impossible for him to gather pebbles, so he took some bread, put it into his pocket, and thought: "As they are leading us into the forest, I'll drop crumbs of the bread along the way and I'll lead my brothers out by following them."

Once again their father and mother led the children into the forest and left them there; again Tom Thumb dropped bread crumbs along the way.

When his older brothers began to cry, Tom Thumb once again promised to get them out of there. But this time he couldn't find the path, because birds had eaten all of the breadcrumbs.

The children walked and walked all around the forest, but didn't find the road. When night fell, they cried and cried, and then they all fell asleep. Tom Thumb woke up before the others, climbed up a tree to have a look around, and spied a little hut. He climbed down, woke his brothers, and led them to the hut.

They knocked and an old woman came out onto the porch and asked what they wanted. They said they'd lost their way in the forest. Then the old woman let them into her house and said: "I feel sorry for you that you came to our house. My husband is an ogre and eats children. If he sees you, he'll eat you. But I feel sorry for you. Hide here under the bed, and I will let you go tomorrow."

The children got frightened and crawled under the bed. Suddenly they heard someone knock at the door and come into the room. Tom Thumb peeked out from under the bed and he saw—a terrible ogre was sitting at the table and shouting to the old woman: "Give me wine." She served him wine, he drank it up, and began sniffing the air. "Why do I sense a human smell in here? Are you hiding someone?" The old woman began to say that no one was there, but the ogre started sniffing more and more and followed the scent to the bed. He began to grope with his arms under the bed, grabbed hold of Tom Thumb's leg, and shouted: "Aha! Here they are!" And he pulled them all out and began to rejoice. He picked up his knife and wanted to slice them all up, but his wife dissuaded him. She said: "You see, how skinny and weak they are. Let us feed them a bit. They'll be fresher and tastier." The ogre obeyed; he ordered her to feed them, and put them to sleep with his young girls.

The ogre had seven young girls who were just as small as the boy's brothers. The girls were all lying and sleeping together in one bed, and each one had a little golden cap on her head. Tom Thumb noticed this and when the ogre and his wife left, he carefully took the caps off the ogres' daughters' heads, and placed them on his own head and those of his brothers. Then he put his own cap and his brothers' caps on the young girls.

The ogre drank wine all night. After he'd drunk a great deal, he felt like eating again. He stood up and went into the main room, where Tom Thumb and his brothers were sleeping, as well as the seven girls. He went up to the boys, felt the golden caps on them, and he said: "In my state of drunkenness, I almost sliced up my daughters." He left the boys alone and went to his daughters, felt their soft caps, and sliced them up, and soon fell asleep.

Then Tom Thumb roused his brothers, opened the door, and escaped into the forest with them.

The children walked all night and all the next day, but still couldn't find their way out of the forest.

The ogre, when he woke up in the morning and saw that he had sliced up his own children instead of the others, put on his magic boots, and ran into the forest to seek out the children.

The ogre kept looking for the children. He didn't find them. He sat down to rest near the place where they were and he fell fast asleep.

The magic boots were such that whoever was wearing them, could take steps, each of which would cover seven versts.

Tom Thumb saw that the ogre was asleep; he snuck up to him, took a handful of gold out of his pocket, and distributed it to his brothers. Then he carefully took off the ogre's boots. After he did so, he put the magic boots on his own feet, told his brothers to hold on tight to each other and to him. He ran so quickly that he immediately emerged from the forest and found their own house.

When they got home, they gave the gold to their father and mother. The parents became rich and didn't try to get rid of the children any more.

The Fool (A Tale in Verse)

A fool decided
To travel to Russia,
To see the people,
To show himself.
The fool saw
Two empty huts;
He looked in the cellar:
In the cellar were devils
With pointy heads,
Eyes like spoons,
Mustaches like a pitchfork,
Arms like rakes,
They play cards,
Throw dice,
Count money.
The fool said to them:
"God help you,
Good people."
Devils don't know how to love—
They grabbed the fool,
Began to beat him,
And trample him,
Scarcely alive
They let the fool go.
The fool arrived
Home, weeping,
Howling loudly,
And his mother abused him,
His wife blamed him,
His sister, too:
"A fool, you're a fool,
You're a stupid Babin,
You shouldn't have talked that way
You should have said:
"May you be damned, enemy,
In the Lord's name!"
The devils would have left,

And you would have ended up with the money
Instead of their money to you
In place of a hidden treasure."
"Fine, woman,
You old woman,
Mother Lukeriya,
Sister Chernava,
In future, I, the fool,
Won't be like that."
A fool decided
To travel in Russia,
To see people,
To show himself.
The fool saw
Four brothers
Milling barley.
He said to the brothers:
"May you be damned, enemy,
In the Lord's name!"
As the four brothers
Grabbed the fool
They began to beat him,
And trample him,
Scarcely alive
They let the fool go.
The fool came
Home, weeping,
Howling loudly,
And his mother scolded him,
His wife blamed him,
His sister, too:
"You're a fool, a fool,
You're a stupid Babin,
You should have said the same
In a different way;
You should have said:
"God help you
May you mill a hundred pounds every day
So you couldn't even carry it!"

"Fine, woman,
You old woman,
Mother Lukeriya,
Sister Chernava,
In future, I won't
Be such a fool."
A fool decided
To travel in Russia,
To see people,
To show himself.
The fool saw
Seven brothers
Burying their mother;
They're all crying,
Wailing loudly.
So he said to them:
God help you,
Seven brothers,
To bury your mother,
May you bury a hundred of them a day,
So you won't even be able to carry them.
The seven brothers
Grabbed the fool,
And began to beat him
And shoving him around,
And rolling him in the mud,
Scarcely alive,
They let the fool go.
The fool is walking
Home, weeping,
Howling loudly,
And his mother scolded him,
His wife blamed him,
His sister, too:
"Fool, you're such a fool,
You should have said the same words
In a different way.
You should have said:
"I wish you a holy eve and incense,

Bestow, oh, Lord God,
The Heavenly kingdom,
Radiant paradise on her."
They would have fed you
There, you fool,
With *kutya* and pancakes."[10]
"Fine, woman,
You old woman,
Mother Lukeriya,
From now on, I won't
Be such a fool."
The fool took off
To travel in Russia,
To see people,
To show himself.
He met a wedding procession—
He said to them:
"The eve and incense,
Bestow, oh, Lord God,
The Heavenly kingdom on them
Radiant paradise on them all."
The groomsmen jumped up,
They grabbed the fool,
Began to beat him,
And trample him,
Struck him on the face.
He left weeping,
He was walking home, wailing.
And his mother scolded him,
His wife blamed him,
His sister, too:
"Fool, you're a fool,
You're a stupid Babin,
You could have said the same
In a different way.
You should have said:

---

10 Boiled rice with raisins and honey (eaten at funeral repast).

May God grant that you,
Prince and princess,
Accept the law,
Live with love,
Bear children."
"From now on,
I won't be such a fool."
A fool decided
To travel in Russia,
To see people,
To show himself.
The fool continued on
And met an old man.
He said to him:
"May God let you,
Follow the law, old man
Live in love,
And bear children."
The old man suddenly grabbed the fool
By his collar,
Began to beat him,
And pummel him,
Hit him with the crutch and broke it.
The fool went home wailing.
And his mother scolded him,
His wife blamed him,
His sister, too:
"You're such a fool,
You're a stupid Babin,
You should have said the same thing
In a different way.
You should have said:
"Bless me,
Holy Father."
"Fine, woman,
You're a fine old woman,
Mother Lukeriya,
From now on, I won't
Be such a fool."

A fool decided
To travel to Russia,
To walk in the forest.
The fool saw
A bear in the woods—
The bear was tearing a cow to pieces
Behind a spruce tree.
He said to him:
"Bless me,
Holy Father."
The bear rushed
At the fool, grabbed him,
Began to mangle him,
Began to hit him,
He left the fool
Barely alive.
The fool came
Home, weeping,
Wailing,
Telling his mother.
And his mother scolded him,
His wife blamed him,
His sister, too:
"You're a fool, a fool,
A stupid Babin;
You should have said the same words
In a different way:
You should have called,
Should have hooted,
Should have cried."
"Fine, woman,
You old woman,
Mother Lukeriya,
Sister Chernava,
From now on, I won't
Be such a fool."
A fool decided
To travel in Russia,
To see people,
To show himself.

He was walking through the wide field—
The fool met a colonel.
The fool called,
And he hooted.
The colonel told
His soldiers,
They grabbed the fool,
Began to beat him,
And they beat him
To death.

Svyatogor-the-Bogatyr (A Tale in Verse)[11]

Svyatogor set out across the broad meadow,
He didn't find anyone there,
With whom he could match his valiant strength.
He felt great strength in himself,
Which was life coursing through his veins.
He felt the weight of his strength, as if a burden.
And Svyatogor-the-radiant said boasting:
"With my own valiant strength,
If I could find a power, I would lift the whole world."
The moment he said those words, Svyatogor caught sight of a traveler—
From a distance in the steppe the traveler was carrying a bag—
And Svyatogor rode toward the traveler.
He was galloping, but the traveler kept walking ahead of him,
At full speed he was unable to catch up to the traveler,
Svyatogor started shouting in a loud voice:
"Hey, you traveler, wait a little.
I can't catch up to you on my fine steed."
From a distance the traveler heard Svyatogor,
He stopped and threw down his bag from his shoulder.
Svyatogor rode up to this bag,
He poked around the bag with his stick—
But the bag wasn't moving as though it was rooted in the ground,

---

11 Svyatogor is a mythical bogatyr (knight/hero) in ancient bylinas of Kievan Rus'. His name
derives from the words for "sacred mountain."

From his steed, Svyatogor kept touching the bag with his fingers—
The bag didn't stir, didn't move.
From his steed, Svyatogor kept grabbing it with his hand and pulling it,
But the bag didn't rise up as though it was growing from the ground,
Then Svyatogor got off his steed, he grabbed the bag,
He adjusted himself and grabbed it with both his hands,
He strained with all of his valiant strength—
Due to straining so much, his pale face turned red with blood,
But he lifted the bag from the ground just a tiny, little bit,
While he himself got stuck in the soil up to his knees
At this point Svyatogor spoke up in a loud voice:
"Tell me the whole truth, oh, passerby,
What's hidden in your bag?"
To these words the traveler said this to him:
"The burden in the bag is from the damp mother earth."
And Svyatogor said back to the traveler:
"And who are you, yourself, what's your name?"
And to that the traveler answered him with these words:
"I'm Mikula; a peasant, Selyaninovich,
I'm Mikula—the damp mother earth loves me."

THE SECOND RUSSIAN BOOK FOR READING

The Little Girl and the Mushrooms (A True Story)

Two little girls were walking home with the mushrooms they had gathered.

They had to cross some railroad tracks.

They thought the train was still far away; they climbed onto the embankment and walked along the rails.

All of a sudden they heard the sound of a train. The elder girl ran back, while the younger girl ran across the tracks.

The elder girl called to her sister, "Don't go back."

But the train was so close and so loud that the younger girl didn't hear her; she thought she was being told to run back. She ran back across the rails, tripped, dropped her mushrooms, and then began picking them up.

The train was already quite close and the driver blew his whistle as loud as he could.

The elder girl shouted: "Leave the mushrooms!" The younger girl thought that she was being told to pick up the mushrooms and crawled along on the tracks.

The driver was unable to stop the train. It whistled as loud as it could, and ran over the little girl.

The elder girl yelled and wept. All the passengers looked out of the train windows; the conductor ran to the end of the train to see what had become of the little girl.

After the train passed by, everyone saw that the girl was lying between the rails with her head down and that she was not moving.

A little while later, after the train had already moved off into the distance, the little girl lifted her head, jumped up onto her knees, picked up the rest of the mushrooms, and ran to join her sister.

The Donkey Wearing a Lion Skin (A Fable)

A donkey put on a lion skin, and everyone thought he was a lion. People and animals ran away from him. A wind came up and made the skin fly open, and the donkey became visible. People came running: they gave the donkey a good beating.

What Sort of Dew Can Be Found on Grass (Description)

When you walk into the forest on a sunny summer morning, "diamonds" can be seen lying in the fields and on the grass. These diamonds twinkle and change color in the bright sunlight—yellow, red, and blue. When you get closer and see what they really are, you can see that it's drops of dew which have collected on the triangular blades of grass and are sparkling in the sun.

The leaves of this grass inside are fuzzy and fluffy, like velvet. The dew rolls down the leaf, but doesn't soak it.

When you carelessly tear off a leaf with a drop of dew, a drop runs down, like a bright ball, you won't see how it slips past the stem. If you tear off such a little cup, carefully raise it to your mouth and drink the dewdrop—it seems to be the tastiest of all beverages.

The Hen and the Swallow (A Fable)

A hen found some snake eggs and began to sit on them to make them hatch. The swallow saw her and said:

"Look, how stupid you are! You'll hatch them, and when they grow, you'll be the first one they hurt."

The Indian and the Englishman (A True Story)

During a war, the Indians captured a young Englishman, took him prisoner, tied him to a tree, and planned to kill him.

An old Indian came up to them and said: "Don't kill him; give him to me."

They gave the prisoner to him.

The old Indian untied the Englishman, took him into his cabin, fed him, and provided a night's lodging.

The next morning the Indian ordered the Englishman to follow him. They walked a long time; when they approached the English camp, the Indian said:

"Your men killed my son; I saved your life; go back to your people and continue killing us."

The Englishman was surprised and said: "Why are you making fun of me? I know that our men killed your son: hurry up and kill me sooner."

Then the Indian said: "When they were about to kill you, I remembered my son, and I felt sorry for you. I'm not making fun of you: go back to your own men and keep killing us, if you wish." And the Indian released the Englishman.

The Reindeer and His Young Calf (A Fable)

Once a calf said to the reindeer:

"Father, you're larger and faster than any dogs; in addition, you have huge horns for defense; why are you so afraid of dogs?"

The reindeer started laughing and said:

"That's true, my child. The one misfortune is this: as soon as I hear dogs barking, I have no time to think: I just start running."

The Waistcoat (A True Story)

A peasant engaged in trade and got so rich that he became a very wealthy man. Hundreds of men worked for him, and he didn't even know them all by name.

Once the merchant lost twenty thousand rubles. The senior salesmen began searching and discovered the one who stole the money.

A senior salesman came to the merchant and said: "I've identified the robber. He should be sent to Siberia."

The merchant said: "Who stole the money?"

The senior salesman replied: "Ivan Petrov; he's confessed to it himself."

The merchant thought for a while and said: "We must forgive Ivan Petrov."

The salesman was surprised and said: "Why forgive him? That way all the other salesmen will do the same thing: they will pinch all of your goods."

The merchant said: "We must forgive Ivan Petrov: when I started trading, he and I were comrades. When I was getting married, I had nothing to wear for the wedding, and he gave me his own waistcoat to wear. "We must forgive Ivan Petrov."

So they forgave him.

The Fox and the Grapes (A Fable)

A fox saw a bunch of grapes hanging high on the vine, and began thinking about how to get them.

It tried and tried, but couldn't reach them. To soothe its irritation, it said: "They're probably not ripe."

Good Luck (A True Story)

Some people arrived at an island where there was a large number of precious stones. The people tried to find more stones: they ate little, slept little, and worked all the time. Only one of them did nothing: he sat in the same place, eating, drinking, and sleeping. When they were getting ready to leave for home, they woke this man up, and asked him: "What will you take home?" He picked up a handful of dirt from under his feet and put it into his bag.

When they all arrived back home, this man took his handful of dirt out of his bag, and in it he found a stone more valuable than all the others combined.

The Maids and the Rooster (A Fable)

A mistress used to wake the maids at night, and as soon as the roosters began crowing, set them to work. It seemed a hardship for the maids; they wondered how to do in the rooster so that he wouldn't wake up their mistress. They killed him, but then things got worse: the mistress was afraid to oversleep and would wake up the maids even earlier.

The Self-Turning Mill (A True Story)

A peasant learned how to fashion mills and began making water mills, windmills, and horse-drawn mills.

Then he decided to make a mill where neither water, nor wind, nor horses would be needed; he wanted to make a mill where a heavy stone would be lowered and by its weight would turn a mill wheel; then it would be raised up and lowered again, so that the mill would work all on its own.

The peasant went to the master and said: "I've designed a self-turning mill that will work all on its own without water and without horses; you wind it up once, it will continue working until you stop it. But I don't have the money for lumber or for cast iron. Master, give me 300 rubles and I'll build such a mill first for you."

The master asked the peasant whether he knew how to read.

The peasant said that he didn't.

Then the master said: "If you knew how to read, I would give you a book about mechanics, and you would see that it's not possible to make such a mill, and that many learned people have lost their minds—trying to design a mill that would turn all by itself."

The peasant didn't believe the master and said: "They write all sorts of nonsense in your books. So a learned mechanic built a hulling mill for a merchant in town, but he messed it up; but when I, an illiterate peasant took a look at it, I remade the hulling part, and it began to work."

The landowner said: "How will you raise your stone after it's descended?"

The peasant said: "It will raise itself when the wheel turns."

The landowner said: "It will rise, but not as high, and the next time, it will rise even lower, and then it will stop, no matter what kind of wheel you make. It's just as if you were sliding down a tall mountain on a sled from and you will climb up a smaller one, but then from the smaller one, you won't be able to get back onto the taller one."

The peasant didn't believe him, went to see a merchant, and promised to build him a mill that didn't need water or horses.

The merchant gave him the money. The peasant kept building and building, and spent all 300 rubles, but his mill didn't work.

Then the peasant sold his land and spent all the proceeds.

The merchant said: "Give me a mill that works by itself without horses, or give me back my money."

The peasant went back to the master and told him the sad story about his trouble.

The master gave him some money and said: "Remain here and work for me: build mills for me, run either by water or horses—you're a master at that, and in the future don't try your hand at something that smarter people than you have failed to do."

The Fisherman and the Fish (A Fable)

A fisherman caught a fish. The fish said to him:

"Fisherman, let me go back into the water: you see how small I am. You won't get much from me. But if you let me go, I'll grow bigger; then you'll catch me again—you'll get much more from me."

The fisherman said:

"I would be a fool to throw you back into the water. No matter how small you are, it's still better than having no fish at all."

A Sense of Touch and Vision (Discussion)

Cross your index finger over your middle finger and then touch a small ball so that it rolls between your two fingers, and close your eyes. It will seem to you that there are two balls. Open your eyes—you'll see there's only one. Your fingers deceive you, but your eyes correct them.

Look (best from the side) at a good clean mirror: it will seem to you that it's a window or a door and that there's something behind it. Touch it with your finger—and you'll see that it's a mirror. Your eyes deceived you, but your fingers correct them.

The Fox and the Billy Goat (A Fable)

A goat got thirsty and felt like having a drink: he walked down the steep slope to the well, drank his fill, and got very heavy. He began to make his way back, but he was unable to do so. So he started to howl. A fox saw him and said:

"You are such a blockhead! If you had as many brains in your head as you have hairs in your beard, then before you climbed down you would have thought about how to get out."

How the Peasant Removed a Rock (A True Story)

On the square in a town lay stood an enormous rock. It took up lots of space and hindered people riding around the town. They summoned engineers and asked them how to remove this rock and how much it would cost.

One engineer said that the rock should be broken up into pieces by blowing it up, and then it could be carried off in parts; he said that it would cost 8,000 rubles; another one said that they should place rollers under the rock and remove it that way; he said it would cost 6,000 rubles.

But a peasant spoke up and said: "I will remove the stone and will ask only 100 rubles for that."

They asked him how he would do it. He replied: "I will dig a large hole next to the rock; I will spread the soil around the square, push the rock into the pit and cover it with the soil."

And that's exactly what the peasant did, and they paid him 100 rubles and another hundred for his clever plan.

The Dog and Its Shadow (A Fable)

A dog was running along a board across a river, and was carrying a piece of meat in its teeth. He saw himself in the water and thought that it was another dog carrying a piece of meat—he dropped his piece and rushed to take away the other dog's meat: but that meat didn't really exist, and a wave carried off his piece. And the dog was left with nothing at all.

Shat and Don (A Fairy Tale)

Old man Ivan had two sons: Shat Ivanych and Don Ivanych. Shat Ivanych was the elder brother; he was stronger and larger, and Don Ivanych was shorter and weaker. Their father showed each of them the road and ordered them to obey him. Shat Ivanych didn't obey his father and didn't proceed along the indicated road; he got lost and disappeared. But Don Ivanych obeyed his father and proceeded in the direction his father had ordered him to go. So he traveled throughout Russia and became famous.

There is a village called Lake Ivan, in the Yepifansky district, in the province of Tula, where there is a lake in the middle of the village. Two streams flow out of the lake in different directions. One stream is so narrow that one can step over it. That stream is called the Don. The other is wide and is called the Shat.

The Don flows straight ahead and the further it goes, the wider it becomes.

The Shat twists in one direction and then another. The Don travels through all of Russia and empties into the Sea of Azov. It contains many fish; wooden barges and steamboats travel on it.

The Shat roams,[1] doesn't leave the province of Tula, and empties into the Upa River.[2]

The Crane and the Stork (A Fable)

A peasant set some nets to catch cranes, because they were knocking down his crops. His nets caught some cranes, but also one stork.

The stork said to the peasant:

"Let me go: I'm not a crane, but a stork; we are the most respected birds. I live on top of your father's house. You can tell by my feathers that I'm not a crane."

The peasant said:

"I caught you with the cranes, so I will kill you with them."

---

1   This is clever word play: *shatayetsya* means roams or wander.
2   The Upa is a river in Tula Province and is one of the main tributaries of the Oka.

The Sudoma (A Tale)[3]

In the province of Pskov, in the district of Porokhovo, there is a little river called the Sudoma; along the banks of this river are two hills, one opposite the other.

The town of Vyshgorod used to stand on one of the hills; on the other in olden times lived the Slavs, who were conducting trials there. The old people maintain that on this hill there used to be a chain hanging down from heaven, and that whoever was in the right, could touch the chain with his hand, and whoever was in the wrong, couldn't reach the chain.

One man borrowed some money from another and then denied it. They brought them both to the Sudoma Mountain and ordered them to grab hold of the chain. The one who had loaned the money, raised his hand and immediately grabbed the chain. It was the guilty man's turn. He didn't deny it, but merely handed his crutch to the man he was suing, so that he could more easily grab hold of the chain with his hands: he stretched out his arms and reached it. People were surprised. What? Were both of them right?

But the guilty man's crutch was hollow: in it was hidden the money that he denied he'd taken. After he'd given his crutch to the man to whom he owed the money, he had actually repaid the money, and therefore could reach the chain.

Thus he deceived everyone. But from that time forward the chain moved up to the sky, but no longer came down. That's what old people say.

---

3 The Sudoma is a river in the Pskov Province of Russia.

The Gardener and His Sons (A Fable)

A gardener wanted to teach his sons how to garden. When he was close to death, he summoned them and said:

"Now, children, when I die, look in the vineyard to see what I hid there."

The children thought that there was a treasure buried there; when their father died, they began digging, and dug up the whole vineyard. They didn't find any treasure, but they did such a good job digging up the vineyard, that more fruit grew there than ever before. Thus they became very wealthy.

The Owl and the Hare (A Fable)

It was growing dark. Owls took wing over the ravine in the forest in search of their prey.

A big gray hare was bounding across the field, and began to smooth his fur. An old owl landed on a branch and watched the gray hare; a young owl said, "Why aren't you trying to catch the hare?" The old one replied: "I'm not strong enough. The hare's too big. If you grab him, he'll carry you off into the thicket." But the young owl said: "Why, I could hold him with one claw, and I hold on tight to the tree with the other claw."

The young owl swooped down on the hare, clutched his back with his claw in such a way that all his claws sank into the hare's fur; he was going to cling to the tree with the other claw. Then he said to himself: "He won't escape." But the hare darted away, and tore the owl into two pieces. One foot remained in the tree; the other was stuck in the hare's back.

The next year a hunter actually killed that very hare, and was amazed to find the talons of a full-grown owl stuck in his back.

The Wolf and the Crane (A Fable)

A wolf swallowed a bone and he couldn't cough it up. He summoned a crane and said:

"Come on, crane, you have a long neck; shove your head down my throat and pull out the bone: I will reward you well."

The crane did as he was asked: he thrust his head in, pulled out the bone, and said:

"Now give me my reward."

The wolf gnashed his teeth and said:

"Isn't it enough reward that I didn't bite off your head when I had it between my teeth?"

The Eagle (A True Story)

An eagle made itself a nest on a large tree, far from the sea, and raised its young.

Once some people were working near that tree and the eagle flew to her nest with a large fish in its talons. The people saw the fish, began to shout, and threw stones at the eagle.

The eagle dropped the fish; people picked it up and went on their way.

The eagle sat on the edge of its nest, and the eaglets raised their heads and began to peep.

Then the eagle flew away from them and perched on an upper branch of the tree.

The eaglets shrieked and peeped even more pitifully.

Then the eagle itself screeched very loudly, stretched her wings, and flew to the sea with difficulty. It returned only late that evening: she flew quietly and low over the ground, and in its talons it held a large fish once again.

When she reached the tree, she looked around—to see if there were any people nearby; then she quickly folded her wings and sat on her nest.

The eaglets raised their heads and opened their mouths, while the eagle tore apart the fish and fed them.

The Duck and the Moon (A Fable)

A duck was swimming along a river, searching for fish, but all day long it didn't find anything. When night fell, it saw the moon reflected in the water; it thought that it was a fish and dove in to catch the moon. Other ducks saw this and began making fun of it.

Since then, the duck was so ashamed and so timid, that when it saw a fish under the water, it didn't even try to catch it, and it died from starvation.

The Bear on a Carriage (A Fable)

An animal-keeper approached a tavern with his bear and tied the bear to the gates, while he went into the tavern to have a drink. The driver of a troika drove up to the tavern, tied up his shaft horse, and also went into the tavern. There were some sweet rolls in the carriage. The bear smelled the rolls, undid the rope, and made his way to the carriage, climbed in, and began to fumble in the straw. The horses turned around and lumbered away from the tavern along the road. The bear grabbed the edge of the carriage with his paws, and didn't know what to do next. The further the horses went, the more excited they became. The bear was holding onto the edges of the cart with his front paws, and kept turning his head first to one side and then to the other. The horses kept glancing back—but kept galloping even faster along the road, down the hill, and then up again. . . . Passersby hardly had time to get out of the way. The horses were galloping in a lather, the bear sat on the cart, holding on to the edges, looking from side to side. The bear saw that things didn't look good—the horses would kill him; he began to roar. The horses began galloping even faster. They kept galloping, and galloped home to their village. Everyone looked to see what was happening. The horses came to rest in their own courtyard, at the gates. The landlady looked—apparently, the landlord was drunk. She came out into the courtyard, but the landlord wasn't on the cart; it was the bear that climbed down. Then the bear jumped off and galloped away across a field and into the forest.

The Wolf and the Sheepdog (A Fable)

A wolf wanted to catch a sheep from a herd and walked through the wind so he would be covered in dust from the herd.

A sheepdog saw him and said:

"It isn't smart that you're covering yourself with dust; your eyes will start hurting."

But the wolf replied: "That's just the problem, doggie: my eyes have been already aching for a long time, but they say that dust from a herd of sheep cures one's eyes very well."

The Vine (A True Story)

During Holy Week a peasant went to see if the ground had thawed.

He went out to his vegetable garden and felt the earth with a stick. The ground was soft. The peasant went into the forest. Buds had already appeared on the large vines. So the peasant thought: "I will plant vines around my garden; when they grow, they will act as a defense!" He took his ax, cut down a dozen vines, sharpened the bigger ends, and planted them in the ground.

All of the vines grew shoots above with leaves; however, under the ground they grew more shoots instead of roots; some caught hold of the ground and took root, while others caught hold awkwardly, collapsed, and died.

By that time the peasant was rejoicing over the success of his vines: six of them had taken root. In springtime the sheep gnawed off four of the vines, leaving only two. The next spring, the sheep chewed off those last two. One was completely gone, while the other recovered, began to root, and grew into a tree. In spring swarms of bees would buzz on the vine. A swarm of bees would often come to rest on the vine, and peasants would collect them. Peasant women and men often had their breakfast and slept under the vine; and kids would climb on it and break twigs off it.

The peasant who planted the vine had died some time ago, but the vine kept growing. The elder son cut branches from it and used them for firewood. The vine kept growing. He would lop off branches all around and make it into the shape of a cone, but in the spring it grew branches again, even though they were thinner ones, but they were twice as big as the previous ones, like the forelock of a colt.

The elder son stopped managing the farm and the villagers moved away, but the vine kept growing in the broad field. Other peasants came and kept cutting it down—but it kept growing. A storm struck the vine; it recovered with branches to the side, and kept growing and flowering. A peasant wanted to cut it down to make a water trough, but he gave up: it was terribly rotten. The vine fell over on its side, and held on with only one side, but it kept growing, and every year bees would fly in to carry away nectar from the flowers.

Once in early spring the lads planned to guard their horses under the vine. It seemed cold to them: so they began to build a fire. They gathered stubble and brushwood. One lad climbed up on the vine, and broke off some branches. They gathered it all in the hollow of the trunk and lit a fire. The vine hissed, its sap was boiling; smoke rose up, and the fire started to spread; the whole inner part of the tree turned black. The young shoots withered, the flowers died. The lads drove their horses home. The burnt vine remained alone in the field. A black crow flew to it, landed on it, and cried: "Well, you've croaked, you old fool: it was high time you did!"

The Mouse under the Barn (A Fable)

A mouse lived under a barn. There was a small hole in the floor of the barn and grain would slip down into the hole. The mouse had a good life, and it wanted to brag about its life. It gnawed a bigger hole and invited other mice to come as guests.

"Come," it said, "and have a good time. I shall treat you. There will be enough food for everyone." When the other mice arrived, they saw that there was no hole at all. The peasant had spotted the large hole in the floor and had repaired it.

How Wolves Teach Their Pups (A Story)

I was walking along the road and behind me I heard a cry. It was a young shepherd boy shouting. He was running across the field and pointing to something.

I looked and there I saw—two wolves running through the field: one full-grown and the other, a pup. The pup was carrying on his back a slaughtered lamb, and held it by the leg with its teeth. The adult wolf ran alongside.

After I saw the wolves, I chased them together with the shepherd and we both started shouting. Hearing our cries, peasants came running with their dogs. As soon as the old wolf saw the dogs and the people, he ran up to the pup, grabbed the lamb, threw it onto its own back, and both wolves ran faster and disappeared from sight.

Then the shepherd boy began to relate what had happened: the large wolf had jumped out of the ravine, grabbed the lamb, killed it, and carried it away.

The young pup ran out to meet him and rushed to the lamb. The old wolf let the young pup carry the lamb, and ran more easily without his load.

Only when misfortune struck, did the old wolf end the lesson and carry the lamb itself.

The Hares and the Frogs (A Fable)

Once the hares gathered and began to complain about their lives: "We are perishing as a result of people, dogs, eagles, and other beasts. It would be better to die just once, than to live and suffer in fear. Let's drown ourselves!"

And the hares raced to the lake to drown themselves. The frogs heard the hares and started plunging into the water. One hare said:

"Wait, lads! Let's not rush to drown ourselves; apparently a frog's life is even worse than ours: they're afraid even of us."

What Auntie Told Us about Her Tame Sparrow, "Zhivchik" (A Story)[4]

A sparrow built a nest behind the shutters of a window of our house and laid five eggs in it. My sister and I watched how the sparrow carried bits of straw and feathers to the shutter and fashioned its nest. Later, after it had laid its eggs there, we were very happy. The sparrow no longer came in carrying straw and feathers, but sat on her eggs. Another sparrow—we were told that one was the husband, and the first one, the wife—would bring his wife worms and feed her.

After a few days, we heard some cheeping from behind the shutter and looked to see what had happened in the nest: there were five tiny, naked birds, without wings or feathers; their beaks were yellow and soft, and their heads were large.

They seemed very ugly to us, and we stopped admiring them; we would merely glance in every once in a while to see what they were doing. The mother bird flew off frequently in search of food, and when she would return the little sparrows would cheep and open their soft yellow beaks, where the mother would insert pieces of worm.

A week later the baby birds had grown, were covered with down, and had become prettier; then we started again observing them. When we came to the shutter one morning to see our little sparrows, we saw that the mother sparrow lay dead next to the shutter. We guessed that she must have been sitting on the shutter for the night and had fallen asleep, and that she got crushed when they closed the shutter.

We picked up the old sparrow and tossed it in the grass. The little ones were cheeping, sticking their little heads up and opening their beaks, but there was no one left to feed them.

My elder sister said: "Now they have no mother, no one to feed them; we'll do it!"

We were delighted, took a basket, put some cotton into it, placed the nest with the little ones on the cotton, and carried it upstairs. Then we dug up some worms, soaked some bread in milk, and began to feed the little birds. They ate with gusto, shook their little heads, cleaned their beaks on the sides of the basket, and all were very happy.

In that way we fed the birds all day long and were very pleased with them. The next day, when we looked into the nest, we saw that the smallest bird was lying dead, and that its feet were tangled in the cotton. We tossed him away and took away all the cotton, so that another baby wouldn't get tangled in it; we

---

4 The sparrow's name means "the lively one."

put grass and moss into the basket. Towards evening two more sparrows spread their feathers, opened their mouths, closed their eyes, and also died.

My sister wept over the sparrows and she began to feed the one remaining baby bird, while we only watched. The last one—the fifth little sparrow, was happy and healthy; we called him "Zhivchik."

Zhivchik lived so long that he'd already started to fly and learned his own name.

When my sister called "Zhivchik, Zhivchik!" he would come, sit on her shoulder, her head, or her hand, and she would feed it.

Then he grew up and began to feed himself. He lived in our attic above, sometimes flew out through the window, but always came back at night to sleep in his own place in the basket.

One morning he didn't fly off anywhere out of his basket; his wings became wet and he spread them wide, like the other sparrows did when they were dying. My sister didn't leave him alone, but took care of him; he wouldn't eat or drink anything.

He was ill for three days and then died on the fourth day. When we saw that he was dead, lying on its back, with crooked claws, we three sisters began to cry so loud that mother came running to see what had happened. When she came in and saw the dead sparrow lying on the table, she understood the cause of our grief. My sister didn't eat for several days, didn't play, but just kept crying.

We wrapped Zhivchik in the nicest rags, put him in a wooden box, and buried him in a hole in the ground. Then we made a funeral mound over him and placed a stone on top of it.

Three Sweet Rolls and One Pretzel (A Fable)

A peasant got hungry. He bought a sweet roll and ate it; but he still wanted more to eat. He bought another sweet roll and ate it; but he still wanted more to eat. He bought a third sweet roll and ate it, too, but he was still hungry. Then he bought some pretzels; after he had eaten one, he felt full. Then the peasant slapped his forehead and said:

"What a fool I am! Why did I eat so many sweet rolls? I should have eaten a pretzel first."

One Thousand Gold Pieces (A True Story)

A wealthy man wanted to give away 1,000 gold pieces to the poor, but didn't know which poor people he should give this money to.

He went to a priest and said: "I want to give 1,000 gold pieces to the poor, but I don't know who I should give it to. Take the money and give it to people you know."

The priest said: "That's a lot of money; I don't know whom to give it to either: perhaps I'll give too much to one person and not enough to another. Tell me what kind of poor person and how much of your money to give them."

The rich man said: "If you don't know to whom to give the money, then God knows: give the money to the first poor person who comes to see you."

A poor man lived in the same parish. He had many children, was sick, and couldn't work. Once the poor man was reading the Psalter and he read these words: "*I have been young, and now am old; yet have I not seen the righteous forsaken, nor his seed begging bread.*"[5]

The poor man thought: "I've been forsaken by God. But I haven't done anything bad. I will go to the priest and ask him, how come such an untruth is written in the Scriptures."

He went to see the priest.

The priest looked at him and said: "This poor man was the first to come to see me," and he gave him all of the rich man's 1,000 gold pieces.

Peter I[6] and the Peasant (A True Story)

Tsar Peter came upon a peasant in the forest. The peasant was chopping wood.

The tsar said: "God help you, peasant!"

The peasant replied: "It's God's help that I need."

The tsar asked: "Do you have a large family?"

"I have four children: two sons and two daughters."

"That's not a very large family. What do you do with your money?"

"I divide my money into three parts: with the first third, I pay my debts; with the second, I invest; and the third, I throw away in the water."

The tsar thought for a while, but didn't understand what the peasant meant.

The peasant explained: "I pay my debts—I feed my father and my mother; I invest my money—I feed my sons; and I throw money away and raise two daughters."

---

5   Psalms 37:25.
6   Peter the Great (1672–1725).

The tsar said: "You have a good head on your shoulders, old man. Now show me how to get out of the forest into the field, since I can't find the road."

The peasant said: "You'll find the road yourself; go straight ahead, then turn right, then left, and then right again."

The tsar said: "I don't understand your directions; you be my guide."

"I have no time to guide you, sir; time is money for us peasants."

"Well, if it costs money, I'll pay you."

"If you'll pay me, let's go."

They got in the small carriage, and off they went.

Along the way, the tsar began asking the peasant; "Have you ever been far away from here, peasant?"

"I've been here and there."

"Have you seen the tsar?"

"I haven't seen the tsar, but I would really like to get a look at him."

"Well, then, as soon as we reach the field,—you'll get a look at him."

"How will I recognize him?"

"Everyone else will take off his hat; only the tsar will keep his hat on his head."

They arrived in the field. When the people saw the tsar, they all took off their hats. The peasant kept looking, but didn't see the tsar.

So he asked, "So where's the tsar?"

Peter Alekseyevich replied to him:[7] "You see there are only the two of us here wearing hats—one of us must be the tsar."

The Mad Dog (A True Story)

A landowner bought a setter pup in town and carried him to his village in the sleeve of his fur coat. The landowner's wife grew to love the pup and kept him in their house. The pup grew and they named him Druzhok.[8]

He went on hunts with the landowner, guarded the house, and played with the children.

Once a stray dog ran into their garden. The dog ran right along the path, its tail lowered, its mouth open, and spit dripping from his tongue. The children were in the garden.

The landowner saw this dog and shouted:

"Children! Run home quickly! This is a mad dog!"

---

7 Ditto.

8 The name means "little friend."

The children heard what their father shouted, but they didn't see the dog, and ran straight towards it. The mad dog was about to attack one of the children, but just then Druzhok threw himself at the mad dog and began fighting with it.

The children ran away, but when Druzhok returned home, he was whining and there was blood on his neck.

Ten days later Druzhok became depressed; he didn't eat or drink, and he rushed to bite a pup. They locked him into an empty room.

The children didn't understand why they locked Druzhok away and they secretly went in to see the dog.

They unlocked the door and began to call Druzhok. He almost knocked them over as he ran out into the courtyard and lay down under a bush. When the mistress saw Druzhok, she called him, but he didn't obey, wouldn't wag his tail, and didn't even look at her. His eyes were dull and spit was dripping from his mouth. Then the mistress called her husband and said:

"Come quickly! Someone let Druzhok out; he's completely rabid. For God's sake, do something!"

The master brought his gun and went up to Druzhok. He aimed it at him, but his hand was shaking as he was aiming. He fired, but instead of hitting his head, he shot him in the rear.

The dog howled and started shaking.

The master went closer to see what was wrong with him.

The whole rear end of the dog was bloody, and both rear legs had been injured.

Druzhok crawled up to the master and began licking his foot. The master started shaking, burst into tears, and ran into his house.

Then they called a hunter: the hunter shot the dog with another gun, killed him, and took it away.

Two Horses (A Fable)

Two horses were pulling two loads. The horse in front was trotting along well, but the rear horse kept stopping. Men began to pile the rear horse's load on the front horse; when they had transferred it all, the rear horse found it easy going, and said to the front horse:

"Toil and sweat! The more you try, the more they'll torture you."

When they reached the inn, the owner said; "Why should I feed two horses, when I can carry everything on one? I had better give the one all the food it wants, and slaughter the other; at least I'll have its hide."

And so he did.

The Lion and the Dog (A True Story)

Wild beasts were on show in London. To see them people had to pay money or bring along stray dogs and cats, which were thrown to the wild animals to eat.

Wanting to see the wild animals, a man caught a little dog in the street and brought it to the menagerie. He was admitted and the little dog was thrown into the lion's cage to be eaten.

The little dog dropped its tail between its legs and hid in a corner of the cage. The lion came over and sniffed it.

Then the little dog rolled over on its back, stuck its paws in the air, and began to wag its tail.

The lion touched it with his paw and turned it over.

The little dog jumped up and stood up on its hind legs in front of the lion.

The lion looked at the little dog, turned his head from side to side, but didn't touch it.

When his master threw him some meat, the lion tore off a piece, and left it for the little dog.

When the lion lay down to sleep in the evening the little dog lay down next to him, putting its head on the lion's paw.

From that time forward, the dog and the lion lived together in the same cage. The lion never harmed the little dog, but ate his own food, slept with the dog, and sometimes even played with it.

One day a gentleman came to the menagerie and recognized his little dog; he told the owner that the dog was his and that he wanted it back. The owner was ready to give it to him, of course; but as soon as they approached the little dog, wanting to take it out of the cage, the lion roared and his mane stood up straight.

So the little dog and the lion lived together in the cage for a whole year.

After a year, the little dog fell ill and died. The lion stopped eating, kept sniffing and licking the little dead dog, and touching it with his paw.

When the lion finally understood that the pup was dead, he suddenly sprang up, his mane rising, thrashed his sides with his tail, threw himself against the wall, and began biting the bars and the floor.

He kept throwing himself about the cage all day, roaring, then he lay down next to the little dead dog, and quieted down. The owner wanted to take the dead dog away, but the lion wouldn't let anyone come near.

Thinking the lion would forget his grief if he had another dog, the owner put another dog into the cage, this one alive. But the lion tore it to shreds at once. Then he put his paws round his little dead friend and lay there without moving for five days.

On the sixth day the lion died.

Equal Inheritance (A Fable)

A certain merchant had two sons. The elder boy was his favorite, and he intended to leave all his wealth to this son when he died. The mother felt sorry for her younger son, and asked her husband not to tell the boys his intention for the time being. She hoped to find some way of making her sons equal. The merchant obeyed her wish and didn't announce his decision.

One day the mother was sitting at the window weeping. A traveler approached the window and asked why she was weeping.

"How can I help weeping?" she said. "In my opinion, there's no difference between my two sons, but their father wishes to leave everything to one and nothing to the other. I've asked him not to announce his decision until I've thought of some way of helping the younger. But I have no money of my own and I don't know what to do in my misery."

Then the traveler said to her, "There's an easy solution to your trouble. Tell your sons that the elder will receive the entire inheritance, and that the younger will get nothing. Then they'll be equal."

The younger son, on learning that he would inherit nothing, went to another country, where he served his apprenticeship and learned a trade. The elder son lived at home and learned no trade, knowing that someday he'd become rich. When the father died, the elder son, who didn't know how to do anything, spent all his inheritance. However, the younger son, who'd learned how to make money in a foreign country, had become rich.

Three Thieves (A True Story)

A peasant was going to town to sell his donkey and his goat.

There was a little bell on the goat.

Three thieves saw the peasant, and one of them said: "I'll steal the goat, and the peasant won't even notice."

The second one said: "And I'll steal the donkey from right under the peasant's nose."

The third robber said: "That's not difficult: I'll steal all the peasant's clothes."

The first robber snuck up to the goat, took off its bell, tied it to the donkey's tail, and led the goat into the field.

At a turn in the road the peasant looked around and saw that his goat was missing; he began to look for it.

Then the second robber went up to him and asked what he was looking for.

The peasant said that his goat had been stolen. The second robber said: "I saw your goat: just now a man with a goat went running into the forest. You can catch him."

The peasant ran off to catch the robber and asked the second robber to watch his donkey. The second robber stole his donkey.

When the peasant returned from the forest and saw that now his donkey was also missing, he started crying and continued on his way.

Along the road near a pond he saw another man sitting and weeping. The peasant asked what was the matter.

The man said that he'd been told to carry a sack of gold to town, but that he sat down to rest by the pond, fallen asleep, and in his dream, tossed the bag into the water.

The peasant asked why he hadn't gone into the water to retrieve the sack.

The man replied: "I'm afraid of water and I don't know how to swim, but I'll give 20 pieces of gold to whoever retrieves my bag." The peasant was delighted and thought: "God gave me good luck that both my donkey and my goat were stolen."

He got undressed, went into the water, but he couldn't find any bag of gold; but, when he came out of the water, all his clothes were gone.

It was the third robber: he had also stolen all the peasant's clothes.

The Father and His Sons (A Fable)

A father instructed his sons to live in harmony: they didn't obey him. He ordered them to bring him a broom and said:

"Break it!"

No matter how hard they tried, they couldn't break it. Then the father untied the broom and told them to keep breaking it twig by twig.

They easily broke off all he twigs one by one.

The father said:

"It's the same with you: if you live in harmony, no one will defeat you; but if you argue among yourselves, anyone can destroy you easily."

Why Is There Wind? (A Discussion)

Fish live in water and people live in air. The fish don't see or hear the water, if they themselves don't move or if the water isn't moving. We also don't see or hear the air if we don't move or if the air isn't moving.

But as soon as we start running, we hear the air—it blows in our face; and sometimes it's even heard, when we are running, like air whistling in our ears. When we open a door into a warm room, the wind always blows from below into the room, and above, it blows from the room into the outside.

When someone is pacing the room, or waving a cloth, we say: "He's creating wind." When someone is lighting a stove, a wind always blows inside it. When there is wind blowing outside, it blows for whole days and nights, sometimes in one direction, sometimes in another. This happens because somewhere on earth the air gets very hot, and in another place it cools down—that's when the wind begins to blow, a breeze moves along the bottom, while on the top, a warm wind blows, just as it blows from outside into the house. And it continues to blow until it warms the place where it was cold, and cools the place where it was hot.

What Is the Wind For? (A Discussion)

Make a cross from two splinters of wood and tie four more splinters around it. Glue a piece of paper over the whole thing. Fasten a bast tail to one end, and fasten a long string to the other, and you've made a kite. Then take your kite, run with the wind, and let it go. The wind will lift it up and carry it high into the sky. The kite will tremble, hum, strain, turn, and flutter its bast tail.

If there were no wind, it would be impossible to fly a kite.

They make four wings out of boards, and secure them to the shaft crosswise; they attach the cogwheel to the shaft in such a way that when it turns, it will catch the cogs and wheels. Then they place the wings facing against the wind: the wings begin to turn, and the shaft and wheels start catching. Then they pour grain between the millstones; the grain gets ground to flour, and drops into a bucket.

If there were no wind, it would be impossible to grind grain in a windmill.

When you are floating in a boat, if you want to move faster, take a long pole and insert it in a hole at the center of the boat; to this pole attach a crossbar. A canvas sail is attached to this pole, with a rope fastened to the bottom of the sail. Then you place the sail where it will catch the wind. And the wind will blow the sail so hard that the boat will lean to one side, the rope will try to tear itself out of your hands, and the boat will sail in the direction of the wind so quickly that the water under the front of the boat will reverberate, and the shores will seem to be rushing backwards past the boat.

If there were no wind, it would be impossible to sail a boat.

In places where people live, the air is bad; if there were no wind, the bad air would remain there. But when the wind blows, it blows away the bad air and brings good, clean air from the forest and the fields. If there were no wind, people would breathe and spoil the air. The air would stay in one place, and people would have to leave that place.

When wild animals wander through the forests and fields, they always go against the wind: they listen using their ears and sense with their nose what's ahead of them. If there were no wind, they wouldn't know which way to go.

Almost all grasses, bushes, and trees, are such that for them to set seeds for grasses, bushes, and trees, it is necessary that pollen be transferred from one blossom to another. The flowers are often located far from one another, and they can't send their pollen from one to another.

When cucumbers grow in hotbeds where there's no wind, people tear off a vine and place it over another so that the pollen would fall on the fruit-bearing blossom, and fertilization would occur. Bees and other insects sometimes carry pollen on their legs from one flower to the next, but it's the wind that carries most of it from one to the other. If there were no wind, half the plants wouldn't produce any seeds.

In warm times, a mist rises above the water. This steam rises higher, and when it cools above, it falls as rain to the earth.

Steam rises above the earth only where there is water—over streams, swamps, ponds, and rivers, most of all, over the seas. If there were no wind, steam wouldn't move, but would gather over the water as clouds and rain would fall again in the same place from the place where they had originated. It would rain over streams, swamps, rivers, and seas, but there would be no rain over fields and forests. The wind spreads the clouds and waters the earth. If there were no wind, then there would be more water where it already stood, and the earth would be parched.

The Very Best Pears (A Fable)

A landowner sent his servant out for some pears and said to him: "Buy me some of the best." The servant came to the shop and asked for some pears. The merchant gave them to him, but the servant said:

"No, give me the very best ones."

The merchant said:

"Try one and you will see that these are very good."

"How will I know," replied the servant, "that they are all good pears, if I try only one?"

He took a little bite from each one and brought them to the landowner. Then the landowner chased him away.

Volga and Vazuza (A Fairy Tale)

There were two sisters: Volga and Vazuza. They began to argue as to which one of them was the wiser, and who will live better.

Volga said: "Why should we argue? We're both of age. Let's get up tomorrow morning and go out, each one going her own way; then we'll see who will travel better and reach the Khvalynskoye Kingdom sooner."

Vazuza agreed, but deceived Volga. As soon as Volga fell asleep, Vazuza took off running straight to the Khvalynskoye Kingdom.

When Volga woke up and saw that her sister had already left, she proceeded neither slowly nor hurriedly on her own path and caught up with Vazuza.

Vazuza was afraid that Volga would punish her; she called herself the younger sister, and asked Volga to get her to the Khvalynskoye Kingdom. Volga forgave her sister and took her with her.

The river Volga begins in the Ostashkovskoye district from the swamps in the Volgo village. There's a small spring there and the River Volga flows out of it. And the River Vazuza begins in the mountains and flows straight, while the Volga keeps winding around.

In spring the Vazuza ice breaks up first and passes through, while the Volga comes later. But when both rivers meet, the Volga is already 30 *sazhens* wide, while the Vazuza is still a small, narrow stream. The Volga passes through all of Russia, three thousand, one hundred and sixty versts, and empties into the Khvalynskoye (Caspian) Sea. And its width during spring tide is twelve versts.

A Calf on the Ice (A Fable)

A calf galloped across the stable and learned to do circles and turns. When winter came, the calf was let out with the other livestock onto the ice and to the water trough. All the cows approached the trough carefully, but the calf took off across the ice, turned up its tail, pricked up its ears, and began to turn circles. On the very first circle its leg gave way and it banged his head on the trough.

It started crying:

"What a wretch I am! I was skipping up to my knees in the straw, but didn't fall; yet here I slipped on the smooth surface."

The old cow said to the young calf:

"If you weren't a calf, you would know that where it's easier to skip, it's harder to hold still."

The Golden-Haired Tsarevna (A Fairy Tale)

In India there lived a tsarevna with golden hair;[9] she had a wicked stepmother. The stepmother grew to hate her golden-haired stepdaughter and persuaded the tsar to send her into exile in the desert. They took her far away into the desert and left her there. Five days later the golden-haired tsarevna returned to her father riding on a lion.

Then her stepmother persuaded the tsar to send her golden-haired stepdaughter into the wild mountains, where only vultures lived. Four days later, the vultures brought her back home.

Then the stepmother sent the tsarevna to an island in the middle of the sea. Fishermen saw the golden-haired tsarevna and on the sixth day they brought her back to the tsar.

Then the stepmother ordered that a deep well be dug in the courtyard; she dropped the golden-haired tsarevna into it and covered her with soil.

In six days, there was a light shining from the place where they had buried the tsarevna, and when the tsar ordered them to dig it up, they found the golden-haired tsarevna.

Then the stepmother ordered that a water trough be hollowed out from a mulberry tree;[10] she locked the tsarevna in it and put it out to sea.

On the ninth day the sea brought the golden-haired tsarevna to the land of Japan, and there the Japanese took her out of the trough. She was still alive.

But as soon as she set foot on the shore, she died, and she was changed into a silkworm.

The silkworm crawled onto a mulberry tree and began eating the leaves. When it had grown somewhat, it suddenly seemed to be dead: it stopped eating and stopped moving.

On the fifth day, in the same amount of time as it took the lion to bring the tsarevna out of the desert, the worm came back to life and began eating mulberry leaves.

---

9 A *tsarevna* is the daughter of a tsar.
10 Berries grow on mulberry trees—similar to raspberries, but the bark is similar to birch trees; silkworms are fed on the leaves. (Tolstoy's note)

After the worm grew a bit more, it died again, and on the fourth day, just as long as it took the vultures to bring back the tsarevna, the worm came back to life and began eating again.

And again it died, and in the same amount of time that the tsarevna returned in a boat, it came back to life.

And it died again for the fourth time and came back to life on the sixth day, when they had dug the tsarevna out of the well.

And again it died, for the last time, and on the ninth day, in the same length of time as it took the tsarevna to land in Japan, it came back to life in the form of a golden silk pupa. The worms die five times and come back to life. A butterfly flew out of the pupa and laid some eggs and from then on, silkworms began to be raised in Japan.

The Japanese raise many worms, and make a great deal of silk; the first dream of the worm is called the dream of the lion; the second, the dream of the vulture; the third, the dream of the boat, the fourth, the dream of the courtyard; and the fifth, the dream of the well.

The Falcon and the Rooster (A Fable)

A falcon was used to its master, and would come back and land on his hand when called; a rooster would run away from his master and cry when people would approach him. So the falcon said to the rooster:

"There's no gratitude in you roosters; one can see that you're of a common breed. You go to your masters only when you're hungry. It is different with us wild birds. We have great strength, and we can fly faster than anybody; still we don't flee from people, but we fly of our own accord to their hands when called. We remember that they feed us."

Then the rooster said:

"You don't run away from people because you've never seen a roast falcon, but over and over again, we see roast roosters."

Heat (Discussion)

I

Why do they place the rails on the railway in such a way that the ends don't connect?

Because in winter the iron contracts from the cold temperature, and in summer, it expands from the heat. If in winter they were to place the rails end to end, in the summer they would expand, press into each other, and rise up.

Everything expands from heat and contracts from cold.

If a screw doesn't fit into a nut, then if you heat the nut, the screw will fit. And if the screw is weak, then heat the screw, and it will become tight.

Why does a glass crack if you pour boiling water into it?

Because the part, which the boiling water heats, expands, while the place which the water doesn't touch, remains as it was before: below the glass wants to expand, but the top won't let it, so the glass cracks.

II

Why, when it snows during the spring thaw, does the snow melt on your hand, but not on your fur coat?

Because the warmth of your face and hand transfers into the snow and melts it: as a result the place on your face where the snow melts, becomes cold.

Why, if you hold a tin cup with cold water in your hands, the water warms up, but your hands feel cold.

Because the warmth from your hands is transferred to the tin, and then into the water.

If you hold the cup with your hands wearing mittens, why doesn't it warm up quickly?

Because your mittens don't let the warmth of your hands transfer to the water, and the tin conducts the warmth of your hands into the water. Iron and tin let heat and cold go through, but a fur coat and wood do not. As a result, iron, tin, and bronze, and any metal warm in the sun faster than wood, wool, and paper, and they also cool down faster.[11] That's why when it's cold, we dress in fur, wool, and in everything that doesn't conduct heat.

Why do they cover the dough with a fur coat, and not with a shield?

Because a fur coat doesn't let heat through, and the dough won't cool, whereas the shield lets heat out and the dough will cool.

Why doesn't snow melt under wood chips and straw, but lies there until mid-summer?

---

11 Metals: gold, silver, copper, iron, lead, mercury, and others. (Tolstoy's note)

Why does ice last longer in cellars, which are covered by straw roofs?

Why, when they want to dry lumber, do they put it under an iron cover, and not under straw?

Why on meadowlands and on stubble, do peasants, to keep their water cool, wrap their pitchers in a towel?

III

Why, when it's windy without frost, do you feel colder than in a frost without wind?

Because the warmth of the body passes into the air and if there's no wind, then the air around the body warms up and remains warmer. But when the wind is blowing, it carries away the warmed air and brings cold air. Once again the warmth of the body passes into the air and warms the air around it, and again the wind carries the warm air away. When the body loses a lot of its warmth, you shiver.

Why, when tea in a mug is hot, do we blow on it?

The Jackals and the Elephant (A Fable)[12]

Some jackals ate all the carrion in the forest, and were left with nothing to eat. So an old jackal came up with a way to find something to feed on. He went to an elephant, and said:

"We had a king, but he became spoiled: he kept ordering us to do things that nobody could do; we want to elect another king, and my people have sent me to beg you to be our king. You will have a good life with us. Whatever you will order us to do, we will do, and we will honor you in everything. Come to our kingdom!" The elephant agreed, and followed the jackal. The jackal brought him to a swamp. When the elephant got stuck fast in it, the jackal said:

"Now give your command! Whatever you command, we will do."

The elephant said:

"I command you to pull me out from here."

The jackal started laughing and said:

---

12 Wild animals, resembling small wolves. (Tolstoy's note)

"Grab hold of my tail with your trunk, and I will pull you out at once."

The elephant said:

"Can I be pulled out by a tail?" But the jackal said to him:

"Why, then, do you command us to do something that's impossible? Did we not chase away our first king for ordering us to do what could not be done?"

When the elephant died in the swamp, the jackals came and ate him up.

Magnet (Description)

In olden times there lived a shepherd; his name was Magnis. One of his sheep went missing. He went into the mountains to look for it. He came to a place where there were just bare rocks. He walked over these rocks and felt that his boots were sticking to them. He touched them with his hand: the rocks were dry and didn't stick to his hands. He walked on them again, and once more his boots were sticking to the rocks. He sat down, took off his boots, took his boot in his hands and began to touch the rocks with this boot.

When he touched them with leather or the sole, they didn't stick, but as soon as he touched them with the nails, his boot stuck to them.

Magnis had a walking stick with an iron tip on one end. He touched the rock with the wooden end, it wouldn't stick; he touched it with the metal end: it stuck so fast he had to yank it away.

Magnis inspected the rock carefully—he saw that it resembled iron, and he brought pieces of it home. From that time forward, they recognized this rock and named it a magnet.

Magnets are found in the ground together with iron ore. Where there is a magnet in the ore, the iron is of the best quality. A magnet looks like iron. If you place a steel needle on a magnet and leave it there for a while, the needle will become a magnet and will begin to attract iron. If two magnets are placed end to end, one end of each will attract the other, while the other end will repel.

If you break a magnetic stick in half, then each half will attract iron with one end and repel it with the other. And if you break it again—the same thing will happen. And you can break it as many times as you would like, one end of each will attract, and the other end will repel. Just like a pinecone, if you break it, one end will be like a navel and the other will be like a cup. And if you do it from the other end, the cup with the navel will meet, but the cup with another cup, will not.

If you magnetize a needle (holding it for a long time on a magnet), and place it in the end of a peg, so that it can turn freely, as soon as you let it go, it will orient itself to point to (noon) the north with one end and to (midnight) the south with the other end.

When people didn't know about magnets, they didn't sail far away on the seas. As they got far out to sea so they couldn't see any land, they could only see the sun and the stars, and knew which way to travel. If it was cloudy, and they couldn't see the sun or the stars, then they themselves wouldn't know which way to sail. The wind would carry the ship and it might crash upon some rocks.

Until they knew about magnets, they didn't sail far from the shores: but after they discovered magnets, they would follow the magnetic needle turning on a peg, so it to could turn freely on its own. With a magnetic needle they began to travel further from the shores, and since then, discovered many new seas.

There is always a magnetic needle (compass) on a boat, and there is a measured rope with knots tied on the end of the ship. The rope is attached in such a way that it uncoils and it's possible to see how far the boat has traveled.

Thus, when one goes on a ship, one always knows where the ship is located: whether it's far from shore, and in what direction it's moving.

The Heron, Fish, and Crawfish (A Fable)

A heron lived by a pond and was getting on in years: it no longer had the strength to catch fish. It began thinking how to live by its wits. It said to the fish: "You fish don't know that a misfortune is awaiting you: I've heard from people—they want to drain this pond and catch all of you fish. I know that there's a fine pond located just beyond this hill. I would like to help you, but I've grown old: it's too difficult to fly." The fish began to beg the heron to help.

The heron said:

"Perhaps I can try to help you; I will carry you across but I can't take you all together, only one at a time."

The fish were delighted; they all begged: "Take me, take me!"

And the heron began to carry them: he would pick up one and carry it into the field, and eat it. And thus he ate a great many fish.

There was an old crayfish living in the pond. When the heron began to carry the fish, he got the point and said:

"Well, heron, now take me to my new home."

The heron picked up the crawfish and carried him away. When the heron reached the field, it wanted to drop the crawfish, but when the crawfish saw all the fish bones lying there, it closed his claws around the heron's neck and choked it, while he himself crawled back to his pond and told all the other fish about it.

A Man Tells How He Rode Horseback (A Story)

We knew this old man, Pimen Timofeich. He was 90 years old. He lived at his grandson's house, and did no work. His back was bent, he walked with a cane, and moved his feet very slowly. He had no teeth at all and his face was wrinkled. His lower lip trembled; when he walked and when he spoke, he smacked his lips and it was impossible to tell what he was saying.

There were four of us brothers, and we all loved to ride horseback. But we didn't have any tame horses to ride. They let us ride only one old horse: and the name of this horse was Voronok.[13]

Once our mother allowed us to go for a ride, and we all went to the stable with the coachman. He saddled Voronok for us, and the first one to ride was my elder brother. He rode for a long time; he rode to the barn and around the garden, and when he was coming back, we shouted: "Now gallop!"

Our elder brother began to kick Voronok with his feet and beat him with his whip, and the horse went galloping past us.

After our elder brother, our second brother mounted the horse and also rode for a long time and also used his whip on Voronok, and he came galloping from behind the hill. He wanted to ride some more, but our third brother kept begging to let him go sooner. Our third brother rode to the barn, and around the garden, and even around the village, and he quickly galloped from near the hill to the stable. When he returned to us, Voronok was breathing heavily and his neck and shoulders were covered with sweat.

When it was my turn, I wanted to surprise my brothers and show them how well I could ride. I started to urge on Voronok with all my strength, but the horse didn't want to move away from the stable. And no matter how much I beat him, he didn't want to gallop, and merely walked, and kept turning back. I was mad at the horse and I beat him with my whip as hard as I could and kicked him with my feet.

I tried to beat him in those places where it was most painful, and broke my whip, and with what was left of it, I began beating the horse's head. But Voronok still didn't want to gallop. Then I turned back, rode up to the coachman, and asked for a stronger whip. But he said to me:

"Enough of riding, sir; dismount. Why torment the horse?"

I was offended and said: "But I didn't get to ride at all. Watch me gallop now. Please give me a better whip. I'll get him moving."

---

13 The horse's name is derived from the Russian word for "raven."

The coachman shook his head and said:

"Ah, sir, you have no pity. Why goad him further? After all, he's 20 years old. The horse is exhausted, breathing with difficulty, and old. He's so very old! He's just like Pimen Timofeich: if you were to sit on Timofeich and wanted to urge him on with your whip? Wouldn't you feel any pity for him?"

I remembered Pimen and obeyed the old man. I climbed down from the horse and, when I looked at him, saw his sweaty sides, labored breathing, and how he shook his mangy little tail, I understood how hard it was for the horse. Before I thought he was just as happy as I was. I felt so sorry for Voronok, that I began kissing his sweaty neck and asking his forgiveness for beating him.

Since then I've grown up and always feel sorry for horses, and always think of Voronok and Pimen Timofeich, when I see someone mistreating a horse.

The Hedgehog and the Hare (A Fable)

Once a hare met a hedgehog and said:

"You're splendid in all respects, except that your legs are crooked, and you stumble."

The hedgehog got angry and said:

"Why are you laughing; my crooked legs are faster than your straight legs. Let me stop by my house, and then let's run a race!"

The hedgehog went home and said to his wife; "I've argued with the hare; we want to run race!"

The hedgehog's wife said: "Clearly you've lost your mind! How can you race against a hare? His legs are very fast, while yours are crooked and slow."

But the hedgehog said: "He has quick legs, but I have a quick mind. Just do what I tell you: let's go out into the field."

So they came across a plowed field. The hedgehog said to his wife:

"Hide at this end of the furrow, while the hare and I start running from the other end; as soon as he starts running, I'll turn back. When he reaches your end, you come out and say, "I've been waiting for you a long time." He can't tell the difference between us; he'll think it's me, not you!"

The hedgehog's wife hid in the furrow, and the hedgehog and the hare started running from the other end.

When the hare took off running, the hedgehog had already run back, and hid in the furrow. The hare arrived galloping up to the other end of the furrow; he looked, and saw the hedgehog's wife sitting there; she saw the hare and said to him: "I've been waiting for you a long time!"

The hare couldn't tell the hedgehog's wife apart from the hedgehog, and thought: "What a miracle! How did he run past me and win?"

"Well," the hare said, "let's run the race again!"

"All right!" said the hedgehog.

The hare set off and ran to the other end of the furrow, and there he saw: the hedgehog was already there, and he said: "Hey, brother, you've only just come; I've been waiting for you a long time."

"What a miracle!" thought the hare. "I galloped here so fast, yet he still overtook me. Well, let's run one more race, and now you won't beat me."

"All right!"

The hare ran as fast as he could; he looked, but there was the hedgehog, sitting and waiting for him.

And so, the hare galloped from one end to the other, until he ran out of strength.

The hare surrendered and said that in the future he would never argue again.

Two Brothers (A Story)

Two brothers went on a journey together. At noon, they lay down to rest in the forest. When they awoke, they saw a stone lying there next to them and something was written on it. They started to figure it out and read:

"Whoever finds this stone, let him proceed straight into the forest toward the sunrise. There will be a river in the forest: let him swim across this river to the other bank. You'll see a bear with bear cubs: take the cubs away from the bear and run up at the mountain, without looking back. On that mountain you'll see a house, and in that house, you will find happiness."

After the brothers had read what was written on the stone, the younger brother said: "Let's go together. Perhaps we can swim across the river, get the bear cubs home, and together we will find happiness."

"I am not going into the forest after bear cubs," said the elder brother, "and I also advise you not to go. In the first place, no one can know whether what's written on this stone is true—perhaps it was written in jest. It's even possible that we haven't read it correctly. In the second place, even if what's written here is true—suppose we go into the forest, night comes, and we can't find the river. We'll be lost. And even if we do find the river, how are we going to swim across it? It may be broad and swift. In the third place, even if we swim across the river, do you think it's easy to take cubs away from the mama bear? She'll kill us, and, instead of finding happiness, we'll perish, and all for nothing. In the fourth place, even if we succeeded in carrying off the bear cubs, we couldn't run up a mountain without stopping to rest. And, most important of all, the stone doesn't tell us what kind of happiness we should find in that house. *It may be that the happiness awaiting us there is not at all the sort of happiness we would want.*"

"In my opinion," said the younger brother, "you're wrong. What's written on the stone could not have been put there without reason. And it's all perfectly clear. In the first place, no harm will come to us if we try. In the second place, if we don't go, someone else will read the inscription on the stone and find happiness, and we'll have lost it all. In the third place, if you don't make an effort and try hard, nothing in the world will succeed. In the fourth place, I don't want people to think I'm afraid of anything."

The elder brother answered him by saying, "Even the proverb says: '*In seeking great happiness, small pleasures may be lost.*' And also: '*A bird in the hand is worth two in the bush.*'"

The younger brother replied, "I have heard: '*He who is afraid of leaves must not go into the forest.*' And also: '*Beneath a stone no water flows.*' In my opinion, we should go."

The younger brother set off, and the elder remained behind.

No sooner had the younger brother gone into the forest, than he found the river, swam across it, and there on the other side was the mama bear, fast asleep. He grabbed her cubs, and ran up the mountain without looking back. No sooner did he reach the top, when people came out to meet him with a carriage to take him into the city, where they made him their king.

He ruled for five years. In the sixth year, another king, who was stronger than he was, waged war against him. The city was conquered, and he was driven out. Again the younger brother became a wanderer, and he arrived one day at the house of the elder brother.

The elder brother was living in a village, neither rich nor poor. The two brothers rejoiced at seeing each other, and at once began telling all that had happened to them.

"You see," said the elder brother, "I was right all along. I've lived here quietly and well, while you, though you may have been a king, have seen a great deal of trouble,"

"I don't regret having gone into the forest and up the mountain,' replied the younger brother. "I may have nothing now, but I shall always have something to remember, while you have nothing to remember at all."

The Water Sprite and the Pearl (A Fable)

A man was riding in a boat and dropped a valuable pearl in the water. He returned to the shore, took a pail, and began to fill it with water and pour it out on the bank. He did so for three days straight.

On the fourth day, a water sprite came out of the sea and asked:

"Why are you scooping up water?"

The man said:

"Because I dropped a pearl."

The water sprite asked:

"Will you stop soon?"

The man said:

"When I've emptied the sea, I'll stop."

Then the water sprite returned to the sea, brought the very same pearl, and gave it back to the man.

The Grass Snake (A Story)

A woman had a daughter named Masha. Masha went to swim with her friends. The girls took off their clothes, left them on the shore, and jumped into the water.

A large grass snake crawled out of the water, and curling up, it lay down on Masha's blouse. The girls came out of the water, put on their clothes, and ran home. When Masha approached her shirt and saw that a grass snake was lying on it, she took a stick and was about to drive the snake away; but the snake raised its head and hissed in a human voice:

"Masha, Masha, promise to marry me."

Masha started crying and said: "Give me back my blouse and I will do anything."

"Will you marry me?"

"I will," she said. And the snake climbed off her blouse and returned to the water.

Masha put on her blouse and ran home. There she said to her mother: "Mama, a grass snake was lying on my blouse and said: 'Marry me or else I won't give you your blouse back.' So I promised him."

Her mother laughed and said: "You must have dreamt it."

A week later a whole den of snakes came crawling to Masha's house.

Masha saw the snakes, got frightened, and said: "Mama, the snakes have come crawling for me."

Her mother didn't believe her, but as soon as she saw them, she got frightened, and locked the vestibule and the door to their hut. The snakes crawled under the gate and into the vestibule, but they couldn't crawl into the hut. Then they crawled back, rolled themselves into a ball, and hurled themselves at the window. They broke the glass, fell on the floor of the hut, and crawled onto shelves, tables, and the stove-bench. Masha hid in a corner on the stove bench, but the snakes found her, and dragged her from there to the water.

Her mother wept and ran after them, but didn't catch up with them. The snakes rushed into the water taking Masha with them.

Her mother wept over her daughter and thought that she had died.

One day the mother was sitting by her window and looking out at the street. Suddenly she saw that her Masha was heading towards her and was leading a little boy by the hand, and was holding a little girl in her arms.

The mother was overjoyed and began kissing Masha and asking her where she'd been and whose children these were. Masha replied that they were her children, that the snake had married her, and that she was living with him in his watery kingdom.

Her mother asked her if she was happy to be living in a watery kingdom; her daughter replied that it was even better than living on the earth.

The mother asked Masha to stay with her, but Masha didn't agree. She said that she had promised her husband to return.

Then the mother asked her daughter:

"How will you get home?"

"I will go there and shout: 'Osip, Osip, come out here and take me.' He will come out onto the shore and take me."

Then her mother said to Masha: "Well, all right, but spend the night here with me."

Masha lay down and fell asleep, and her mother took an axe and went to the water.

She got to the shore and began to cry, "Osip, Osip, come out here."

The snake swam up to the bank. Then the mother struck the snake with her axe and cut off his head. The water became red from the blood.

The mother went home; her daughter woke up and said: "I'm going home, Mama; I feel bored here." And she left.

Masha took her little girl in her arms, and her little boy by the hand.

When they got to the shore, she began to call: "Osip, Osip, come out here and take me." But no one came out of the water.

Then she looked at the water and saw that it was red and a snake's head was floating in it.

Then Masha kissed her son and daughter and said to them:

"You have no father, and you also won't have a mother. You, my daughter, will be a swallow: fly above the water. You, my son, will be a nightingale; sing at twilight; and I will be a cuckoo bird, and will cry cuckoo over my dead husband." And they all flew off in different directions.

The Sparrow and the Swallows (A Story)

One day I was out in the courtyard, looking at a swallow's nest under the eaves. As I watched, both swallows left the nest and flew away.

While they were away, a sparrow flew down from the roof, hopped onto the edge of the nest, looked around, and darted into the nest. Then it stuck its head out and chirped.

Soon after, one of the swallows returned. It wanted to enter the nest, but as soon as it saw the visitor, it twittered, beat its wings, and flew away.

The sparrow sat there, chirping.

All of a sudden a little flock of swallows appeared. Each swallow flew up to the nest, as though to have a look at the sparrow, and then flew off again.

The sparrow was not frightened. It turned its head this way and that and continued to chirp.

The swallows kept flying up to the nest, bustled about, and flew off again.

There was a reason why the swallows were flying up to the nest: each brought a little glob of mud in its beak, and together they were gradually closing up the entrance to the nest.

Again and again they flew up and away, making the opening smaller and smaller as they added more and more mud to it.

At first, the sparrow's neck could be seen, then only its head, then its beak, and at last nothing at all could be seen. The swallows had closed the nest completely. Then they flew off and began circling over the house, whistling shrilly.

Cambyses and Psamtik (History)[14]

When the Persian tsar Cambyses conquered Egypt and took the Egyptian tsar Psamtik prisoner, he ordered that Psamtik should be led out into the square with other Egyptians along with two thousand men, together with Psamtik's

---

14 Cambyses II, who flourished sixth century BCE, was the Achaemenid king of Persia (reigned 529–522 BCE), who conquered Egypt in 525. Psamtik (d. 610 BCE), governor, later king

daughter; he ordered them to dress her in rags and to send her with buckets to fetch water; he sent the daughters of most distinguished Egyptians dressed in similar clothes with her. When the daughters walked past their fathers, howling and weeping, the fathers burst into tears as they looked at their daughters. Only Psamtik didn't cry; he merely cast his eyes down.

After the girls had passed by, Cambyses brought out Psamtik's son along with other Egyptians. They all had ropes tied around their necks and bits between their teeth. They were being led out to be killed.

Psamtik saw this and understood that his son was to be taken to his death. But just as he did at the sight of his daughter, while other fathers were weeping, he merely cast his eyes down.

Then his former comrade and relative walked past Psamtik.

He had previously been wealthy, but now like a pauper, he begged for alms from the soldiers. As soon as Psamtik saw him, he called him by name, slapped himself on the forehead, and began sobbing. Cambyses was surprised at what Psamtik did, and sent to ask this way:

"Psamtik! Your lord Cambyses asks why you didn't weep, as your daughter was humiliated and your son was led to his death, yet you felt so sorry for a beggar who's not even your relative."

Psamtik replied:

"Cambyses! My own grief is so great, that it's impossible to cry about it, but I feel sorry for my comrade because in his old age he's fallen from wealth into poverty."

When the other captive tsar, Cyrus,[15] who was present there, heard Psamtik's words, his own grief seemed even greater to him, and he burst into tears; and all the Persians who were also there began crying.

And Cambyses himself began to feel pity, and ordered Psamtik's son returned to him, and Psamtik himself brought before him. But they didn't find his son alive—he'd already been killed—but Psamtik himself was brought to Cambyses, who pardoned him.

The Shark (A Story)

Our ship was anchored off the coast of Africa. It was a fine day, with a fresh breeze blowing from the sea; but towards evening the weather changed: it

---

(reigned 664–610 BCE) of ancient Egypt, expelled the Assyrians from Egypt and reunited the country.

15 Cyrus: (600–530 BCE); commonly known as Cyrus the Great, was the founder of the Achaemenid Persian Empire.

became stuffy and hot air from the Sahara Desert was blowing at us, as if from a red-hot stove.

Before sunset, the captain went on deck, and shouted: "Swim time!"—and in a minute the sailors jumped into the water, lowered the sail into the water, tied it up, and made a bath in the sail.

There were two young boys on the ship with us. They were the first to jump into the water, but they felt confined in the sail and decided to have a swimming race on the high seas.

Both, like lizards, stretched out in the water and with all their strength swam to the place where there was a barrel above the anchor.

At first one boy overtook his comrade, but then he began to lag behind. The boy's father, an old gunner, stood on the deck, admiring his son. When his son began to lag behind, the father shouted to him: "Don't give up! Push on ahead!"

Suddenly, from the deck, someone shouted: "Shark!"—and we all saw the back of a sea monster in the water.

The shark was heading straight for the boys.

"Back! Back! Turn back! Shark!" shouted the gunner. But the boys didn't hear him; they swam on, laughing and shouting even more merrily and louder than before.

The gunner, pale as a ghost, looked at the children without moving.

The sailors lowered a boat, jumped into it and, plying their oars, raced with all their might toward the boys; but they were still far away from them, while the shark was no more than twenty paces from the boys.

At first the boys didn't hear what was being shouted and didn't see the shark; but then one of them looked back: we all heard a piercing scream, and the boys swam in different directions.

This scream seemed to wake the gunner. He took off and ran to the cannons. He turned the gun carriage, leaned on the cannon, took aim, and grabbed the fuse.

We all, no matter how many of us were on the ship, froze with fear and waited to see what would happen.

A shot rang out and we saw that the gunner had fallen next to the cannon and covered his face with his hands. We didn't see what happened to the shark and the boys because for a moment smoke clouded our eyes.

But when the smoke cleared over the water, at first a quiet murmur was heard from all sides; then this murmur became stronger. Finally, a loud, joyful cry rang out.

The old gunner opened his eyes, got up, and looked out at the sea.

The yellow belly of the dead shark was floating above the waves. Within a few minutes the boat sailed up to the boys and brought them back safely on board the ship.

Why Windows Sweat and Why Dew Forms
(An Explanation)

When water dries up, what happens to it?

All things expand in heat. Water expands in heat and divides into such tiny bits that it's impossible to see them, and then passes into the air. These little bits float around in the air and are invisible, as long as the air is warm. But if the air cools, the steam cools right away and it becomes visible.

If you heat a bathhouse really hot and pour water on the bricks, the water will turn into steam and the bathhouse will be dry. If you pour on more water, the same thing happens: it disappears again. If the bathhouse is hot, a tub of water vanishes in the air. The tub of water will remain in the warm air of the bathroom and be invisible. The air of the bathroom will absorb the entire tub of water. But if you keep adding more water, the air will become saturated and won't be able to accept any more; the extra water will turn into drops. It can hold one tub, but additional water will overflow.

If you bring hot bricks into the same unheated bathhouse and start pouring water on them, you'll pour on a small tub; it will disperse and it won't be visible—the air will absorb it. But if you start pouring in another small tub, the water will turn into drops. In the same bathhouse, when the air was hot, it absorbed a tub; but when it is cold it can absorb only a container.

If you blow on a glass, little drops will form on it. And the colder it is the more drops will form. Why is that? Because a person's breath is warmer than the glass and it contains a great deal of moisture. As soon as the breath touches the cold glass, it turns into water.

A sponge holds water, and the water is invisible until you squeeze the sponge; but as soon as you do, the water flows out. The same way, the air also holds water while it is hot; but when it cools, the water will flow out.

If you bring a cold pot from the cellar during the summer, water droplets will form on it right away. Where did this water come from? It was there all the time. Only when it was warm, the water was invisible, but as the heat passed from the air to the cold pot, the air surrounding the pot cools down, and droplets formed. The same thing happens on windows. It's warm in the room, and steam is contained in the air; but when the windows cool from the outside, and inside next to the windows, the air cools down, and droplets form.

This is how dew is formed. As the ground cools down at night, the air above it also cools, and the steam comes out of the cool air in the form of water drops and they settle on the ground.

Sometimes it happens that it's cold outside, but warm inside, and the windows don't sweat; sometimes it's warm outside, but it's not as warm inside—and the windows sweat.

Sometimes it's warm at night, and there's lots of dew: and then there's a cool night, and there's no dew.

Why does this happen? Because there is both dry air and moist air.

A dry wind occurs without warming up, and can still raise a lot of steam; moist air occurs and without heat, it can't absorb any more water. Dry air is like a sponge, still not saturated with water, while moist air is like a sponge all saturated with water. If the air is a little cooler, and you squeeze the sponge, the water will start to flow. In moist air every object, if it's colder than the air, will be soaked; whereas in dry air, every wet object will dry out. Steam is emitted from it and the air absorbs it.

The Bishop and the Robber (A True Story)

They had been searching for a certain robber for a long time. One time he changed his clothes and came into the town. The police recognized him and chased after him. The robber was running away and got to a bishop's house; the gates were open and he went into the courtyard.

A novice asked him what he wanted.

The robber didn't know how to reply and said at random: "I need to see the bishop."

The bishop received the robber and asked on what business he'd come.

The robber replied: "I'm a robber; they're after me; hide me, or I'll kill you."

The bishop said: "I'm an old man, and I'm not afraid of death; but I feel sorry for you. Go into that room; you're tired; get some rest, and I'll send you some food."

The police didn't dare enter the bishop's house, and the robber stayed to spend the night.

After the robber had rested, the bishop went in to see him and said: "I feel sorry for you for being cold and hungry, and because you are being chased like a wolf, but I feel most sorry that you have done a lot of evil and are destroying your soul. Stop doing these evil deeds!"

The robber replied: "No, I won't be able to break out of the habit of doing evil deeds. I've lived as a robber and I will die like one."

The bishop left him, opened all the doors, and went to bed.

That night the robber woke up and began pacing through all the rooms. He was surprised that the bishop hadn't locked anything up and had left all the doors open.

The robber began to look around—to see what he could steal; he saw a large silver candlestick and thought: "I'll take this item—it costs a lot of money—but I'll leave, and won't kill the old man." And that's what he did.

The police hadn't deserted the bishop's house and stood watch all the time. As soon as the robber came out, they surrounded him and found the candlestick he was hiding under his coat.

The robber began to deny it, but the police said: "You can deny your previous evil deeds, but you can't contest the fact that you've stolen this candlestick. Let's go to see the bishop—he'll confirm your guilt."

They brought the robber to the bishop, showed him the candlestick, and asked him: "Is this your candlestick?" He replied, "It is."

The police said: "It was stolen from you, and here's the robber."

The robber said nothing; his eyes roamed just like a wolf's eyes.

The bishop made no reply, returned to his room, took a match to the first candlestick, gave it to the robber, and said: "Why, my friend, did you take only one candlestick? I gave them both to you."

The robber began crying and said to the police: "I'm a robber and a bandit: take me away."

Then he said to the bishop: "Forgive me, for Christ's sake, and pray to God for me."

Yermak (History)

During the reign of Ivan the Terrible there were wealthy merchants named Strogonov and they lived in Perm, near the river Kama.[16] They found out that around the Kama for a distance of 140 versts there was good land: fields that had not yet been plowed, and forests that had not yet been cut. There were many wild beasts in the forests, lakes along the river teeming with fish; no one lived there, except some Tatars, who would sometimes visit.

So the Strogonovs wrote a letter to the tsar:

"Grant us this land, and we will build towns, gather men together, populate it, and prevent the Tatars from passing through it."

The tsar consented and granted them the land. The Strogonovs sent out agents to collect people. Many people came who were out of work. The Strogonovs assigned lands and forest to all who came, gave cattle to each, and

---

16 Ivan Vasilyevich (1530–1584) was the first Russian ruler to assume the title of "tsar."

agreed not to tax them during their lives; they only required of them that, if necessary, they would go fight the Tatars. Thus this land was settled by Russians.

Twenty or so years passed. The Strogonov merchants grew richer and richer, and this territory of one hundred and forty versts became too small for them. They wanted still more land. Now there were lofty mountains a hundred versts distant, the Urals, and they had heard that beyond these mountains there was some excellent land. The owner of this land, which was boundless, was a Siberian prince named Kuchum.

In former times Kuchum had pledged his allegiance to the Russian tsar, but later on he began to revolt, and was now threatening to destroy the Strogonov towns.

And again the Strogonovs wrote to the tsar: "You granted us land, and we have brought it under your sway; now the thieving little Tsar Kuchum has revolted against you, and he wants to take this land away and destroy us. Order us to take the territory that lies beyond the Ural Mountains; we will conquer Kuchum and bring all his land under your sway."

The tsar consented, and replied: "If you have the power, take possession of Kuchum's land. But do not lure many people away from Russia."

As soon as the Strogonovs received this letter from the tsar they sent their agents to collect still more people. And they gave orders to recruit more Cossacks from the Volga and the Don.

Now at that time there were many Cossacks roving along the Volga and the Don. They formed bands numbering two hundred, three hundred, or six hundred men, elected their atamans or leaders, and sailed up and down in boats, seizing and plundering merchant ships, and wintering in a stronghold on the banks.

The Strogonovs' agents came to the Volga and began to make inquiries: "Who are the most famous Cossacks here?" And the reply came: "There are many Cossacks, And they make our life miserable. There is Mishka the Circassian, and Sarui-Azman . . . but there is no one worse than Yermak Timofeyich, the ataman.[17] He has an army of a thousand men, and not only the people and the merchants fear him, but even the tsar's army dares not engage him."

And the stewards went to the ataman Yermak and tried to persuade him to join the Strogonovs. Yermak received the stewards, listened to their words, and promised to come with his army by the feast of the Assumption.

By the time of the Feast of the Assumption about six hundred Cossacks,[18] with their ataman Yermak, the son of Timofey, came to Strogonov. At first Strogonov

---

17 Cossack chieftain.
18 The Feast of the Assumption is widely celebrated on August 15 all over Christendom. This holy day marks the occasion of the Virgin Mary's bodily ascent to heaven at the end of her life.

sent them out against the neighboring Tatars. The Cossacks defeated them. Later, when there was nothing else to do, the Cossacks began to roam the neighborhood and pillage. Strogonov summoned Yermak, and said: "I'm not going to keep you any longer, if you are going to act so lawlessly." And Yermak replied: "I'm sorry, but it's not so easy to manage my men; they have had their fun. Give us some work to do. "And Strogonov said: "Go beyond the Urals, fight with Kuchum, and conquer his land. Even the tsar will reward you." And he showed Yermak the tsar's missive. Yermak was delighted; he called together his Cossacks, and said:

"You make me feel ashamed before the master here. You're always up to some lawlessness. If you don't stop, he'll dismiss you, and then where will you go? The tsar has a great army on the Volga; they'll take all of us prisoners, and it will go poorly with us on account of the bad deeds we've done. But if you find it dull here, then here is some work for you to do."

And he showed them the tsar's letter permitting Strogonov to conquer the land beyond the Urals. The Cossacks talked it over and agreed to go.

Yermak returned to Strogonov, and the two began to confer on how best to organize the expedition.

They figured out how many boats would be needed, how much grain, powder, lead; how many cattle, firearms; how many Tatar prisoners to serve as interpreters; and how many German gunsmiths.

Strogonov said to himself: "Though this is going to cost me dearly, still I must provide him with all he asks; otherwise they'll settle down here and ruin me."

So Strogonov agreed, got everything together, and fitted out Yermak and his Cossacks.

On the first of September, Yermak and his Cossacks started to row up the river Chusovaya in thirty-two boats, each carrying twenty men. For four days they rowed upstream and entered the Silver River. This was as far as they could go by boat. They made inquiries of the guides, and learned that at this point, they had to climb over the mountains, proceed about two hundred versts by land, and then there would again be some other rivers. The Cossacks stopped here; they built a town and unloaded all their belongings, threw aside their boats, constructed carts, loaded them up, and set out on their journey across the mountains. The whole region was forest and no one lived there. For ten days they went across the country and reached the Zharovnya River. There they halted again and set to work building boats. When they were ready, they started on their voyage down the river. They sailed for five days, and reached regions still more delightful: fields, forests, and lakes. There was also an abundance of fish and game, and the game was not afraid of them. After they sailed for one day more, they reached the Tura River. There they began to meet the inhabitants, and saw Tatar towns.

Yermak sent some Cossacks to inspect one small town, bidding them find out what sort of a place it was and whether it had many defenders. Twenty men went on this expedition; they threw all the Tatars into a panic, and captured the whole town and all their cattle. They killed some Tatars and captured some prisoners.

Through interpreters, Yermak asked the Tatars what kind of people they were, and under whose sway they lived. The Tatars replied that they belonged to the tsardom of Siberia and their tsar was Kuchum.

Yermak let the Tatars go, except three of the most intelligent, whom he retained as guides to show him the way.

They sailed on. The further they sailed, the wider the river was becoming all the time, and the countryside grew better and better.

They kept meeting more and more people. But the inhabitants were not very strong, and the Cossacks captured all the towns along the river.

In one town they took a large number of Tatars prisoners, including one person of authority, an old Tatar. They asked him who he was. He said: "I'm Tauzik, a servant of my tsar Kuchum; I am his head man in this town."

Yermak questioned Tauzik about his tsar. "Was his city of Sibir far away? Did Kuchum have a large army? Was he very wealthy?" Tauzik told him all. "Kuchum is the greatest tsar in all the world. His city of Sibir is the biggest town in the world. In it," said he, "there are as many men and cattle as there are stars in the sky. The tsar Kuchum's army is beyond number; all the other tsars banded together couldn't vanquish him."

Yermak said: "We Russians have come here to vanquish your tsar Kuchum, to take his town, and to bring him under the sway of the Russian tsar. We have a very large army. Those who have come with me are only the vanguard, but those who follow us in boats are beyond number, and they all have guns. And our guns will shoot through a tree, not like your bows and arrows. Just look here!"

And Yermak shot at a tree and split it; the Cossacks began to fire off their guns from all sides. Tauzik fell on his knees with fright, and Yermak said to him: "Now go back to your tsar Kuchum and tell him what you've seen. Let him submit to us; if he doesn't, we'll destroy him." And he let Tauzik go.

The Cossacks sailed on. They entered the great river Tobol, and all the time they were drawing nearer and nearer to the city of Sibir. They came to the mouth of the little river Babasan. Behold! On the bank stood a town, and around the town were many Tatars.

An interpreter was sent to the Tatars to inquire who those men were. The interpreter came back with the answer: "This army has been assembled by Kuchum. The general who commands the army is Kuchum's own son-in-law,

Mametkul. He sent me here and commanded me to say to you, 'Go back, or else he will slaughter all of you.'"

Yermak collected his Cossacks, went on shore, and began to fire at the Tatars. As soon as they heard the noise of the firing, they started fleeing. The Cossacks set out in pursuit of them; some they killed, others they captured. Mametkul himself barely escaped.

The Cossacks sailed on. They came out upon a broad, swift river, the Irtuish. They sailed down this river for one whole day and arrived at a handsome town, and there they stopped. The Cossacks marched into the town. As soon as they reached it, the Tatars began shooting arrows at them and wounded three Cossacks. Yermak sent his interpreter to say to the Tatars: "Surrender your town, or else we'll slaughter you." The interpreter returned, saying:

"Kuchum's servant, Atikh Murza Kachara, lives here. He has a great army, and he declares that he will not surrender the town."

Yermak gathered his Cossacks and said: "Now, lads, if we don't take this town, the Tatars will start celebrating and won't let us pass. Therefore, the sooner we frighten them, the easier it will be for us. All of you come on! Throw yourselves on them all at once!" And thus they did. There were many Tatars there, and brave fellows they were!

As the Cossacks rushed forward, the Tatars began shooting arrows from their bows. They overwhelmed the Cossacks with their arrows. Some of them were killed, others, wounded. The Cossacks got furious, and they reached the Tatars; they killed all they fell upon.

In this little town the Cossacks found many treasures, cattle, rugs, furs, and much mead. Afterwards they buried their dead, rested a while, took their plunder, and sailed on. They had not sailed very far when, behold! On the bank there stood something like a town, and there was an army that seemed to stretch as far as the eye could see; the entire army was surrounded by a ditch, and the ditch was protected by a palisade. The Cossacks stopped. They began thinking. Yermak called a council: "Well, lads, what shall we do?"

The Cossacks were disheartened. Some said: "We must sail by." Others said: "We must turn back."

They grew desperate and blamed Yermak, saying: "Why did you bring us here? They've killed so many of us already, and wounded even more, and now we'll all perish here." They began to shed tears.

Yermak said to his sub-ataman, Ivan Koltso: "Well, now, Vanya, what do you think?" And Koltso replied: "What do I think? If we're not killed today, then we will be killed tomorrow; and if not tomorrow, then we'll die for nothing at home. My advice is, leap onshore, head straight for the Tatars, and God will decide."

And Yermak exclaimed: "Aye! You're a brave fellow, Vanya! That's what we must do! Hey! You lads! You're not Cossacks, but old women! Apparently, it was only catching sturgeon and scaring Tatar women—that's all you're good for. Don't you see for yourselves? If we go back, we'll be killed! If we row by, we'll be killed! If we stay here, we'll be killed! Where should we go back to? If you work hard, it gets easier afterward! Lads, you resemble a healthy mare that my father had. On her way downhill she would pull and on level ground she would pull; but when it came to going uphill, she would balk, turn around, and wait for it to get easier. Then my father took a stake and beat her. And the mare twisted, kicked, and broke the cart. Then father took her out of the harness and killed her. Now, if she'd pulled, she wouldn't have been thrashed. So it is with us, lads. There's only one thing left for us to do: head straight for the Tatars."

The Cossacks laughed, and said: "Apparently you're wiser than we are, Timofeich. There's no point in even asking us fools. Take us wherever you wish. We can't die twice, but we have to die once."

And Yermak said: "Now listen, lads. This is the way we'll do it. They haven't seen all of us yet. We'll split into three bands. Those in the middle will march straight at them, and the other two divisions will make a flank movement from the right and from the left. Now when the middle division begins to engage them, they'll think that we're all there, and they'll come out. Then we'll hit them from the flanks. That's the way, lads. And if we beat them, there'll be nothing left to fear. We'll become tsars ourselves."

And that was what they did. As soon as the middle division went forward under Yermak, the Tatars began to yell and rush out. Then the wings joined the battle, the right under Ivan Koltso, the left under the ataman Meshcheryak.

The Tatars were panic-stricken and took to their heels. The Cossacks slaughtered them. And no one at all dared oppose Yermak any longer. Thus he made his entrance into the town of Sibir. And there, Yermak took up his residence exactly as if he'd been tsar.

The neighboring princes began coming to Yermak with salutations; the Tatars returned and began settling down in Sibir. Kuchum and his son-in-law, Mamutkil, however, dared not make a direct attack on Yermak; they kept going around in circles, planning how to destroy him.

In springtime, at the time of the floods, some Tatars came running to Yermak, and said: "Mametkul is coming to attack you again; he's gathered a great army, and is now on the Vagaya River."

Yermak hastened over rivers, swamps, streams, and forests, crept up with his Cossacks, fell on Mametkul, killed many of the Tatars, took Mametkul himself prisoner, and brought him back to Sibir. Now there remained only a few Tatars who were not subdued; that summer Yermak marched against those who would not submit; on the Irtysh and the Ob rivers, Yermak brought so much land under subjugation that you couldn't circle it in two months.

After he had conquered all this land, he sent a messenger to the Strogonovs with a letter, in which he said: "I have taken Kuchum's city, I have Mametkul in captivity, and have brought all the people under my sway. But it has cost me many Cossacks. Send us more men, so that we may have more fun. The wealth in this land is limitless in extent." And he also sent costly furs: fox, martens, and sable.

Two years passed. Yermak still held Sibir, but no reinforcements had arrived from Russia: Yermak's Russian forces were shrinking.

One time the Tatar Karacha sent a messenger to Yermak, saying: "We have submitted to your sway, but the Nogay are harassing us; let some of your brave men come to our aid. We'll conquer the Nogay together. And we'll swear an oath that we won't harm your men."

Yermak had faith in their oath, and sent Ivan Koltso to them with forty men. As soon as these men arrived, the Tatars fell upon them and killed them; and this still further reduced the number of Cossacks.

Another time some Bukhara traders sent word to Yermak that they were on their way with merchandise, which they wished to bring to his town of Sibir, but that Kuchum and his army were in their way, and wouldn't let them pass.

Yermak took fifty men and went out to clear the road for the Bukharans. But when he reached the Irtysh River, he didn't find any Bukharans. They prepared to spend the night there.

The night was dark and rainy. No sooner had the Cossacks retired for the night, than the Tatars rushed out from every side, threw themselves on the sleeping Cossacks, and began to mow them down. Yermak leapt up and began to fight. He was wounded in the arm with a knife. Then he ran to the river. The Tatars went after him. He threw himself into the river. And that was the last they saw of him; his body was never found and no one knew how he died.

A year later, the tsar's troops came, and the Tatars made peace.

Sukhman (A Story in Verse)

> While gentle Prince Vladimir's
> Feast was in progress
> For his boyars, princes, and bold young warriors,
> Everyone was boasting at the feast:
> One was bragging about his golden treasures,
> Another, his fine steed,

A strong one was bragging about his strength.
A foolish one, was bragging about his young wife, and
A clever one, his aged mother.
The bogatyr, Sukhman Odikhmantyevich,
Sat alone, deep in thought,
Not bragging about anything.
Then, Prince Vladimir, the bright sun,
Pacing alone around the room,
Shook his golden curls,
And said to Odikhmantyevich:
"Why, Sukhmantyushka, you've become so thoughtful,
You don't eat or drink,
You don't carve up a white swan,
And you don't brag of anything at the feast!"
Sukhman said the following:
"If you order me to brag,
I'll deliver into your hands,
A white swan, not bloodied,
Not wounded, but alive."
And Sukhman stood up on his swift legs,
Saddled his fine steed,
Rode out to the blue sea,
To the blue sea, to the peaceful creeks.
Sukhman rode up to the first creek,
But didn't come upon any white swans.
He rode to the second creek,
But didn't see any goose-swans,
And at the third creek,
No gray geese or white swans,
And Sukhmantyushka got to thinking:
"How will I return to the splendid city of Kiev [Kyiv]?
What will I say to Prince Vladimir?"
And he headed for the mother Dnepr River;
He looked, and saw that it was flowing not as always,
Not as always, not as previously,
But the water was muddied by sand.
And then Sukhman asked the Dnepr River:
"Why are you flowing, thus, mother Dnepr,
Not as always, not as previously,
And your water is muddied by sand?"

And the mother Dnepr River replied:
"I'm flowing not as before,
Not as always, not as previously,
Because forty thousand wicked Tatars
Stand behind me, behind the Dnepr River,
From morn 'til night they build a bridge,
What they build by day, I destroy at night,
And I'm running out of strength."
Then Sukhman said the following:
"It's not my youthful bragging,
Not to engage the Tatar forces."
And he let his fine steed run,
And galloped over the Dnepr River,
And his fine steed didn't even get his hooves wet,
Sukhman ran up to the powerful oak tree,
To the powerful, strong oak,
The oak tree with the twisted roots,
And he uprooted it.
White sap ran from the thick end of the oak;
He grabbed the oak at the top,
And drove his steed straight at the Tatars.
Sukhmantyushka began to turn around
And wave his cudgel,
As he waved it ahead—a street formed,
As he turned it back—a little lane appeared.
Odikhmantyevich killed all the Tatars,
Three Tatar kids escaped,
They hid under bushes and willows by the Dnepr River,
Sukhman rode up to mother Dnepr,
The three Tatar kids shot three arrows
At Odikhmantyevich from under the bushes,
Into his fair body, into his sides.
Sukhmantyushka-the-bright yanked out the arrows
From his sides, from his bloody wounds,
He plugged them up with poppy leaves,
And killed the three Tatar kids with a knife.
Sukhman rode back to Prince Vladimir.
Tied his steed to a post in the courtyard.
Sukhman entered the dining room.
There was Prince Vladimir, the handsome sun,

Pacing around the room all alone,
He said to Odikhmantyevich:
"Well, then, Sukhmantyushka, didn't you bring me
A white swan, unbloodied?"
Sukhman said the following words:
"Hail, Prince Vladimir, I wasn't busy with any swans
Beyond the Dnepr River.
I met a force of forty thousand men
Beyond the Dnepr River:
The evil Tatars were going to Kiev,
Building a bridge from morn 'til night,
And the Dnepr River ripped it out at night,
But the river kept running out of strength,
I released my steed and attacked the Tatars,
I killed all of them, to the last man."
Prince Volodimir,[19] the bright sun,
Didn't believe these words.
He ordered his faithful servants
To take Sukhman by his fair arms,
And lock him up in the deep dungeon:
And he sent Dobrynyushka to the Dnepr
To report on Sukhman's deeds.
Dobrynyushka stood up on his swift legs,
And harnessed his faithful steed,
And rode out into the field to mother Dnepr River,
And saw—40,000 men
Lying there, all dead.
And there was an oak tree lying on the ground, with its roots
All broken into splinters,
Dobrynyushka picked up the oak pulled from the ground,
He brought it back to Vladimir,
And this is what Dobrynyushka said:
"Odikhmantyevich was bragging about the truth,
I saw, beyond the Dnepr River,
Forty thousand evil Tatars lying there,
And Odikhmantyevich's oak club,
Shattered into splinters."

---

19 An alternate spelling of Vladimir.

Then Prince Vladimir ordered his servants
To go to the deep dungeon,
And bring Odikhmantyevich out immediately,
To bring him to Vladimir so he can see him with his own eyes;
He then spoke these words:
"For his great deeds,
I will pardon the brave lad,
I will love him, and grant him
Towns and their surroundings,
And villages and their surroundings,
And a large fortune of gold."
His faithful servants went to the deep dungeon
To fetch Odikhmantyevich,
They said these words to him:
"Come out from the dungeon, Sukhman:
Prince Vladimir pardons you
For your great deeds,
And wants to grant you
Towns and their surroundings,
Villages and their surroundings,
And a large fortune of gold."
Sukhman came out into the fresh air,
And he said the following:
"Hail, Prince Vladimir, our bright sun,
You didn't pardon me in time,
You didn't favor me in time,
And now your clear eyes
Won't see me any longer."
And Odikhmantyevich pulled out
The poppy leaves from his bloody wounds,
And the bright light Sukhmantyushka said:
"Flow, oh river of my blood,
Of my hot blood,
Of my hot blood, shed in vain,
Flow Sukhman, oh the river Sukhman,
Become a sister to the Dnepr River."

THE THIRD RUSSIAN BOOK FOR READING

The Tsar and the Falcon (A Fable)

Once on a hunt the tsar released his favorite falcon after a hare and went galloping after it.

The falcon caught the hare. The tsar took it away, and started to look for some water to quench his thirst. The tsar found some water on a hillside. But it trickled out, only one drop at a time. So the tsar drew his cup from his saddle, and placed it under the water.

The water trickled into the cup, and when the cup was full, the tsar put it to his lips, and was about to drink. Suddenly while sitting on the tsar's hand, the falcon flapped its wings and spilled the water.

Again the tsar placed the cup under the spring. He waited a long time, until it was filled to the brim, and again, when he started lifting it to his lips, the falcon started flapping its wings and spilled the water.

When for the third time the tsar managed to get his cup filled, and was lifting it to his lips, the falcon spilled it once more.

The tsar grew angry, slammed the falcon with all his might against a stone, and killed it.

Then the tsar's servants appeared; one of them ran up to the spring to find a more plentiful supply of water and to fill the cup quickly.

But the servant brought no water back; he returned with an empty cup, and said:

"That water isn't fit to drink; there's a snake in the spring, and it's poisoned all the water. It's a good thing the falcon spilled the cup. Had you drunk the water, you would have died.

The tsar said: "I paid the falcon back cruelly; he saved my life, but I killed him."

The Fox (A Fable)

A vixen was caught in a trap; she tore off her tail and got away. And she began thinking: how could she conceal her shame? She summoned other foxes and tried to convince them to chop off their tails. "A tail," she said, "is completely useless, merely an extra weight we drag around with us."

One fox said: "Oh, you wouldn't be saying that if you yourself weren't lacking a tail!"

The tailless fox held her tongue and walked away.

Harsh Punishment (A Story)

A man went to the market and bought some beef. There they tricked him: they gave him some spoiled beef and, in addition, cheated him about the weight.

On his way home with the beef he kept cursing. He ran into the tsar who asked him: "Why are you cursing?"

He replied, "I'm cursing the man who deceived me. I paid for three pounds of beef, and was given only two; plus it was spoiled. The tsar said, "Let's go back to the market and point out to me the man who deceived you." The man went back and showed the tsar who'd deceived him. The tsar made the merchant weigh the meat in his presence, and saw that the man had in fact been deceived. So the tsar asked, "How do you want me to punish the merchant?" The man said: "Order that he cut as much flesh from his back as he stole from me."

So the tsar said: "All right. Take a knife and cut a pound of flesh from the merchant's back. But beware: make sure that the weight is accurate, because if you cut off more or less than a pound, you will be the guilty one."

The man fell silent and went home.

The Wild Donkey and the Tame Donkey (A Fable)

A wild donkey saw a tame donkey, went up to him, and began to praise his way of life: his coat was so smooth and his feed was so tasty. Then, as they loaded up the tame donkey, and the driver began to urge him ahead with a stick from behind, the wild donkey said: "No, brother; now I don't envy your way of life; I see that you earn your way through hard labor."

The Hare and the Hound (A Fable)

A hare once asked a hound: "Why do you bark when you chase us? You would be much more likely to catch us, if you ran without barking. Whereas when you bark, you just drive us into the hunter's hands; he can hear where we're running, and hurries to meet us with his gun, shoots, kills us, and doesn't give you anything."

The dog replied: "That's not the reason I bark. I bark simply because when I catch your scent, I get angry, and because I'm just about to catch you. I myself don't know why, but I can't keep from barking."

The Deer (A Fable)

A deer approached a stream to get a drink, saw his reflection in the water, and began to admire his fine antlers—they were large and branched; but when he looked at his legs, he said: "But my legs are poor and feeble." All of a sudden, a lion jumped out and threw himself on the deer. The deer set off galloping across the open field. He was getting away, but when he got to the forest, his antlers got tangled in the branches, and the lion grabbed him. When the deer was about to die, he said: "How foolish I am! The legs that I thought were poor and feeble are what was saving me, and those antlers I was admiring, are the cause of my death."

Hares (A Description)

Hares feed at night. During winter forest hares feed on the bark of trees, while field hares feed on winter crops and grass, and the threshing floor hares eat the grain in the granary. Through the night hares make a deep, visible track through the snow. Men, dogs, wolves, foxes, ravens, and eagles love to hunt hares. If a hare were to walk straight ahead, it would be easily caught in the morning by following its tracks; but God has made hares cowardly, and their cowardice saves them.

At night a hare goes fearlessly through the forests and fields, leaving straight tracks; but as soon as morning comes, its enemies wake up, and it hears the barking of dogs, the squeaking of sleighs, the voices of peasants, or the crashing of a wolf through the forest; then it begins to rush from side to side in fear. It jumps forward, gets frightened of something, and runs back following its own tracks. It hears something again, leaps at full speed to one side, then runs away from its previous tracks. Again something makes a noise, and the hare turns back, and leaps to one side. When it's daylight, the hare lies down.

In the morning hunters try to follow the hare's tracks, but they get confused by its double tracks and long leaps, and marvel at the hare's cunning. But the hare didn't mean to be cunning. It's merely afraid of everything.

The Dog and the Wolf (A Fable)

A dog fell asleep at the rear of a courtyard. A wolf ran up wanting to eat him. The dog said: "Wolf, don't eat me yet: I'm lean and bony now. Wait a while—my master's going to celebrate a wedding; then I shall have plenty to eat. I'll grow fat. It'll be better to eat me then."

The wolf believed the dog and went away. When the wolf came a second time, he saw the dog stretched out on the roof. The wolf said to him:

"Well, did they celebrate the wedding?"

The dog replied:

"Listen, wolf! If you ever catch me asleep again in the front yard, don't wait for the wedding."

The Tsar's Brothers (A Fairy Tale)

A tsar was walking along the street. A beggar came up to him and asked him for alms.

The tsar didn't give him anything.

The beggar said: "Tsar, you've obviously forgotten that God is father to all of us: we're all brothers and we have to share all that we have."

The tsar stopped and said: "You speak the truth: we're all brothers and we have to share everything," and he gave the beggar a gold coin.

The beggar took the gold coin and said: "You've given me too little; is that how one shares with his brothers? You must share half. You have a million rubles, but you gave me only one."

Then the tsar said: "You're right: I have a million rubles and gave you only one, but I have as many brothers as I have rubles."

The Blind Man and the Milk (A Fable)

A man born blind asked a sighted man: "What color is milk?"

The sighted man said: "The color of milk is the same as that of white paper."

The blind man asked: "Well, does that color rustle in one's hands like paper?"

The sighted man said: "No, it's as white as flour."

The blind man asked: "Well, is it as soft and powdery as flour?"

The sighted man said: "No, it's simply as white as a white hare."

The blind man asked: "Well, is it as fluffy and soft as a hare?"

The sighted man said: "No, it's as white as snow."

The blind man asked: "Well, is it as cold as snow?"

No matter how many examples the sighted man gave, the blind man was unable to understand what the white color of milk was like.

The Gray Hare (Description)

A gray hare was living in the winter near a village. When night came, he pricked up one ear, listened for a while; then pricked up his other ear, wiggled his whiskers, sniffed, and sat up on his hind legs. Then he took a leap or two over the deep snow, sat on his hind legs again, and started looking around. The hare couldn't see anything but snow. The snow lay in waves and sparkled like sugar. Over the hare's head hovered a frosty vapor, and through this vapor one could see large, bright stars.

The hare had to cross the highway in order to reach a threshing floor it knew of. On the highway one could hear sleigh runners squeaking, horses snorting, and sleigh seats creaking.

The hare stopped again near the road. Peasants were walking alongside their sleighs, with the collars of their caftans raised. Their faces were barely visible. Their beards, mustaches, and eyelashes were all white. Steam rose from their mouths and noses. Their horses were sweaty and hoarfrost was sticking to their sweat. Their horses jostled under their collars and dove in and out of snowdrifts. The peasants ran behind the horses and in front of them, striking them with their whips. Two peasants walked beside each other, and one of them was telling the other how a horse of his had once been stolen.

When the carts passed by, the hare leapt across the road and quietly headed for the threshing floor. A dog following the cart caught sight of the hare. It began to bark and darted after the hare. The hare took off toward the threshing floor over the snowdrifts, which held it back; but the dog got stuck in the snow after the tenth leap, and stopped. Then the hare, too, stopped and sat up on his hind legs for a while, and then slowly headed for the threshing floor.

On his way he met two other hares on the sown winter field. They were feeding and playing. The hare played a while with his companions, dug in the frosty snow with them, ate some of the winter crops, and went on.

In the village everything was quiet; all the lights were out. All one could hear was a baby's cry in a hut and the crackling of frost in the cabin logs. The hare made his way to the threshing floor, and there found some companions. He played awhile with them on the cleared floor, ate some oats from the open granary, climbed on the kiln over the snow-covered roof and across the wicker fence, and then headed back to his ravine.

Dawn was glimmering in the east; the stars grew less bright, and frosty vapor was rising more thickly from the earth. In the nearby village women woke up and were on their way to fetch some water; peasants were bringing feed from the barn; children were shouting and crying. There were more carts going along the road and peasants were talking loudly to one another.

The hare leapt across the road, went to his old lair, picked out a high place, dug the snow away, went back into his new lair, lowered his ears onto his back, and fell fast asleep with his eyes wide open.

The Wolf and the Bow (A Fable)

A hunter went out to hunt with a bow and arrows. He killed a goat. He threw it over his shoulders and carried it along. On his way he saw a boar. He threw down the goat, took a shot at the boar, and wounded him. The boar rushed at the hunter and ripped him to death; but he himself also died on the spot. A wolf smelled the blood and came to the place where the goat, the boar, the man, and his bow were all lying.

The wolf rejoiced, and thought: "Now I shall have enough food to eat for a long time; but I won't eat everything all at once, but little by little, so that nothing will be lost. First I'll eat the tougher things, and then I'll munch on what's softer and sweeter."

The wolf sniffed at the goat, the boar, the man, and then said: "This is all soft food, so I'll eat it later; first let me start on these sinews of the bow." And he began to gnaw on the sinews. When he bit through the first string, the bow sprang back and struck him on his belly. The wolf died on the spot and other wolves came and ate up the man, the goat, the boar, and the first wolf.

How the Peasant Divided the Geese (A Fairy Tale)

A poor peasant ran out of bread. He decided to ask his master for some. But, so as not to go empty handed, he caught a goose, cooked it, and brought it to the master. The master accepted the goose and said to the peasant: "Thank you for the goose, but I don't know how to divide it. I have a wife, two daughters, and two sons. How will I share the goose without causing offense? Then the peasant said, "I'll divide it." He took a knife, cut off the head of the goose, and said to the master: "You're the head of household so you get the head." Then he cut off the back of the goose and said to the master's wife: "You sit at home and take care of the house, so you get the hind part." Then he cut off the feet of the goose and gave them to the two sons, and said: "You get the feet to follow in your father's footsteps." And to the daughters, he gave the wings. "You," he said, "will soon fly the coop, so here is a wing for each of you, and I'll take whatever's left." And he took the rest of the goose for himself.

The master laughed and gave the poor man both bread and some money.

A rich peasant found out that the master had given the poor peasant both money and bread. He roasted five geese and took them to his master.

The master said, "Thank you for the geese. But I have a wife, two sons, and two daughters; there are six of us all together—how shall we divide your geese equally?"

The rich peasant got to thinking, but he couldn't come up with any ideas. Then the master sent for the poor peasant and had him divide the geese. The poor peasant gave one goose to the master and his wife, and said, "With this goose, that makes three of you; he gave one to the daughters and said, "This makes three of you with this goose"; he gave one to the sons and said, "This makes three of you with this goose"; and he took two geese for himself: "There," he said, "I make three with these two geese. It's all equal."

The master laughed again and gave the poor peasant some more bread and more money, and chased the rich peasant away.

The Mosquito and the Lion (A Fable)

A mosquito flew up to a lion and said: "You think you're stronger than I am? Not likely! What does your strength amount to? You can scratch with your claws and gnaw with your teeth: that's how women fight with men. I'm stronger than you: if you like, let's go to war!" And the mosquito started buzzing and began biting the lion on its bare cheeks and nose. The lion began to smack its face with its paws and scratch it with his claws: the lion soon had blood all over its face and was exhausted.

The mosquito began buzzing with joy and flew away. Later it got tangled in a spider's web and the spider began to suck its blood. So the mosquito said: "I overpowered the strong beast, the lion, but I'm perishing at the hands of a wretched spider."

The Apple Trees (A Story)

I planted two hundred young apple trees, and for three years I dug around them in the spring and the fall, and in the winter I wrapped them with straw to protect against the hares. In the fourth year, when the snow melted, I went to take a look at my apple trees. They had grown stouter during the winter: the bark was shiny and filled with sap; all the branches were sound, and at all the tips and axils there were pea-shaped flower buds. Here and there buds were bursting, and the purple edges of petals could be seen. I knew that all the buds would become blossoms and produce fruit, and I was delighted as I looked at the apple trees. But when I took off the wrapping from the first tree, I saw that down at the ground the bark had been nibbled away like a white ring, down to the wood itself. The mice had done that. I unwrapped a second tree, and the same thing had happened there. Of the two hundred trees not one was unharmed. I smeared pitch and wax on the nibbled spots; but when the trees were all in bloom, the blossoms fell off right away; out came small leaves, but they, too, dropped off. The bark became wrinkled and turned black. Out of the two hundred apple trees only nine were left. On these nine trees the bark had not been gnawed through all the way around, but strips of bark had been left hanging on the white ring. On these strips, where the bark held together, knots were growing; although the trees had suffered, they survived. All the rest were ruined; shoots came out below the rings, but they were all wild.

The bark of a tree is like a man's arteries: blood flows through them to the whole body; and through the bark, sap goes up the tree and reaches the branches, leaves, and flowers. The whole inside of a tree may be taken out, as is often the case with old willows, and yet the tree will live as long as the bark is alive; but when the bark is ruined, the tree is finished. If a man's arteries are severed, he will die; in the first place, it's because blood will leak out; in the second place, it's because the blood won't circulate throughout the body.

Even a birch dries up this way when children bore a hole in it to drink its sap, and then all the sap flows out.

That's how the apple trees were ruined because the mice gnawed the bark all around, and the sap couldn't rise from the roots to the branches, leaves, and flowers.

The Horse and the Masters (A Fable)

A gardener had a horse. It had to work a lot and got little to eat; so it began praying to God for another master. And so it happened. The gardener sold the horse to a potter. The horse was glad, but the potter had even more work for it to do. Once again the horse complained of its lot, and began praying that it might get a better master. And this prayer, too, was answered. The potter sold the horse to a tanner. When the horse saw the skins of horses in the tanner's yard, it began to howl:

"Woe is me, the wretched one! It would have been better if I could've stayed with my previous masters. Apparently they've sold me now not for my work, but for my skin."

Bedbugs (A Story)

One time I stopped at an inn to spend the night. Before I went to bed, I took a candle and inspected all the corners of the bedroom and the walls; when I saw that there were bedbugs in all the corners, I began thinking of how I could settle down for the night so that the bedbugs wouldn't get to me.

I had a folding bed with me, but I knew that if I placed it even in the middle of the room, that bedbugs would crawl from the walls onto the floor and from the floor, up the legs of the folding bed, and from there onto me; therefore I asked the owner for four wooden cups, poured water into them, and placed a cup under each of the four legs of the bed. I lay down, put the candle on the floor, and began to watch, hoping to see what the bedbugs would do. There were lots of bedbugs, and they had already picked up my scent; I saw how they crawled across the floor and climbed onto the edge of the cup; some bedbugs fell into the water, while others turned around and went back.

"I've outsmarted you," I thought. "Now you won't get me." I was about to blow out the candle, when all of a sudden I felt something biting me. I looked around: it was a bedbug. How did it get to me? Not a minute had passed, when I found another. I started to look around and tried to determine how they'd managed to get to me.

For a long time I couldn't understand, but finally I glanced up at the ceiling and there I saw—a bedbug crawling across it; as soon as it was above my bed, it let go of the ceiling and dropped down on me. "No," I thought, "It's impossible to trick you." I put on my coat and left the room.

The Old Man and Death (A Fable)

Once an old man cut some wood, and started hauling it away. He had a long way to carry it; he soon grew tired, put down his bundle, and said: "Oh, if only death would come for me!" Then death came and said: "Here I am. What do you need?" The old man was frightened, and said: "Help me lift my bundle!"

How the Geese Saved Rome (History)

In the year 390 BC wild Gallic tribes attacked the Romans. The Romans were unable to withstand the attack, and some of them ran away from the city altogether, while others locked themselves inside a fortress. The fortress was called the Capitol. Only senators remained in the city. The Gauls entered the city, killed all the senators, and burned Rome down. Only the Capitol was left standing in the middle of the city—which the Gauls couldn't breach. They wanted to plunder it because they knew that the Capitol contained lots of riches. But it stood on a steep hill: on one side there were walls and gates, and on the other side, a steep ravine. At night the Gauls stealthily crawled out from the ravine and advanced on the Capitol. They supported each other from below, and handed each other spears and swords.

Thus they managed to clamber onto the top of the ravine—and not a single dog heard them.

They were already mounting the wall, when suddenly some geese sensed that there were people nearby: they began honking and flapping their wings. One Roman citizen woke up, rushed to the wall, and knocked a Gaul into the ravine. He fell and pulled some others down after him. Then the Romans came running and began to throw logs and stones into the ravine and killed many Gauls. Soon help reached Rome, and the Gauls were driven off.

From then on the Romans celebrate that day as a holiday in memory of those events. Priests walk around the city wearing their robes; one of them carries a goose and someone drags a dog on a leash behind him. People approach the goose and bow to it and to the priest: they give the goose gifts, while they beat the dog to death with sticks.

Why Trees Crackle during Frosty Weather (A Discussion)

Because there's moisture in the trees, and this moisture freezes, like water. When water freezes, it expands; and when it has no place to go, it makes the trees split.

If you pour water into a bottle and let the water in the bottle freeze, the water expands and breaks the bottle.

When the water becomes ice, there is so much strength in this ice, that if you fill an iron cannon with water and it freezes, the ice will split the cannon.

Why doesn't ice contract from the cold like iron, but expands when it freezes? Because, when water freezes, its particles connect with each other in a different way and there are more empty spaces between them.

Why doesn't water contract when it freezes? So that water in rivers and lakes wouldn't freeze down to the bottom.

Ice expands from the cold, and it becomes lighter than water and it floats; it freezes only from below and becomes thicker and thicker, but it never freezes all the way to the bottom. But if water were to contract in freezing weather, the way iron does, then the upper level of the water would freeze in the river and would sink, because the ice would be heavier than the water. Then the upper top level would freeze again and sink, and thus the rivers and lakes would freeze from the bottom to the top.

Moisture (A Discussion)

I

Why does a spider sometimes make a compact web and then sit in the middle, yet sometimes it leaves its nest and spins a new web?

A spider makes a web according to the weather—what it is and what it will be. Looking at a spider, you can predict the weather; if the spider is sitting and hiding in the middle of its web and doesn't leave it, it will rain. If he leaves his nest and makes a new web, then there will be a change in the weather.

How can the spider know in advance what the weather will be?

The spider's senses are so subtle that when dampness just begins to collect in the air, and we don't yet feel it, and to us, the weather seems fine—to a spider, it's already raining.

Just like when a naked person immediately feels the dampness, and a clothed person doesn't notice it, it's raining for the spider, while for us, it's merely about to rain.

II

Why in autumn and winter do doors swell and fail to close, while in summer they dry out and close easily?

Because in autumn and winter wood absorbs water like a sponge, and it expands, and in summer water evaporates as steam and it contracts.

Why does weak wood—aspen—swell more, while oak swells less?

Because in strong wood—oak—there is less open space and water has nowhere to go; while in weak wood—aspen—there is more empty space and water has extra room. In rotten wood there's even more empty space and therefore rotten wood swells most of all and becomes softer.

Beehives are made of weak, rotten wood: the best ones are made from rotten willow. Why is this? Because the air will pass through rotten wood and it's easier for the bees to breathe there.

Why do damp planks warp?

Because they dry out unevenly. If you put one side of a damp board against the stove, the water evaporates, and the wood shrinks on that side and will pull the other side after it; but the damp side can't shrink, because it contains water—and the whole board will bend.

In order for the floorboards not to warp, they are cut into pieces from dry wood, and these pieces are boiled in water. When all the water boils dry, they are glued together, and they never warp (for example, parquetry).

Various Connections of Particles (A Discussion)

Why are cart bolsters cut and wheel hubs turned not from oak, but from birch? Bolsters and hubs have to be strong, and oak is not more expensive than birch. That's because oak splits lengthwise, while birch does not split, but falls to pieces.

Although oak particles are more firmly connected than birch, they are connected in such a way that the wood splits lengthwise, while birch does not.

Why are wheels and runners made from oak and elm, and not from birch and linden?

Because, when oak and elm are steamed in a bath, they bend and do not break, while birch and linden split apart in all directions.

This is for the same reason again, that is, that the particles of the wood in the oak and in the birch are connected in a different way.

The Lion and the Fox (A Fable)

A lion, growing old, was no longer able to catch any animals and he decided to live by his cunning. He went into a cave, lay down, and pretended to be sick. The other animals came to visit him, and he ate those that ventured into his den. The fox figured out the trick. It stood at the entrance of the cave, and said: "Well, lion, how are you feeling?"

The lion answered: "Not well. But why don't you come in?"

The fox replied: "I won't come in because I can tell by the tracks that many other animals have gone in before me, but not one of them has come out."

The Righteous Judge (A Story)

An Algerian ruler by the name of Bawakas wanted to find out for himself whether it was true, as he'd been told, that in one of his towns there lived a righteous judge, who could immediately recognize the truth and no rogue could deceive him. Bawakas dressed up as a merchant and set off on horseback for the town where that judge lived. By the gate into the town a cripple came up to Bawakas and began to beg for alms. Bawakas gave him some money and was about to ride on, when the cripple caught hold of his cloak.

"What do you want?" asked Bawakas. "Haven't I given you some alms?"

"Yes, you have," said the cripple, "but do me another favor: carry me on your horse to the square, or I'll be crushed by the horses and camels."

Bawakas sat the cripple behind him and carried him to the square. Then Bawakas stopped his horse. But the cripple didn't dismount. Bawakas said:

"Why are you sitting there? Get down; we've arrived."

But the beggar said:

"Why should I get down, now it's my horse; and if you won't give up the horse of your own free will, let's go to the judge."

People had gathered round them and were listening to their argument; they all shouted:

"Go to the judge, he'll settle your dispute!"

Bawakas and the cripple went to see the judge. There were other people there, too, and the judge called them by turn to settle their disputes.

Before it was Bawakas's turn, the judge called up a scholar and a peasant. They were quarrelling over a wife. The peasant said she was his wife, and the scholar said she was his. The judge heard them out, paused for a moment and said:

"Leave the woman with me and come back tomorrow."

When they had left, a butcher and an oil-seller came in. The butcher was covered with blood, and the oil-seller, with oil. The butcher was holding money in his hand, and the oil-seller was holding the butcher's arm. The butcher said:

"I bought some oil from this man and drew out my purse to pay, but he grabbed my arm and tried to take away my money. And that's how we've come to you—I'm holding a purse in my hand, and he's holding my arm. But the money is mine, and he's a thief."

But the oil-seller said:

"That's not true. The butcher came to me to buy some oil. After I'd poured him a full jug, he asked me to change a gold piece. I got the money and put it on the counter; but then he took it, and tried to run off. I caught him by the arm and brought him here."

The judge paused for a moment and said:

"Leave the money here with me and come back tomorrow."

When it was the turn of Bawakas and the cripple, Bawakas recounted what had happened. The judge heard him out and then turned to the cripple. The beggar said:

"That's not true. I was riding on my horse through the town, and he was sitting on the ground and asked me to give him a ride. I put him on my horse and took him where he wanted to go; but he wouldn't get off and said that it was his horse. That's not true."

The judge thought for a moment and said:

"Leave the horse with me and come back tomorrow."

The next day many people gathered to hear the judge's verdicts.

The first to come up were the scholar and the peasant.

"Take your own wife," the judge said to the scholar, "and give the peasant fifty strokes with a stick."

The scholar took his wife, and the peasant was punished forthwith.

Next the judge called the butcher.

"The money is yours," he said to the butcher. Then he pointed to the oil-seller and said: "He should be given fifty strokes with a stick."

Then Bawakas and the cripple were summoned.

"Would you know your horse from twenty others?" the judge asked Bawakas.

"I would."

"And you?"

"I would, too," said the cripple.

"Come with me," the judge said to Bawakas.

They went into the stable. Bawakas immediately pointed to his own horse among the other twenty.

Then the judge called the cripple into the stable and ordered him to point to his horse. The cripple recognized the horse and pointed to it. Then the judge sat down and said to Bawakas:

"The horse is yours: take it. And the cripple is to be given fifty strokes with a stick."

After the trial, the judge went off home and Bawakas followed him.

"What's the matter? Aren't you happy with my decision?" asked the judge.

"I'm very happy with it," said Bawakas. "But I would like to know how you could tell that the wife belonged to the scholar, not to the peasant, that the money belonged to the butcher, not the oil-seller, and that the horse was mine, not the cripple's."

"I found out about the wife like this: in the morning I summoned her to me and asked her to fill my inkwell with ink. She picked up the inkwell, washed it quickly, and deftly poured in the ink. So she was obviously used to doing this. Had she been the peasant's wife she would not have known how to do it. So, it turns out that the scholar was right. I found out about the money like this: I put the money in a cup of water and looked at it this morning to see whether there was any oil on the surface. If the money had belonged to the oil-seller, it would have had oil on it from his hands. There was no oil on the water, so obviously the butcher was telling the truth. It was harder to find out about the horse. Both the cripple and you immediately pointed to the same one from the other twenty horses. But I didn't take you both into the stable to see whether you would recognize the horse, but to see which one of you the horse would recognize. When you walked up to it, it turned its head and moved towards you; but when the cripple touched it, it flattened its ears and raised its leg. So I knew that you were the true owner of the horse."

Then Bawakas said:

"I am not a merchant, but the ruler Bawakas. I came here to see whether it was true what's said about you. Now I see that you are indeed a wise judge. Ask me for anything you like, and I will reward you."

"I need no reward . . ." said the judge. "I'm happy that my tsar has praised me."

The Deer and the Vineyard (A Fable)

A deer was being pursued by hunters and it hid in a vineyard. When the hunters had passed by without noticing it, the deer began to munch on the grape leaves. The hunters noticed the leaves rustling, and they wondered: "Is there perhaps an animal under the leaves?" They fired a shot and wounded the deer. As it was dying, the deer said, "It serves me right, since I wanted to eat the same leaves that saved me!"

The Tsar's Son and His Comrades (A Story)

A tsar had two sons. He loved his elder son and bestowed his entire kingdom on him. Their mother felt sorry for her younger son and argued with her husband. The tsar was angry with her for this and they quarreled over it every day. So the younger tsarevich thought: "It would be better for me to leave home and go away somewhere." He said farewell to his father and mother, dressed in simple clothes, and went off to travel the world.

Along his way he met a merchant. The merchant told the tsarevich that at one time he'd been wealthy, but that all his goods had sunk in the sea, and that he was going to foreign parts to seek his fortune.

They continued on together. On the third day they met with another comrade. They got to talking, and the new friend said that he was a peasant; he had a house and a piece of land, but there was a war going on; his fields had been trampled and his house had been burned—and he now had nothing to live on; he was going to foreign lands to seek work.

They all went on together. They arrived at a large town and sat down to have a rest. Then the peasant said: "Well, friends, enough of having fun; now we've come to town; it's time for us to get down to work, each one as he knows best.

The merchant said: "I know how to trade. If I had a little money, I could do a lot of trading."

And the tsarevich said: "I don't know how to work or how to trade, I know only how to reign. If I had a kingdom, I would reign well."

And the peasant said: "I need neither money nor a kingdom; as long as my legs work and my hands move—I can survive and can feed you, too. Meanwhile, if you wait for money or a kingdom, you'll starve to death."

And the tsarevich said: "A merchant needs money, I need a kingdom, you need strength to work: money, a kingdom, and strength, all come to us from God. If God wants it, He'll grant me a kingdom, and to you, strength; and if He doesn't want it, He won't give you strength or grant me a kingdom."

The peasant didn't stay to listen, but hastened into town. There he got a job hauling firewood. In the evening they paid him for his work. He brought the money home to his comrades and said: "While you were planning to reign, I already earned some money."

The next day the merchant asked for some money from the peasant and went into town.

At the market the merchant found out that in town there was little oil, and that any day they were expecting a new supply. The merchant went to the harbor and began looking at the ships. While he was there, a ship with the oil arrived. The merchant went on board the ship before anyone else, found the captain, bought all the oil, and put down a deposit. Then the merchant ran back into town, resold the oil, and, for his troubles, earned ten times more than the peasant had given him. He brought the money back to his comrades.

The tsarevich said: "Well, now it's my turn to go into town. You were both fortunate; perhaps I will also have good luck. Nothing is too hard for God—He provided the peasant with work and the merchant, with profit; may He grant a tsarevich a kingdom."

The tsarevich went into town and saw people wandering the streets crying. He started asking why they were crying. They told him: "Don't you know that last night our tsar died, and we won't be able to find another one as good as he was."

"What did he die of?"

"Our villains must have poisoned him."

The tsarevich laughed and said: "That can't be."

Suddenly one man looked at the tsarevich more carefully and noticed that he spoke with a foreign accent and was dressed in clothes different from those of other people in town. He cried: "Lads! This man has been sent to us by our villains to snoop about our town. Perhaps he's the one who poisoned the tsar. You see, he speaks with an accent and he's laughing, while we're all crying. Seize him, and take him to prison."

They seized the tsarevich, took him off to prison, and didn't give him anything to eat for two days. On the third day they came for him and took him to court. Many people gathered to hear how he would be tried.

At the trial they asked the tsarevich who he was and why he'd come to their town. He replied: "I'm the son of a tsar; my father gave his entire kingdom to my older brother; my mother intervened for me, and as a result, my father quarreled with her. I didn't want that and said farewell to my father and mother, and began wandering. Along the way I met two comrades: a merchant and a peasant—and together we came to your town. While we were sitting and resting outside of town, the peasant said now that we needed work, each of us, would do whatever he could do; the merchant said that he knew how to trade, but that he had no money; and I said, that I knew only how to reign, but had no kingdom. The peasant said that we would starve to death, waiting for money and a kingdom; but he had strength in his hands and he was able to feed himself and the two of us. So he went into town, earned some money, and brought it back to us. The merchant took this money, engaged in trade, and earned ten times the original amount: I went into town, where you arrested me, locked me in prison for no reason, and you haven't given me anything to eat for two days. And now you want to execute me. I'm not afraid of anything because I know that it all comes from God, and that if He wants, then you'll kill me for no good reason, and if He wants, you will make me tsar."

After he said all of this, the judge was silent and didn't know what to say. Suddenly, one person from among the people cried: "God has sent us this tsarevich. We won't find a better tsar! Let's choose him as our tsar!"

And they all chose him as their tsar.

After they chose him, the tsarveich sent for his two comrades. When they were told that a tsar was summoning them, they grew afraid: they thought that they had committed some crime. But they couldn't run away, and were brought to the tsar. They fell at his feet, but the tsar ordered them to stand up. Then they recognized their comrade. The tsar related to them everything that had happened and said: "Don't you see that I was right? Both bad and good—everything comes from God. And it's no more difficult for God to grant a kingdom to a tsarevich, than a profit to a merchant, and work to a peasant."

He rewarded them and allowed them to remain in his kingdom.

The Little Jackdaw (A Fable)

Once a hermit saw a falcon in the forest. The falcon brought a piece of meat to a nest, tore it into little pieces, and began to feed the little jackdaw.

The hermit was surprised how it could be that a falcon was feeding a jackdaw and it thought: "The little jackdaw, even it isn't forgotten by God; God taught this falcon to feed the strange orphan. Obviously, God feeds all His creatures, while we think only of ourselves. I shall cease worrying about myself, and will no longer lay in food. God doesn't desert any of His creatures, and He also won't desert me."

And thus he did: he sat down in the forest and didn't get up from his place. He just kept praying. For three days and three nights he sat without eating or drinking. On the third day, the hermit was so weak that he couldn't even raise his arms. He fell asleep from weakness and dreamt of an old man. The old man seemed to approach him and said: "Why don't you lay in any supplies? You think that you will please God, but you're sinning. God structured the world so that each creature would secure what he needs. God ordered the falcon to feed the little jackdaw, because the jackdaw would perish without the falcon; but you can work. You want to test God, and that's a sin. Wake up and go to work, as you did before."

The hermit woke up and resumed his life as he had previously been living.

How I Learned to Ride Horseback (The Story of a Landowner)

When we were living in town, we used to study every day; only on Sundays and holidays, my brothers and I would go out to play. Once my father said: "The older children must learn how to ride. They should be sent to riding school!"

I was the youngest of the brothers and asked: "May I learn to ride, too?"

My father said: "You'll fall off." I began to beg him that I should also be taught, and I almost cried. My father said: "All right, you may go, too. But watch out! Don't cry when you fall off. He who doesn't fall off a horse at least once will never learn to ride."

When Wednesday came, all three of us were taken to a riding school. We entered through a large porch, and from there, went to a smaller one. Beyond the porch was a very large room: it had sand instead of a floor. And in this room gentlemen and ladies were riding, and also boys like us. That was the riding school. It was not very bright inside, there was a smell of horses, and you could hear the riders snap their whips and yell at their horses; the horses struck their hooves against the wooden walls. At first I was frightened and couldn't see very well. Then our valet called the riding master and said: "Give these boys some horses: they'll be learning to ride." The master said: "All right!"

Then he looked at me, and said: "This one is too young." But the valet said: "He's promised not to cry when he falls down." The master laughed and walked away.

Then they brought in three saddled horses; we took off our coats and went down a staircase to the riding school. The master was holding a horse by a cord,[1] and my brothers rode around on him. At first they rode at a slow pace, later, at a trot. Then they brought in a pony. It was a red horse, and his tail was cut off. He was called Chervonchik.[2] The master laughed, and said to me: "Well, young gentleman, get on your horse!" I was both happy and scared, and tried to act in such a manner so that no one would notice. For a long time I tried to get my foot into the stirrup, but couldn't do it because I was too small. Then the master lifted me up in his arms and put me in the saddle. He said: "The young master is not heavy, only about two poods: he couldn't be more than that."

At first he held me by the hand, but I saw that my brothers were not being held, and so I begged him to let go of me. He said: "Aren't you afraid?" I was very frightened, but I said that I wasn't. I was so afraid because Chervonchik kept dropping his ears. I thought he was angry with me. The master said: "Well be careful, don't fall!" and he let go of me. At first Chervonchik went at a slow pace, and I sat up straight. But the saddle was slippery, and I was afraid I would slip off. The riding master asked me: "Well, are you steady in the saddle?" I said: "Yes, I am." "If so, then go at a slow trot!" and the master clicked his tongue.

Chervonchik started at a slow trot, and began to jerk me up and down. But I kept silent, and tried not to slip off to one side. The master praised me: "What a cavalier, splendid!" I was very pleased.

Just then the master's friend came up to him and began talking with him; the master stopped watching me.

Suddenly I felt that I had slipped a little to one side on my saddle. I wanted to straighten myself up, but was unable to do so. I wanted to tell the master to stop my horse, but I thought it would be a disgrace if I did, and so I kept silent. The master wasn't looking at me; Chervonchik was running at a trot, and I slipped even more to one side. I looked at the master and thought that he'd help me, but he was still talking with his friend, without looking at me, and he kept repeating:

---

1 Cord—a rope for driving a horse in a circle. (Tolstoy's note)
2 The word is the equivalent of "Ruddy."

"Well done, cavalier!" I was now completely on one side, and was very scared. I thought that I was lost, but I felt ashamed to cry. Chervonchik shook me up and down once more: I slipped off entirely and fell to the ground. Then Chervonchik stopped; the riding master looked at the horse, and saw that I wasn't on him. He said: "I declare, my young cavalier has fallen off!" and he came over to me. When I told him that I wasn't hurt, he laughed and said: "A child's body is soft." I felt like crying. I asked him to put me on the horse again, and he lifted me up. After that, I didn't fall off again.

Thus we rode twice a week at the riding school and I soon learned to ride well and was not afraid of anything.

The Axe and the Saw (A Fable)

Two peasants went into the forest for wood. One had an axe, the other, a saw. They chose a tree and began to argue. One said—the tree should be chopped down. The other said—it should be sawed down.

A third peasant said: "I'll settle this: If the ax is sharp, it's better to chop it down; if the saw is even sharper, it's better to saw it down. He took the ax and began chopping down the tree. But the ax was so blunt that it couldn't chop anything.

He picked up the saw: he discovered that the saw was bad, too, and couldn't cut anything. Then he said: "Stop arguing: the ax won't chop and the saw won't cut. First you should sharpen the ax and fix the saw, and then you can argue." But these two peasants got even angrier at each other because one had an unsharpened ax, and the other had a dull saw, and they began fighting.

A Soldier's Wife's Way of Life (A Peasant's Story)

We lived in poverty on the edge of a village. There was my mother, my nanny (elder sister), and my grandmother. My grandmother had a braid and wore an ancient woolen skirt; she wrapped her head in some sort of old rag, and a small sack hung down from under her neck. My grandmother loved me and felt sorry for me more than my mother. My father was a soldier.[3] They said that he drank a great deal, and that was why they sent him away to serve. As if in a dream I remember that he used to come home to us when he was on leave. Our cottage was small and propped up in the middle with a tree, and I recall how I climbed

---

3   Recruits in the Russian army served for a period of twenty-five years.

onto this support, tumbled down, and struck my head on a bench. A scar has remained on my forehead up to now.

There were two small windows in our cottage, and one was always plugged up with a rag. Our courtyard was narrow and open. An old washtub sat in the middle of it. In the courtyard stood only one old lopsided horse; we didn't have a cow, but we had two poor sheep and one lamb. I always slept next to this lamb. We ate bread and water. There was no one there to do any work; my mother always complained about her stomach, my grandmother, about her head, and she always stood at the stove. My nanny was the only one who worked for herself, but not for the family; and she bought her own clothes and planned to get married.

I remember that mother became sicker, and then gave birth to a little boy. They put mama in the entryway. My grandmother borrowed some grain from the neighbor and sent Uncle Nefed to fetch the priest. And my sister went to gather folks for the christening.

People came; they brought three loaves of bread. The relatives began to arrange the tables and to cover them with tablecloths. Then they brought benches and a bucket of water. They all took their places. When the priest came, the godfather and godmother stood in front, and Aunt Akulina held the infant. They started to pray. Then they got out the infant and the priest submerged it in water. I got frightened and cried out: "Give me the infant!" But my grandmother got angry with me and said: "Be quiet or I'll beat you."

The priest immersed the infant in the water three times and gave him to Aunt Akulina. She wrapped him up in a calico cloth and took him to his mother in the entryway.

Then everyone sat down at the tables, Grandmother served two cups of kasha, poured on some vegetable oil, and served all the people. After everyone had eaten, they got up from the tables, thanked my grandmother, and left.

I went to my mother and said:

"Mama, what's his name?"

Mother said, "Same as you." The infant was skinny; his little feet and tiny hands were paltry, and he kept crying. Whenever I woke up at night, he was still crying, and mama was singing him lullabies. She was groaning, but kept singing.

Once I woke up at night and heard my mother weeping. Grandmother got up and said: "What's the matter? Christ be with you!" Mother said: "The little boy died." Grandmother lit a fire in the stove, washed the infant, put a clean shirt on the baby, tied the belt, and put him under the icons. When day broke, Grandmother left the cottage and went to find Uncle Nefed. He brought two old boards and started making a coffin. He made a little coffin and placed the infant in it. Then mother sat down next to the coffin, keening and wailing in a soft voice. Then Uncle Nefed put the coffin under his arm and carried it out to bury.

The only joy we had was when we gave nanny away in marriage. Peasants came to us once and brought a loaf of bread and some wine. They began to offer some wine to mother. She drank it. Uncle Ivan cut off a piece of bread and offered it to her. I stood next to the table and wanted some bread. I bent down to mother and whispered to her. She started laughing, and Uncle Ivan said: "What does he want? Some bread?"[4] Then he sliced off a large piece for me. I took it and went into the pantry. Nanny was sitting there. She starting asking me: "What are the peasants saying out there?" I said: "They're drinking the wine." She started laughing and said: "They're marrying me off to Kondrashka."

Soon they gathered again to celebrate our marriage. Everyone got up early. Grandmother heated the stove, mama made *pirozhki*, and Aunt Akulina washed the beef.

Nanny got dressed up in her new fur slippers, put on a red *sarafan*,[5] a nice kerchief, and didn't do anything. Then, when the hut was warm, mother also got dressed up, and many people came to visit—it was a full house.

Then three pairs of horses with bells drove into our courtyard. On the last pair sat the bridegroom Kondrashka wearing a new caftan and a tall hat. He climbed down from his cart and went into the hut. They put a new fur coat on nanny and brought her out to her bridegroom. They sat him and his bride at a table and the old women began singing songs in their honor. Then they got up from the table, prayed to God, and went out to the courtyard. Kondrashka seated nanny in one cart and he sat in the other. After everyone was in a cart, they crossed themselves, and departed. I went back into the hut and sat down by the window to wait for them to return. Mother gave me a piece of bread; I ate it, and then fell asleep. Later my mother woke me up and said: "They're coming!" She gave me a rolling pin and told me to sit at the table. Kondrashka entered the hut with nanny, followed by lots of people, more than before. There were also people outside, all looking at us through the windows. Uncle Gerasim was the best man; he came up to me and said: "Get out." I was frightened and wanted to do so, but grandmother said: "You show him the rolling pin and say: 'What's this?'" So I did. Uncle Gerasim put some money into a glass and poured some wine on it, then gave it to me. I took the glass and gave it to grandmother. Then we got up and let them all sit down.

Then they began to serve wine, aspic, and beef; they began singing songs and dancing. They served Uncle Gerasim some wine; he drank a little and said: "The wine is bitter." Then nanny took hold of Kondrashka's ears and began kissing

---

4   The Russian word for bread (*khleb*) has a large number of affectionate forms.
5   Russian peasant woman's sleeveless dress.

him. They sang and danced a long time; then everyone left and Kondrashka took Nanny to his house.

After this we began living in even greater poverty. We sold our horse and our last two sheep, and often we didn't have any bread to eat. Mother went to borrow money from our relatives. Soon grandmother passed away, too. I remember how mother keened and wailed: "My own dear mother! Who did you leave me to, bitter and luckless? Who did you leave your unfortunate child to? Where will I get some sense? How can I live out my life?" And she wept and mourned for a long time.

Once I went with some other kids up to the big road to look after the horses and I saw—there came a soldier with a sack over his shoulder. He came up to us kids and asked: "What village are you from, lads?" We replied: "From Nikolskoye." "And tell me, does the soldier's wife Matryona still alive there?" And I said: "Yes, she's alive; she's my mother." The soldier looked at me and asked: "Have you seen your father?" I replied: "He's gone to be a soldier, and I haven't seen him." The soldier said, "Well, let's go. Take me to Matryona; I've brought her a letter from your father." I said, "What letter?" And he said: "Let's go and you'll see." "Well, then, let's go."

The soldier went with me, at such a fast pace, that I could hardly keep up with him. And we came to our house. The soldier prayed to God and said: "Greetings!" Then he took off his coat, sat down on the windowsill, and began surveying the hut and said: "Is this all the family you have?" Mother was bashful and said nothing, merely looked at the soldier. He asked: "Where's your mother?" and he started crying. Now my mother ran up to my father and started kissing him. I also climbed up on his lap and began feeling him all over with my hands. He stopped crying and began laughing.

Then people came and my father greeted everyone and said that he had permission to leave the service.

As soon as they brought home the cattle, nanny came and exchanged kisses with my father. Mother started laughing and said: "You don't recognize your own daughter?" Father called her over again, kissed her, and asked how she was getting on. Then mother went to make some eggs and sent nanny for some wine. Nanny brought a bottle, stopped up by paper, and placed it on the table. Father said: "What's this?" And mother said: "Some wine for you." And he said: "I haven't had a drink in five years; but bring me some eggs." He prayed to God, sat down at the table, and started to eat. Then he said, "If I hadn't stopped drinking, I wouldn't be a noncommissioned officer, and wouldn't have brought anything home, but now, thank the Lord." He took a purse with money out of his sack and gave it to mother. Mother was overjoyed, hastened, and went to hide the money.

Then, when everyone had dispersed, Father lay down to sleep on the back stove-bench; he placed me next to him, and mother lay down at our feet. They talked for a long time, almost until midnight. Then I fell asleep.

In the morning, mother said: "Oh, I have no firewood!" Father asked; "Is there an ax?" "There is, but it's dented and not very good." Father put on his boots, took the ax, and went outside. I ran after him.

Father pulled the pole off the roof and placed it over a log, raised the ax, and chopped swiftly, brought the wood into the hut, and said: "Here's some firewood for you, light the stove; today I'll go buy us a cottage with some trees in the courtyard. We also have to buy a cow."

Mother said: "Oh, you need a lot of money for all that."

And father replied: "We'll work. This little man is growing!" Father said, pointing to me.

Then father prayed to God, ate some bread, got dressed, and said to mother: "If there are fresh eggs: bake them in the ashes for dinner" And he left the house.

Father didn't return for a long time. I began to ask mother if I could go after him. She didn't let me. I wanted to leave, but she didn't allow it and gave me a beating. I sat down on the stove-bench and started crying. Then father came into the hut and he asked: "Why are you crying?" I said: "I wanted to go after you, but mother wouldn't let me, and she gave me a beating." And I started crying even worse. Father started laughing, went up to mother, and pretended to beat her, saying, "Don't beat Fedka, don't beat Fedka!" Mother pretended to cry; father started laughing and said: "Fedka and you cry very easily. Then father sat down, seated me next to him, and cried, "Well, now, mother, give us something to eat: we're very hungry."

Mother gave us some kasha and eggs, and we began eating. Mother said: "Well, then, what happened?" And father said: "I bought it: eighty rubles in silver coins, white as glass. In just a little while we'll buy some wine for the peasants, and they'll bring it for me some Sunday."

And from then on, we began living well.

The Cat and the Mice (A Fable)

A house was overrun with mice. A cat made its way into this house and began catching them. The mice saw that things were looking bad, and they said: "Mice, let's not come down from the ceiling anymore; the cat can't get up there." When the mice stopped coming down, the cat decided that he would have to catch them with a trick. He held onto the ceiling with one paw, hung down from it, and pretended he was dead. One mouse looked at him and said: "No, my friend, even if you became a bag, I wouldn't get near you."

Ice, Water, and Steam (An Explanation)

Ice is sometimes hard as stone. If a stick freezes in ice, it's impossible to pull it out of the ice until the ice melts. When ice is cold, loaded carts will ride on top of it and they won't sink; and throw ten poods of iron on them, the ice still won't crack.

The colder the ice, the stronger it is. When the ice warms up, it gets weaker, and becomes like kasha; whatever has frozen in it can now be taken out; it cracks beneath one's feet and can't even hold one pood of iron. When the ice warms up even more, it turns into water. It's easy to pick any object out of the water, and water won't hold anything up except wood. If you heat the water more, it will hold even less. It's easier to swim in cold water than in warm water. In hot water even wood will sink.

If one keeps heating the water, it will disperse, as steam; and steam can hold nothing at all, and goes in all directions.

If one boils water under a lid, the water evaporates and then forms droplets under the lid, flows down, and becomes water once again. If you collect this water and subject it to freezing, it will become ice again.

If you heat water, it becomes steam; freeze water and it becomes ice. The same water can become airborne when it's heated, and hard, when it freezes.

There is no heat in ice; there is a little heat in water, and a great deal of heat in steam.

If you put a block of ice on top of ice, the block doesn't get warm and doesn't get cold.

But if you pour some water on ice, the ice warms up, while the water cools down. The ice will melt if there's lots of water, and the water will freeze, if there's lots of ice.

And if you direct steam onto ice, the ice will warm up, and the steam will cool down: the ice will melt and become water, and the steam will get cooler, and will also turn into water.

If the water is cold and the air is cold, then the water won't warm up and the air won't cool down. But if the air is warm, and the water is cold, what will happen? The heat will pass from the air into the water, and the water will become warmer and warmer, while the air will become cooler and cooler, until they reach the same temperature.

If the air is warmer than the water, the water will warm up, while the air will cool down; and if the water is warmer, then the air heats up, and the water will cool down.

If frozen water forms in the air from liquid water—that means that the water is warmer than the air; and it will keep cooling down, while the air will keep warming up.

If in the air, airborne water becomes liquid water—that means the air is cooler than the airborne water, and the water will be cooling down, and the air will be warming up.

If hard water becomes liquid water in the air—that means the air is warmer, and it will cool down, become hard, but ice will melt.

If steam forms in the air from water, the water will dry up—that means the air is warmer, it will cool down, and water will keep heating up.

It's not possible to heat with ice, but one can heat with water and steam. Here's how one can heat with water: bring water into a cold house. After the water freezes, carry the ice outside. It will freeze again—then carry it out again. And the house will become warmer, and it will become so warm that the water won't freeze. Why does this happen? Because as the water freezes, it sheds excess heat into the air, and it will continue to do so, until the air warms up, and the water stops freezing.

Here is how one heats with steam: steam is released in a cold house. The steam will start getting cooler; it will flow downwards as drops and will turn into water. This water is taken out and the house becomes warmer.

Why will this happen? Because as soon as the steam becomes water, it releases its excess heat into the air.

When ice forms out of water, and when water forms from steam, then the warmth passes into the air from the water and from the steam—and the air becomes warmer. But when water forms from ice, and steam forms from water, then the warmth of the air passes into the water and the steam—and the air becomes colder.

If you want to cool a warm room, bring some ice in and let it melt. Why will the air become colder? Because the ice, for it to become water, absorbs heat from the air.

If you want to cool down, pour some water and allow it to dry up. Why does this happen? Because steam forms from the water. And so that steam forms from the water, it absorbs a great deal of warmth from the air.

As a result, it becomes colder, when it's raining, and warmer when it's about to rain. When it's raining, water dries up, becomes steam, and absorbs heat. But when it's only about to rain, then the steam passes into the air, and it cools down and turns into clouds: and from them it's warm.

That's why we say, "It's muggy."

The Quail and Her Chicks (A Fable)

Some peasants were cutting down a meadow, and there, under a tussock, was a quails nest.

The mama quail flew down to the nest with food and saw that the grass had been cut all around the meadow. She said to her chicks: "Well, children, a disaster has occurred! Now be silent and don't move, or else you'll be lost. I'll move you this evening." But the chicks rejoiced that it had become brighter in the meadow, and they said: "Mother is old and therefore she doesn't want us to rejoice." And they began to cheep and whistle.

Some children brought the peasants dinner at the scene of the mowing: they heard the chicks and tore off their heads.

Bulka (An Officer's Story)

I had a bulldog, and his name was Bulka. He was completely black, except for the tips of his front paws, which were white.

All bulldogs' lower jaws are longer than the upper jaw, and the upper teeth set into the lower; but in the case of Bulka, the lower jaw was protruding so far forward that a finger could be inserted between the upper and lower teeth. Bulka had a broad face and big, black, shining eyes. His teeth and white canines were always visible. He looked like a Negro. Bulka had a gentle disposition and wouldn't bite; but he was very strong and tenacious. Whenever he took hold of anything, he put his teeth together and hung on like a rag, and it was impossible to make him let go; he was like a pair of pincers.

One time he was sent to hunt a bear; he seized the bear by the ear, and hung on like a bloodsucker. The bear pounded him with his paws, squeezed him, shook him from side to side, but couldn't get rid of Bulka; then the bear tucked in his head in his attempts to crush Bulka, but the dog hung on until they could splash cold water over him.

I took him home when he was just a puppy, and reared him myself. When I went to the Caucasus, I chose not to take along him along with me, and I left secretly, and gave orders to keep him chained up. At the first posting station I was just about to start off with a fresh team of horses, when suddenly I saw something black and shining dashing along the road. It was Bulka wearing his brass collar. He was rushing along with all his might toward the station. He leapt up on me, licked my hand, and then lay down in the shadow under my cart. His tongue lolled out at full length. He kept drawing it back in, swallowing his spittle, and then thrusting it out again. He'd been racing there and couldn't catch his breath; his sides were actually straining. He twisted from side to side, and pounded the ground with his tail.

I learned afterwards that, when he discovered I had gone, he broke his chain, jumped out of the window, and dashed over the road following my trail, and had just run twenty versts in the heat of the day.

Bulka and the Wild Boar (A Story)

One time in the Caucasus we went boar hunting, and Bulka ran to go with me. As soon as the hunting dogs got to work, Bulka dashed off in the direction of their barking and disappeared in the woods. This was during the month of November; at that time wild boars and pigs are usually very fat.

In the forests of the Caucasus, frequented by wild boars, grow all manner of fruits, wild grapes, pine cones, apples, pears, blackberries, acorns, and rose apples. And when all these fruits ripen, and the frost loosens them, the wild boars feed on them and grow fat.

At this time of year a wild boar becomes so fat that he can't run very far when pursued by the dogs. After they've chased the boar for two hours, he ducks into a thicket and there comes to rest. Then the hunters run to the place where he's resting and shoot him. By the barking of the dogs one can tell whether the boar's taken cover or is still running. If he's running, then the dogs bark with a yelp, as if someone were beating them; but if he's taken cover, they bay with a long howl, as if at a man.

On this expedition I had been running through the forest for a long time, without once coming across the track of a boar. At last I heard the protracted howl and whine of the hounds and turned my steps in that direction. I was already near the boar. I could hear a sound in the thicket. This was made by the boar's pursuit by the dogs. But I could tell by their barking that they'd not yet brought him to rest, but were only chasing around him. Suddenly I heard something rushing behind me, and looking around, I saw Bulka. He'd evidently lost the scent of the hunting dogs in the forest and had become confused; but now he had heard their baying, and like myself, was also rushing in their direction. He was running across a clearing in the tall grass, and all I could see of him was his black head, and his tongue sticking out between his white teeth. I called him, but he didn't look around; he dashed by me, and was lost to sight in the thicket. I hurried after him, but the farther I went, the denser the underbrush. The branches knocked my hat off and lashed my face; the thorns of briers hooked onto my coat. By this time I was very near the barking dogs, but I couldn't see anything.

Suddenly I heard the dogs barking louder; there was a tremendous crash, and the boar, which was trying to break his way through, began to screech. And this made me think that now Bulka had reached the scene and was attacking him. I put forth all my strength, and made my way through the underbrush to the spot. Here, in the very thickest of the woods, I caught a glimpse of a spotted hunting hound. He was barking and howling without moving from the spot. Three paces from him I saw something black struggling.

When I came nearer, I saw that it was the boar, and I heard Bulka uttering shrill screams. The boar began grunting and thrusting himself on the hound, which, with his tail between his legs, backed away from him. I had a fair shot at the boar's side and head. I aimed at his side and fired; I could see that I hit him. The boar uttered a squeal, turned away from me, and dashed through the thicket. The dogs ran barking and yelping on his trail. I made my way through the thicket after them. Suddenly I heard and saw something under my very feet. It was Bulka. He was lying on his side, squealing. Under him was a pool of blood. I said to myself, "My dog is done for," but now I had no time for him, and I rushed on. Soon I saw the boar. The dogs were attacking him from behind, and he was snapping first to one side, then the other. When the boar saw me, he made a dash at me. I fired for the second time, with the gun almost touching him, so that his bristles were singed. The boar gave one last grunt, stumbled, and fell on the ground with all his weight.

When I reached him, he was already dead; only here and there his body twitched, or shuddered a little. But the dogs, with bristling hair, were tearing at his belly and his legs; others were licking his blood from where he was wounded.

At that point I thought of Bulka, and I hastened back to look for him. He was crawling toward me, groaning. I went to him, knelt down, and examined his wound. His belly was torn open, and a whole mass of his bowels protruded from his belly and lay on the dry leaves. When my comrades joined me, we put Bulka's intestines back inside and sewed up his belly. While we were doing this and puncturing the skin, he kept licking my hands.

We fastened the boar to a horse's tail, in order to bring it out of the woods, and we put Bulka on the back of a horse, and thus brought him home. Bulka was sick for about six weeks, but at last he recovered.

Pheasants (A Description)

In the Caucasus woodcocks are called *fazani*, or pheasants. They are so abundant that they're cheaper than domestic fowl. Pheasants are hunted with the *kobylka*, with the *podsada*, or with a dog.[6]

This is the method of hunting with the *kobylka*. You take some canvas and stretch it over a frame; in the middle of the frame you put a joist, and make a hole in the canvas. This canvas-covered frame is called a *kobylka*. Just after sunrise you go out into the forest with it and with a gun. You carry the *kobylka* in front of you, and through the hole you keep a lookout for pheasants. In the early morning the pheasants go out in search of food. Sometimes you come across a whole family; sometimes just a hen with her chicks; sometimes the cock with his hen; sometimes several cocks together.

The pheasants see no person; they're not afraid of the canvas and let one come very close. Then the hunter sets down his *kobylka*, puts the muzzle of his musket out through the hole, and shoots at his leisure. The following is the method of hunting with the *podsada*: You let a common domestic dog loose in the woods, and follow him. When the dog comes upon a pheasant, he chases it. The pheasant flies up into a tree and the dog begins to bark at it. The hunter goes in the direction of the barking and shoots the pheasant in the tree. This mode of hunting would be easy if the pheasant would fly to an isolated tree, or would sit on an exposed branch so as to be in full sight. But the pheasants always choose a tree in the densest part of the thicket, and when they see the hunter, they hide in the branches. It's not only hard to make your way through the thicket to the tree where the pheasant's perched, and it's also hard to get sight of him. When it's only one dog barking under the tree, the pheasant isn't afraid; he sits on a limb, even cocks his head, and flaps his wings. But the instant he sees a human, he stretches himself out along the limb, in such a way that only an experienced hunter would be likely to spot him, while an inexperienced one would stand underneath and see nothing.

When the Cossacks sneak up to pheasants, they always keep their faces hidden behind their caps, and don't look up, because the pheasant is afraid of a man with a musket, but most of all, he's afraid of seeing his eyes.

Pheasants are hunted with dogs in the following way: the hunters take a setter and follow him around in the woods. The setter catches the scent where early in the morning the pheasants had been out feeding, and he begins to follow their trail. No matter how many times the pheasants have crossed their tracks, a good setter will always pick out the last one, leading from the place where they were feeding.

---

6 Both Russian terms are explained in the text below.

The farther the dog gets on their track, the stronger the scent becomes, and thus he reaches the place where the pheasant has stopped for the day to rest or walk in the grass. When he comes close, it seems to him that the pheasant is directly in front of him, and now he begins to move more and more cautiously, so as not to scare the bird; from time to time he will stop to make his leap and grab it. When the dog gets very close to the bird, the pheasant flies up, and the sportsman shoots it.

Milton and Bulka (A Story)

I got myself a setter to hunt pheasants. This dog's name was Milton. He was big, thin, and gray, with spots, had long lips and ears; he was also very strong and intelligent. He and Bulka never quarreled. Never did any other dog dare pick a quarrel with Bulka. All Bulka had to do was show his teeth once, and other dogs would put their tails between their legs and run away. One time I was going out hunting pheasants with Milton. Suddenly Bulka came bounding after me into the woods. I tried to drive him away, but in vain. It was a long way to go home for the sake of getting rid of him. I came to the conclusion that he wouldn't interfere, and I continued on my way; but as soon as Milton smelled a pheasant in the grass and started on the trail, Bulka dashed ahead and began to interfere. He was eager to get the pheasant before Milton. If he heard anything in the grass, he would leap and jump about; but his sense of smell was not that keen, and he couldn't keep to the trail, so he would watch Milton, and follow wherever Milton went. As soon as Milton picked up a trail, Bulka would dash ahead. I tried to call Bulka back, I even beat him, but I could do nothing. As soon as Milton found a trail, he would dash ahead and get in the way. I was about to go home, because I felt that my day of hunting was ruined, but Milton knew better than I did how to throw Bulka off the track. This was the way he did it: as soon as Bulka ran ahead of him, Milton would leave the scent, turn in a different direction, and pretend that he was still hunting for it. Bulka would then run to where Milton was pointing, and Milton, glancing up at me, would wag his tail, and set out again. Milton would purposely run ten feet away from the right trail for the purpose of deceiving Bulka. Then he would lead me straight ahead again, so that throughout the whole hunt he kept deceiving Bulka, and didn't let him spoil my sport.

The Turtle (A Story)

One time I went out hunting with Milton. Just as we reached the forest he began to pick up a scent. He stretched out his tail, pricked up his ears, and began sniffing. I got my musket ready and started after him. I supposed that he was on the track of a partridge, a pheasant, or a hare. But Milton didn't turn off into the woods; instead he ran into a field. I followed him and looked ahead.

Suddenly I caught sight of what he was after. In front of him a small turtle, the size of a hat, was making its way. Its bald, dark-gray head and long neck were thrust out like a pistil. The turtle was moving along with its bare legs, and its back was entirely covered by its shell.

As soon as it saw the dog, it drew in its legs and head, and flattened itself into the grass, so that only its shell was visible. Milton grabbed it and tried to bite it; but he couldn't get his teeth through it, because a turtle has the same sort of shell over its belly as over its back, with mere openings in front, on the side, and at the back for sticking out its head, legs, and tail.

I rescued the turtle from Milton, and examined the markings on its back, saw how its shell was formed, and how it managed to conceal itself in it. When you hold one in your hands and look under the shell, only then can you see something within, black and alive. I tossed the turtle down on the grass and went on, but Milton didn't want to leave it; he seized it in his teeth and followed me. Suddenly Milton whined and dropped it. The turtle in his mouth had extended one claw and scratched his mouth. He was so angry at it that he began to bark, picked it up again, and trotted after me. I told him again to drop it, but Milton wouldn't obey me. Then I took the turtle from him and threw it away. But he wouldn't give it up. He began in all haste to dig a hole with his paws, and then he pushed the turtle into the hole, and covered it up with soil.

Turtles live both on land and in the water, like grass snakes and frogs. They produce their young from eggs and lay their eggs on the ground; but they don't sit on them; the eggs themselves hatch out like fishes' spawn and become little turtles. Turtles are often small—no larger than a saucer; and then, again, they can be big, reaching a length of seven feet and a weight of seven hundred twenty pounds. These large turtles live in the sea.

One single female turtle in the spring will lay hundreds of eggs. The shell of a turtle is its ribs. In humans and other animals each rib is separate, but in the case of the turtle, the ribs form the shell. It's also a peculiarity that in all other animals the ribs grow underneath the flesh, but in the case of the turtle, the ribs grow outside, and the flesh is underneath them.

Bulka and the Wolf (A Story)

At the time when I was about to leave the Caucasus, war was still raging and it was hazardous to travel by night without an escort.

I was eager to start as early as possible in the morning, and therefore didn't go to bed at all.

A friend of mine came to keep me company; we spent the whole evening and night sitting in front of my hut on the street of the Cossack outpost.

It was a misty, moonlight night, and so light that one could see to read, though the moon itself was invisible.

In the middle of the night we suddenly heard a little pig squealing in a court-yard on the other side of the street. One of us cried: "That's a wolf strangling a young pig."

I ran into my hut, grabbed my loaded musket, and hurried out into the street. Everyone was standing at the gates of the yard where the young pig was squealing, and they shouted to me, "Over here!" Milton came leaping after me, evidently thinking that since I had my gun, I was going hunting; and Bulka pricked up his short ears and bounded from side to side, as if inquiring what he should grab hold of. As I was running toward the wattle fence, I saw a wild animal coming directly at me from the other side of the yard. It was a wolf. He ran up to the fence and leapt on top of it. I moved away and got my gun ready. As soon as he jumped down from the fence on my side, I leveled my gun at him, almost touching him, and pulled the trigger; but the gun only made a "click" and didn't fire. The wolf didn't stop, but ran down the street. Milton and Bulka set out in pursuit. Milton was close to the wolf, but evidently didn't dare seize him; while Bulka, though he put forth all the strength of his short legs, couldn't catch up with him. We ran as fast as we could after the wolf, but the wolf and the dogs were now out of sight. But soon near the ditch at the corner of the outpost we heard barking and whining, and through the moonlit mist we could make out something was kicking up dust: the dogs were tackling the wolf. When we reached the ditch, the wolf was already gone, and both the dogs returned to us with their tails erect and with angry-looking mugs. Bulka growled and rubbed his head against me; he evidently wanted to tell me about it, but didn't know how to do so.

We examined the dogs and found a small wound on Bulka's head. He had probably overtaken the wolf in front of the ditch, but didn't have time to tackle him; the wolf had snapped at him and run off. The wound was small, so that we knew it was not dangerous.

We returned to the hut, sat down, and talked over what had happened. I was annoyed that my musket had misfired, and I couldn't help thinking that, if it had gone off, the wolf would have fallen on the spot. My friend was surprised that a wolf had managed to make its way into the courtyard. An old Cossack declared that there was nothing surprising about it, and that it wasn't a wolf, but a witch, who'd cast a spell over my gun! Thus we sat and talked. Suddenly the dogs sprang up, and in the middle of the street, we saw right in front of us the very same wolf; but this time, at the sound of our voices, he made off so swiftly that the dogs couldn't catch up with him.

After this the old Cossack was entirely convinced that it was no wolf, but a witch; I wondered if perhaps it might have been a mad wolf, because I'd never heard or known of a wolf to return among humans after it had been chased away.

Just to make sure, I scattered gunpowder over Bulka's wound and set it on fire. The powder blazed up and cauterized the sore spot.

I cauterized the wound with the powder to destroy the mad virus, if it hadn't yet reached his bloodstream. If the saliva was poisonous and reached the dog's bloodstream, I knew that it would spread all over his body, and there would be no way to cure him.

What Happened to Bulka in Pyatigorsk (A Story)

From the outpost, I didn't return directly to Russia, but stopped at Pyatigorsk and spent two months there. I gave Milton to the old Cossack hunter, but I took Bulka to Pyatigorsk with me.

Pyatigorsk, or "Five Mountains," is so called because it's built on Mount BeshTau. *Besh* in the Tatar language means five, and *Tau*, means mountain. A sulfur hot spring flows from this mountain. This water is as hot as boiling water, and over the spot where the water flows from mountain surfaces, steam is always rising, just as it does from a samovar. The whole region where the city is situated is very charming. The hot springs flow down from the mountains, while at the bottom the little river Podkumok flows. The hillsides are covered with forests; around them there are fields, and on the horizon rise the mighty Caucasus mountains. The snow on these mountains never melts, and they're always as white as sugar. One mighty mountain is Elbrus, like a loaf of white sugar; it can be seen from every point when the weather is clear. People come to these hot springs for medical treatment; summer cottages and canopies are built over the springs, while gardens and paths are laid out all around. There is music playing in the morning; people drink the waters, take the baths, or stroll.

The city itself stands on the mountain, and below the city is a suburb.

I lodged in a little house in this suburb. It stood in a courtyard, and there was a little garden in front of its windows. In the garden were my landlord's bees, not in hollow tree trunks as in Russia, but in round basket hives. The bees there were so peaceful that Bulka and I always used to sit out in the garden, among the hives in the morning. Bulka used to run there, marvel at the bees, smell them, and listen to their buzzing; but he moved so carefully that the bees didn't bother him and left him alone.

One morning I came home from taking the waters and sat drinking my coffee in the latticed garden. Bulka began scratching behind his ears and rattling his collar. This noise disturbed the bees, and I removed the collar from Bulka's neck. After a little while I heard a strange and terrible uproar in the direction of the city on the mountain. Dogs were barking, yelping, and howling, men were yelling, and this whole tumult was coming down the mountain and seemed to be coming closer and closer to our suburb. Bulka had ceased his scratching, and had laid his broad head with his white teeth exposed between his white front paws; his tongue was hanging out, as was his way; he was lying peacefully beside me. When he heard the uproar, he seemed to understand what it was all about; he pricked up his ears, bared his teeth, jumped up, and began growling. The noise was coming nearer. It seemed as if all the dogs in the whole city were yelping, whining, and barking. I went out to the gate to look, and my landlady joined me there. I asked: "What's all that?" She replied: "Prisoners are coming from the jail to beat the dogs to death. There are too many dogs running loose, and the city authorities have ordered that all dogs in the city be killed."

"What! Would they kill my Bulka if they saw him?"

"No. They've been ordered to kill only those dogs without collars."

Just as I was speaking, the prisoners had already approached our yard.

Soldiers marched out in front, followed by four convicts in chains. Two of the convicts had long iron hooks in their hands, and the two others had clubs. When they came in front of our gate, one of the prisoners caught a stray dog with a hook, dragged him into the middle of the street, and the other prisoner began to beat him with his club. The whelp squealed horribly, and the convicts shouted something and roared with laughter. The convict with the hook turned the little dog over and, when he saw that it was dead, he pulled out his hook and began searching for other victims. At this moment Bulka leaped headlong at the convict, just as he had at the bear. I remembered that he was without a collar, and I cried, "Back, Bulka!" and I shouted to the convicts not to beat my dog. But the convict saw Bulka, guffawed, and skillfully speared him with his hook, and caught him under the thigh. Bulka tried to break away, but the convict pulled him toward him, and shouted to the other, "Beat him!" The other prisoner was already swinging his club, and Bulka would surely have been killed, but as he struggled, the skin on his haunches gave way, and, putting his tail between his legs, and with a frightful wound in his thigh, he came running at full speed through the gate, into the house, and hid under my bed.

What saved him was the fact that the skin on the place where the hook seized him tore out entirely.

The End of Bulka and Milton (A Story)

Bulka and Milton met their deaths at about the same time. The old Cossack did not understand how to treat Milton. Instead of taking him along only when he went after birds, he began taking him to hunt boars. That same autumn a *sekach* boar gored him.[7] No one knew how to sew up his wound, and Milton died.

Bulka also didn't live long after his rescue from the convicts. Soon afterwards, he began to mope and to lick everything that came his way. He would lick my hand, but not as in former days, when he meant to caress me. He licked long, and energetically thrust out his tongue, and then he began to grab my hand with his teeth. Evidently he felt the impulse to bite my hand, but tried to refrain. I stopped giving him my hand. Then he began licking my boot and the table leg, and then biting the boot or the table leg. This went on for two days, and on the third day, he disappeared, and no one ever saw him or heard of him again.

It was impossible for him to have been stolen, and he could not have run away from me. This happened about six weeks after the wolf had bitten him. It must have been true that the wolf was rabid. Bulka also became rabid and went off. He was afflicted with what hunters call *stechka*, the first stage of madness. It is said that madness is first indicated by spasms in the throat. Rabid animals want to drink, but they can't, because water makes the spasms more intense. Then they lose control of themselves out of pain and thirst, and begin to bite. Probably these spasms were just beginning with Bulka, when he showed an inclination to lick everything, and then to bite my hand and the table leg.

I traveled over the whole region and made inquiries about Bulka, but I could learn nothing about where he'd gone or how he'd died. If he'd run and bitten any one as mad dogs do, I would have heard about him. But probably he went out somewhere into the thick woods, and died there all alone. Hunters say that when an intelligent dog is attacked by madness, he runs off into the field or woods, and there searches for an herb, which he needs, rolls over in the dew, and tries to cure himself. Evidently Bulka was unable to get well. He never returned, and disappeared forever.

---

7   A *sekach* is a two-year-old wild boar, with sharp, straight tusks. (Tolstoy's note)

The Birds and the Nets (A Fable)

A hunter set out a net near a lake and caught a number of birds. The birds were large, and they lifted the net up and flew away with it. The hunter ran after them. A peasant saw the hunter running, and said: "Where are you running? Do you really think one can catch up with the birds, while on foot?" The hunter said: "If it was only one bird, I wouldn't catch it, but now I will."

And so it happened. When evening came, the birds headed away for the night, each in a different direction: one to the woods, another to the swamp, a third to the field; and together with the nets they all fell to the ground, and the hunter caught them.

Intuition (An Explanation)

A human sees with his eyes, hears with his ears, smells with his nose, tastes with his tongue, and touches with his fingers. One man's eyes see better, another's eyes see worse. One hears from a distance, and another is deaf. One has keen senses and can smell something from a distance, while another smells a rotten egg and doesn't even notice that it's rotten. One can recognize a thing by touch, and another can't tell the difference between wood and paper. One will take a substance in his mouth and find it sweet, while another will swallow it without knowing whether it's bitter or sweet.

The same way the various senses differ in strength in different animals. But in all animals the sense of smell is stronger than it is in humans. When a human becomes familiar with a thing, he looks at it, listens to the noise it makes, now and then smells it or tastes it; but, above all, a man has to touch it, to identify it.

But nearly all animals need to smell a thing more than anything else. Horses, wolves, dogs, cows, and bears don't recognize a thing until they smell it.

When a horse is afraid of something, it snorts—it's clearing its nose so as to smell better, and doesn't stop being afraid until it has smelled the object well.

A dog frequently follows its master's track, but when it sees him, it doesn't recognize him and begins to bark, until it smells him and finds out that what looked so frightening, is really his master.

Oxen see other oxen beaten, and hear them roar in the slaughterhouse, and still don't understand what's going on. But an ox or a cow needs only find a spot where there's ox blood, and smell it, and it will understand and will start roaring and stamping its feet, and can't be driven away from the spot.

An old man's wife had fallen ill; he went to milk the cow himself. The cow snorted—she realized that it wasn't her mistress, and would not give him any milk. The mistress told her husband to put on her fur coat and kerchief—then the cow gave milk; but when the old man opened the coat, the cow smelled him and stopped giving milk again.

When hunting hounds follow an animal's trail, they never run on the track itself, but always run to one side, about twenty paces from it. When an inexperienced hunter wants to direct the dog to the scent, and sticks its nose into the track, it will always jump to one side. The track itself smells so strong to the dog that it can't make out whether the animal has run forward or returned back. It runs to one side, and only then discovers in what direction the scent grows stronger, so it can follow the animal. The dog does precisely what we do when somebody speaks very loudly in our ears; we take a step away, and only then do we make out what's being said. Or, if what we're looking at is too close, we take a step back and only then can we make it out.

Dogs recognize each other and make signs to each other by means of their smell.

The smell is even more sensitive in insects. A bee flies directly to the flower that it wants to reach; a worm crawls to its leaf; a bedbug, flea, and a mosquito, can catch the scent of a human from hundreds of thousand insect paces away.

If the particles, which separate from a substance and enter our noses are very small, then how tiny must those particles be that reach the organs of smell of insects!

The Dogs and the Cook (A Fable)

A cook was preparing a dinner. Some dogs were lying at the kitchen door. The cook killed a calf and threw the guts out into the yard. The dogs picked them up and ate them, and said: "He's a good chef: he cooks well."

After a while the cook began to clean peas, turnips, and onions, and threw out the refuse. The dogs rushed for it, but turned their noses up, and said: "Our cook has gone bad: he used to cook well, but now he's no longer any good."

But the cook paid no attention to the dogs, and continued to prepare dinner in his own way. The dinner was prepared, and the family enjoyed it and praised the cook for it, but not the dogs.

The Founding of Rome (A History)

There was a tsar who had two sons: Numitor and Amulius. When he was dying, he said to his sons: "How do you want to divide my kingdom between you?

Who will get the kingdom, and who will get all my riches?" Numitor took the kingdom, and Amulius got the riches. When Amulius got the riches, he became envious that his brother was his tsar, and he began to give gifts to the soldiers and persuade them to banish Numitor and to make him tsar instead. That's what the soldiers did, and Amulius became tsar. Numitor had a daughter. She gave birth to twins—two little boys. They were both large and handsome.

Amulius was afraid that people wouldn't come to love these twins and when they grew up, and they wouldn't be chosen as tsars. He summoned his servant Faustulus, and said to him: "Take these two boys and toss them into the river."

The river was called the Tiber.

Faustulus placed the children in a cradle, took them to the riverbank, and left them there. Faustulus thought that they would die there. But the River Tiber flooded its banks, picked up the cradle, carried it, and placed it next to a tall tree. That night a she-wolf came and began to feed the twins with her milk.

The boys grew up and became strong and handsome. They lived in the forest not far from the town where Amulius lived. They learned to hunt wild beasts and feed on them. People got to know them and loved them for their beauty. The bigger twin was named Romulus, and the smaller one, Remus. Once the shepherds of Numitor and Amulius were grazing their livestock not far from the forest and they had a quarrel; Amulius's shepherds drove away Numitor's flock. The twins saw this and ran after the shepherds, caught up with them, and took their livestock.

Numitor's shepherds were angry with the twins about this; they chose a time when Romulus was away; they seized Remus and brought him to Numitor in town and said: "Two brothers have appeared in the forest and are taking away cattle and plundering. We caught one of them and brought him here." Numitor ordered that Remus be taken to the tsar Amulius. The tsar said: "They have offended my brother's shepherds. Let him be their judge." They brought Remus to Numitor again. Numitor summoned him and asked: "Where are you from and who are you?"

Remus replied: "We are two brothers: when we were little, we were carried in a cradle to a tree on the banks of the Tiber, and there we were fed by wild beasts and birds. And we grew up there. And to learn who we really are—we have kept our cradle. There are brass stripes on it and something is written on them."

Numitor was surprised, and thought: "Aren't they perhaps my own grandsons?" He kept Remus with him and sent for Faustulus to question him.

Meanwhile Romulus was looking for his brother and couldn't find him anywhere. When the shepherds told him that his brother was taken into town, he took the cradle with him and went into town after him. Faustulus recognized the cradle right away, and told the people that these were the grandsons of Numitor and that Amulius wanted to drown them. Then the people got angry at Amulius and killed him; they chose Romulus and Remus to be their tsars. But Romulus and Remus didn't want to live in that town and left their grandfather Numitor to be tsar there. They themselves went back to that spot under the tree where they had been fed by the she-wolf, alongside the River Tiber, and there they built a new city called Rome.

God Sees the Truth, but Waits to Speak (A True Story)

In the town of Vladímir there lived a young merchant named Aksyonov. He had two shops and a house of his own.

Aksyonov was a handsome, fair-haired, curly-headed fellow, full of fun, and he was a good singer. While still quite a young man, he'd taken to drink, and was disorderly when he'd had too much; but after he married, he gave up drinking, except now and then.

One summer Aksyonov was going to the fair in Nízhny;[8] as he was saying good-bye to his family, his wife said to him:

"Ivan Dmitryevich, don't set off today; I had a bad dream about you."

Aksyonov laughed and said:

"You're afraid that when I get to the fair, I'll go on a spree."

His wife replied:

"I don't know what I'm afraid of; all I know is that I had a bad dream. I dreamt you returned from town and, when you took off your cap, your hair was all gray."

Aksyonov laughed. "That's a good sign," said he. "See if I don't sell all my goods, and bring you some presents from the fair."

So he said good-bye to his family, and drove away.

When he'd traveled halfway there, he met a merchant whom he knew, and they put up at the same inn for the night. They had some tea together, and then went to bed in adjoining rooms.

It was not Aksyonov's habit to sleep late; wishing to travel while it was still cool, he woke his driver in the middle of the night, and told him to harness the horses. Then he made his way across to the landlord of the inn, paid his bill, and continued on his way.

---

8   Nizhny Novgorod Fair is the most famous fair in Russia. Its history begins with Makarevskaya Fair, which was held in Nizhny in the nineteenth century. Then it was the main trading platform of the country where prices for goods for the coming year were set.

When he had gone about twenty-five miles, he stopped for the horses to be fed. Aksyonov rested a while in the passageway of the inn, then stepped out onto the porch, and, ordering a samovar to be heated, got out his guitar and began to play.

Suddenly a troika drove up with tinkling bells, and an official alighted, followed by two soldiers. He came right up to Aksyonov and began to question him, asking who he was and where he came from. Aksyonov answered him fully, and said, "Won't you have some tea with me?" But the official went on questioning him and asked, "Where did you spend last night? Were you alone, or with a fellow merchant? Did you see that other merchant this morning? Why did you leave the inn so early?" Aksyonov wondered why he was being asked all these questions, but he described all that had happened, and then added, "Why do you question me as if I were a thief or a robber? I'm traveling on business of my own, and there is no need to question me."

Then the official, calling in the soldiers, said, "I'm the police officer of this district, and I'm questioning you because the merchant with whom you spent last night has been found with his throat cut. Show your belongings and you will be searched."

They entered the house. The soldiers and police officer took Aksyonov's luggage and searched it. Suddenly the officer drew a knife out of a bag and cried, "Whose knife is this?"

Aksyonov looked, and seeing a bloodstained knife taken from his bag, he grew frightened.

"Why is there blood on this knife?"

Aksyonov tried to answer, but could hardly utter a word; he merely stammered: "I—I don't know—that knife—it's not mine."

Then the police officer said:

"This morning the merchant was found in bed with his throat cut. You're the only person who could have done it. The house was locked from the inside, and no one else was there. There's a bloodstained knife in your bag, and your face betrays you! Tell me how you killed him, and how much money you stole from him?"

Aksyonov swore he hadn't done it; that he hadn't seen the merchant after they had tea together; that he had no money except for eight thousand rubles of his own; and that the knife wasn't his. But his voice kept breaking off, his face turned pale, and he trembled with fear as if he were guilty.

The police officer ordered the soldiers to bind Aksyonov and put him in the cart. As they flung him into it with his feet tied together, Aksyonov crossed himself and wept. His money and goods were taken from him, and he was sent to the nearest town and imprisoned there. Inquiries as to his character were made in

Vladímir. The merchants and other inhabitants of that town said that in former days he used to drink and carouse, but that he was a good man. Then the trial came: he was charged with murdering a merchant from Ryazan, and robbing him of twenty thousand rubles.

His wife was in despair, and didn't know what to believe. Her children were all still quite little; one was a baby at her breast. Taking them all with her, she went to the town where her husband was in jail. At first she wasn't allowed to see him; but, after much begging, she obtained permission from the officials, and was taken to him. When she saw her husband in prison dress and in chains, locked up with thieves and criminals, she fainted and didn't come to for a long time. Then she drew her children close to her and sat down next to him. She gave him news from home and asked what had happened. He told her all, and she asked, "What can we do now?"

"We must petition the tsar not to let an innocent man perish."

His wife told him that she'd already sent a petition to the tsar, but that it had not been accepted.

Aksyonov did not reply, but only looked depressed.

Then his wife said, "It was not for nothing that I dreamt your hair had turned gray. Do you remember? You shouldn't have started out that day." And running her fingers through his hair, she said: "Vanya dearest, tell your wife the truth: Did you do it?"

"So you suspect me, too!" said Aksyonov. He hid his face in his hands and began to weep. Then a soldier came to say that his wife and children had to leave; Aksyonov said good-bye to his family for the last time.

When they were gone, Aksyonov started recalling what had been said, and when he remembered that his wife had also suspected him, he said to himself, "It seems that only God can know the truth; it is to Him alone I must appeal, and from Him alone can I hope for mercy."

And from then on Aksyonov wrote no more petitions; he gave up all hope and only prayed to God.

Aksyonov was condemned to be whipped and sent to the mines. He was flogged with a knout, and when his wounds were healed, he was driven to Siberia with other convicts.

For twenty-six years Aksyonov lived as a convict in Siberia. His hair turned white as snow, and his beard grew long, thin, and gray. All his mirth disappeared; he stooped; he walked slowly, spoke little, and never laughed; but he prayed often.

In prison Aksyonov learned to make boots, and earned a little money, with which he bought *The Lives of the Saints*. He read this book when there was enough light in the cell; on Sundays in the prison church he read the lessons and sang in the choir; his voice was still strong. The prison authorities liked Aksyonov for his meekness, and his fellow prisoners respected him: they called him "Granddad," and "The Saint." When they wanted to petition the prison authorities about anything, they always asked Aksyonov to be their spokesman; when there were quarrels among the prisoners they went to him to sort things out and to judge the matter.

No news reached Aksyonov from home. He didn't even know if his wife and children were still alive.

One day a fresh gang of convicts was brought to the prison. In the evening the old prisoners gathered round the new ones and started asking what towns or villages they came from, and why they'd been sentenced. Among the rest Aksyonov sat down near the newcomers, and listened with a downcast air to what was being said.

One of the new convicts, a tall, strong man of sixty, with a closely cropped gray beard, was telling the others why he'd been arrested.

"Well, friends," he said, "I ended up here for nothing. I only took a horse that was tied to a sledge: I was arrested and accused of stealing. I said that I'd only taken it to get home more quickly, and had then let it go; besides, the driver was a personal friend of mine. So I said, 'It's all right.' 'No,' said they, 'you stole it.' But how or where I stole it they couldn't say. Once I really did something wrong, and ought by rights to have come here long ago, but that time I wasn't found out. But now I've been sent here for nothing at all. . . . Eh, but I'm telling you lies; I've been to Siberia before, but I didn't stay long."

"Where are you from?" asked someone.

"From Vladímir. My family is of that town. My name is Makar, and they also call me Semyonich."

Aksyonov raised his head and asked: "Tell me, Semyonich, do you know anything about the merchant family Aksyonov from Vladímir? Are they still alive?"

"Know them? Of course, I do. The Aksyonovs are rich, though their father's in Siberia: he's a sinner like us, it seems! As for you, Granddad, how come you're here?"

Aksyonov didn't like to speak about his misfortune. He only sighed, and said, "For my sins I've been in prison these last twenty-six years."

"What sins?" asked Makar Semyonich.

But Aksyonov said only, "Well, well—I must have deserved it!" He would have said no more, but his companions told the newcomer how Aksyonov came to be in Siberia: how someone had killed a merchant, had put a knife among Aksyonov's things, and Aksyonov had been unjustly condemned.

When Makar Semyonov heard this, he looked at Aksyonov, slapped his knee, and exclaimed, "Well, this is amazing! Really amazing! But how old you've grown, Granddad!"

The others began asking him why he was so surprised, and where he had seen Aksyonov before; but Makar Semyonov didn't reply. He only said: "It's amazing that we should meet here, lads!"

These words made Aksyonov wonder whether this man knew who'd killed the merchant; so he said, "Perhaps, Semyonich, you've heard about that affair, or maybe you've even seen me before?"

"How could I help not hearing? The world's full of rumors. But that was a long time ago, and I've forgotten what I heard."

"Perhaps you've heard who killed the merchant?" asked Aksyonov.

Makar Semyonov laughed and replied, "It must have been the person in whose bag the knife was found! If someone else had hidden the knife there, 'A person's not a thief till he's caught,' as the saying goes. How could anyone put a knife into your bag while it was under your head? It surely would have awakened you?"

When Aksyonov heard these words, he felt sure this was the man who had killed the merchant. He stood up and walked away. All that night Aksyonov lay awake. He felt terribly unhappy, and all sorts of images rose in his mind. First there was the image of his wife as she was when he parted from her to go to the fair. He saw her as if she were present; her face and her eyes arose before him; he heard her speak and laugh. Then he saw his children, quite little, as they were at that time: one with a little cloak on, another at his mother's breast. And then he remembered himself as he used to be—young and merry. He remembered how he sat playing the guitar on the porch of the inn where he was arrested, and how carefree he'd been. In his mind's eye, he saw the place where he'd been, the executioner, and people standing around; the chains, the convicts, all the twenty-six years of his prison life, and his premature old age. The thought of all this made him so wretched that he was ready to kill himself.

"And it's all that villain's doing!" thought Aksyonov. And such anger overtook Makar Semyonov that he longed for vengeance, even if he himself should perish for it. He kept repeating prayers all night, but could get no peace. During the day he did not go near Makar Semyonov, nor did he even look at him.

Two weeks passed in this way. Aksyonov couldn't sleep at night, and was so miserable that he didn't know what to do.

One night, as he was walking around the prison, he noticed some soil that came rolling out from under one of the cots on which the prisoners slept. He stopped to see what it was. Suddenly Makar Semyonov jumped out from under the cot, and looked up at Aksyonov with a frightened face. Aksyonov tried to go past without looking at him, but Makar grabbed his hand and told him that he'd been digging a hole under the wall, getting rid of the dirt by putting it into his tall boots, and emptying it out every day on the road when the prisoners were driven to their work.

"But you keep quiet, old man, and I will help you escape, too. If you blab they'll flog the life out of me, but I'll kill you first."

Aksyonov trembled with anger as he looked at his enemy. He drew his hand away, saying, "I have no wish to escape, and you've no need to kill me; you killed me a long time ago! As to telling on you—I may do so or not, as God directs."

The next day, when the convicts were led out to work, the convoy soldiers noticed that Makar Semyonov emptied some dirt out of his boots. The prison was searched, and the tunnel was located. The warden came and questioned all the prisoners to find out who'd dug the hole. They all denied any knowledge of it. Those who did know wouldn't betray Makar Semyonich, knowing he'd be flogged almost to death. At last the warden turned to Aksyonov, whom he knew to be an honest man, and said:

"You're a truthful old man; tell me, before God, who dug the hole?"

Makar Semyonov stood as if he were quite unconcerned, looking at the warden and not even glancing at Aksyonov. Aksyonov's lips and hands trembled, and for a long time he couldn't utter a word. He thought, "Why should I hide the person who ruined my life? Let him pay for what I've suffered. But if I tell, they'll probably flog the life out of him, and what if I suspect him wrongly? And, after all, what good would that be to me?"

"Well, old man," repeated the warden, "tell us the truth: Who's been digging under the wall?"

Makar Semyonov stood there as if nothing had happened and looked at the warden, but didn't look at Aksyonov. Aksyonov's feet and lips were trembling, and for a long time he was unable to speak. He thought: "If I hide him, what can I forgive him for when he's destroyed me? Let him pay for my suffering. But if I tell on him, they'll flog him. What if I suspect him for no reason? Will it be any easier for me?"

The warden repeated his question: "Well, old man," repeated the warden, "tell us the truth: Who's been digging under the wall?"

Aksyonov glanced at Makar Semyonov, and said:

"I don't know and I didn't see anything."

So they never found out who was digging under the wall.

That night, when Aksyonov lay down on his bed and was just beginning to doze, he heard someone came into his cell quietly and sit down on his bed. He peered through the darkness and recognized Makar.

"What more do you want from me?" asked Aksyonov. "Why have you come here?"

Makar Semyonov remained silent. So Aksyonov sat up and said, "What do you want? Go away, or I'll call the guard!"

Makar Semyonov bent close over Aksyonov, and whispered, "Ivan Dmtriyevich, forgive me!"

"For what?" asked Aksyonov.

"It was I who killed the merchant and hid the knife among your things. I meant to kill you too, but I heard a noise outside; so I hid the knife and escaped through the window."

Aksyonov was silent, and didn't know what to say. Makar Semyonov got off his bed, bowed low, and said: "Ivan Dmitriyevich," he said, "forgive me! For the love of God, forgive me! I'll confess that it was I who killed the merchant; you'll be released and will return home."

"It's easy for you to talk," said Aksyonov, "but I've suffered for you all these twenty-six years. Where could I go to now? My wife is dead, and my children have long since forgotten me. I have nowhere to go. . . ."

Makar Semyonov wouldn't stand up, but kept beating his head on the floor. "Ivan Dmitriyevich, forgive me!" he cried. "When they flogged me with the knout it was not so hard to bear that as it is to see you now . . . yet you took pity on me, and didn't tell. For Christ's sake, forgive me, wretch that I am!" And he began to sob.

When Aksyonov heard him sobbing he, too, began to weep and said:

"God will forgive you!" said he. "Maybe I am a hundred times worse than you." And with these words his heart grew light, and the longing for home left him. He no longer had any desire to leave the prison, but only hoped that his final hour would come soon.

In spite of what Aksyonov had said, Makar Semyonov confessed his guilt. But when the order for Aksyonov's release came, he was already dead.

Crystals (A Discussion)

If you pour salt into water and stir, the salt will begin to dissolve and will disappear entirely; but if you pour more and more salt into it, in the end the salt will stop dissolving, and no matter how much you may stir it, the salt will remain in the water as white powder. The water is saturated with salt and can't hold any more. But heat the water, and it will take more; and the salt, which didn't dissolve in cold water, will do so in hot water. But pour in even more salt, then even the hot water won't absorb it. And if you heat the water even more, the water will evaporate as steam, and more salt will be left behind. Thus, for everything that dissolves in water, there is a limit after which the water won't hold any more. More will be dissolved in hot than in cold, but in each case, when it is saturated, it will not take any more. The thing will be left, but the water will evaporate in steam.

If the water is saturated with saltpeter, and more saltpeter is added, and if it's heated and allowed to cool without being stirred, the extra saltpeter won't remain as a powder at the bottom, but will collect in little six-sided columns, and will settle at the bottom and along the sides, one column next to another. If the water is saturated with saltpeter and is put in a warm place, the water will evaporate in steam, and the extra saltpeter will again collect in six-sided columns.

If water is saturated with table salt, heated, and allowed to evaporate in steam, the extra salt will not settle out as powder, but as little cubes. If the water is saturated both with salt and saltpeter, the extra salt and saltpeter will not mix, but each will settle in its own way: the saltpeter in columns, and the table salt in cubes.

If water is saturated with lime, or with some other salt, and anything else, each substance will settle out in its own way. When the water evaporates in steam: one in three-sided columns, another in eight-sided columns, a third in bricks, a fourth in little stars—each in its own way. These figures are different for each solid material. At times these forms are as large as one's hand—such stones can be found in the ground. At other times these forms are so small that they can't be seen with the naked eye; but each material has its own form.

If, when the water is saturated with saltpeter, and little figures are forming in it, a corner of one of these little figures is broken off with a needle, new pieces of saltpeter will emerge and will repair the broken end as it ought to be—into a six-sided column. The same will happen to table salt or any other material. All the tiny particles turn around and attach themselves with the correct side, as necessary.

When ice freezes, the same process takes place.

A snowflake flies, and no pattern can be seen in it; but the moment it settles on anything dark and cold, on cloth or fur—you can discern its pattern; you will see a little star, or a six-cornered little figure. On the windows the steam doesn't freeze in any old form, but always as a star.

What is ice? It's cold, solid water. When liquid water becomes solid, it forms itself into figures and the heat leaves it. The same takes place with saltpeter: when it changes from a liquid into a solid, the heat leaves it. The same is true of table salt, or melted cast iron, when it changes from a liquid into a solid. Whenever something changes from a liquid into a solid, heat leaves it, and it forms patterns. And when it changes from a solid to a liquid it absorbs heat, the cold leaves it, and its patterns are dissolved.

Bring in melted iron and let it cool down; bring in hot dough and let it cool down; bring in slaked lime and let it cool down—it will warm the room. Bring in ice and let it melt—it will cool the room. Bring in saltpeter, table salt, or anything that dissolves in water, and put it into water, and it will grow cold. In order to freeze ice cream, salt is added to the water.

The Wolf and the Goat (A Fable)

A wolf saw a goat grazing on a rocky mountain, and he couldn't get at her; so he said to her: "You should come down here, lower! This place is flatter and the grass is much sweeter to eat."

But the goat answered: "That's not the reason you're not calling me to come down, wolf: you're not worried about my food, but about your own food."

Polycrates of Samos (History)

Once there was a Greek tsar named Polycrates.[9] He was lucky in all respects. He conquered many cities and became very wealthy. Polycrates described his entire happy life in a letter to his friend Amasis in Egypt.[10] Amasis read the letter and wrote in a reply to Polycrates: "It's pleasant to know one's friend is enjoying his good fortune. But I don't like your happiness. In my opinion, it's better when a man is successful in one field, but not in another—so it alternates. Listen to me and do this: take whatever is dearest to you and throw it somewhere where people won't get to it. Then you will have happiness alternating with unhappiness."

Polycrates read this and listened to his friend. This is what he did: he had an expensive ring; he took this ring, gathered many people, and boarded a boat with all of them. Then he ordered the boat to set sail for the sea. And when they had traveled far from the island, in the presence of all the people on board, he took off his ring, threw it into the water, and returned home.

---

9 Polycrates (flourished sixth century BCE) was the tyrant (c. 535–522 BCE) of Samos in the Aegean Sea.

10 Amasis, also called Ahmose II (flourished sixth century BCE), pharaoh in Egypt who reigned 570–526 BCE.

Five days later a fisherman happened to catch a very large, magnificent fish, and he wanted to give it as a present to the tsar. He went to Polycrates at his court, and when the tsar came out to see him, the fisherman said: "Tsar, I caught this fish and brought it to you because only a tsar should eat such a splendid fish." Polycrates thanked the fisherman and invited him to dinner. The fisherman presented the fish to the tsar; the cooks cut the fish and found in it the very same ring that Polycrates had thrown into the sea.

When the cooks brought the ring to Polycrates and said where they'd found it, Polycrates wrote another letter to his friend Amasis and told him how he'd thrown the ring into the sea, and how it had been found. Amasis read the letter and thought: "That's not a good sign; clearly it's impossible to escape one's fate. It's better for me to part from my friend, so that I won't have to feel sorry for him later." And he wrote to tell Polycrates that their friendship was over.

At that time there was a man named Oroetus.[11] He was angry at Polycrates and wanted to destroy him. Oroetus conceived of the following scheme. He wrote to Polycrates that the Persian tsar Cambyses had offended him and wanted to kill him and that he supposedly got away from him. Oroetus wrote the following to Polycrates: "I have great riches, but I don't know where to live. Accept me with all my riches, and together we will become the most powerful tsars. And if you don't believe that I have so much wealth, send someone to see."

Polycrates sent his servant to see whether it was true that Oroetus brought so many riches. When the servant came, Oroetus deceived him: he took many boats and loaded stones into all of them; then he placed some of his gold on top of the stones.

When the servant saw these boats, he believed that they were all filled with gold. And that's what he told Polycrates.

Then Polycrates wanted to go to Oroetus himself to see his riches. That same night Polycrates's daughter had a dream in which her father was hanging in the air. His daughter asked him not to go to Oroetus: but her father got angry and said that he wouldn't give her away in marriage unless she would stop talking. His daughter replied: "I'd gladly forego marriage, but don't go to Oroetus: I'm afraid that something bad will happen to you."

Her father didn't listen and went anyway. When he arrived, Oroetus seized him and had him hanged until he was dead. Thus his daughter's dream had come true. Polycrates's great happiness ended in great misfortune.

---

11 Persian satrap of Lydia, appointed by King Cyrus the Great, responsible for the death of Polycrates of Samos, killed by order of king Darius I the Great (sixth century BCE).

Volga-Bogatyr (A Story)[12]

When tiny little stars
Spread across the heavens,
When the clear bright moon
Shone in the lofty sky—
And the beautiful sun illuminated
Our holy mother Rus'
There was born a brave young man
Radiant Volga—Sir Buslaevich;
Due to his bogatyr-like birth
The damp mother earth trembled,
The blue sea was stirred up,
And fish hid in the depths of the sea,
Wild beasts hid themselves in thickets,
The Turkish Empire trembled,
When Volga was turning seven years old—
He wanted to gain great wisdom.
He went to study with the wise men,
And his studies turned to knowledge:
Volga came to understand all wisdom:
The first wisdom he learned—
How to turn into a bird;
He learned another bit of wisdom—
How to turn into a fish;
Learned a third bit of wisdom—
How to turn himself into a gray wolf.
When Volga turned fifteen,
He chose a retinue for himself;
He gathered a brigade—
Of youngsters, his equals—
Thirty brothers minus one,
He himself was the thirtieth.
When Volga got with his retinue
To the steep bank near Kiev,

---

12 The hero's name differs from the name of the river by the addition of soft sign, which is difficult
to render in transliteration.

Volga Buslaevich said:
"You, my brave retinue,
Thirty brothers minus one,
I myself am the thirtieth—
Listen to your big brother,
Do what you're ordered to do:
Tie the silk nets
And drop them into the blue sea."
His retinue obeyed Volga right away,
They tied the nets of silk
And dropped them into the blue sea.
Volga turned into a fish,
A large-toothed pike,
He swam into deep waters,
Scared away all the red fish,
Then Volga took a stand with his retinue
On a steep bank near Kiev,
And Volga Buslayevich said:
"You, my brave retinue,
Thirty brothers minus one,
Myself included as the thirtieth—
Listen to your big brother,
Do what you're ordered to do
Weave silk ropes,
Place them all over the forest,
On the paths of wild animals."
Here his retinue obeyed Volga;
It wove silk ropes,
Spread them all over the forest,
Volga turned himself into a wild animal,
A long-legged gray wolf
He took off into the thick forest,
Into deep broken branches, into thickets,
He scared away a marten,
Drove the wild beasts into a noose.
When Volga stood with his retinue
On a steep bank near Kiev,
Volga Buslayevich said:
"We caught all the fish

From the deep blue sea,
And we trapped a marten
From the dense, dark forests,
Is there a brave lad,
Who'll go to the Turkish Empire,
To the tsar Sultan Beketych,
To inform his royal council?"
The brave lads began to hide,
The big ones behind the middle-sized ones,
The middle-sized ones behind the smallest,
There was no reply from the smallest.
And Volga Buslayevich said:
"Volga himself will have to go."
Volga turned himself into a bird,
Flew high up to the sky.
He arrived in the Turkish Empire,
And sat on the windowsill.
The tsar Saltan Beketovich was sitting
With his tsaritsa Davidyevna,
And they were talking:
Saltan Beketovich said:
"You, my beloved wife,
The youthful bright Davidyevna,
I wish to make war on Holy Rus',
I want to capture the splendid city of Kiev,
I want to present a Russian town
To each of my sons;
I want to bring you a luxurious coat
Made of sable fur."
Davidyevna replied to him:
"Hail, oh, Tsar Saltan Beketovich!
In vain do you prepare
To make war on the Russian lands.
Or don't you know that
All is not the way it used to be in Russia?
The beautiful sun has illuminated
The holy Russian lands:
A brave young warrior was born there,
The bogatyr Volga Buslayevich,

He's sitting by the window right now and listening to
Our secret conversations.
You won't capture the magnificent city of Kiev,
And you won't grant a Russian town
To each of your nine sons.
You will lose your head to
That Volga Buslayevich."
Saltan didn't believe those words,
And he grew angry at the tsaritsa,
Slapped her across her face,
And drove Davidyevna out of his sight.
Volga Buslayevich speculated,
Wrapped himself in ermine,
Ran into the deep cellar.
He stretched silk bowstrings
Nibbled on the taut bows,
From tempered arrowheads
He removed the iron pieces
And buried them in the ground
He turned into a bird again
And rushed back towards Kiev,
Gathered his retinue,
And approached the Turkish Empire.
The kingdom was well fortified
With a high stone wall
With sturdy gates in the wall,
With gilded damask steel swords,
With brass hooks and bolts,
The vault over the gate
Made of expensive fish teeth,
Engraved with a fine notch
Along tiny complicated, little cuts
At times could a small insect crawl through?
At this point the retinue became discouraged:
"How shall we get through these stone walls?
Should we, good lads,
Lose our heads in vain?"
Volga Buslayevich came up with a solution:
He turned himself into a small insect,

And his good men into insects,
He made it through with his retinue,
Through the gate made with fish teeth,
Once over the wall Volga Buslayevich
Turned the insects
Into men dressed in battle gear.
And Volga Buslayevich spoke:
"Listen to your big brother,
Do what he orders you to do
In the splendid Turkish Empire,
Cut down the young and old.
Destroy all to the very root:
Leave only thirty
Of the loveliest maidens."
Here the retinue obeyed Volga:
In the splendid Turkish Empire,
Cut down the young and old.
Destroy all to the very root:
They didn't leave any seeds for reproduction;
They left only thirty
Of the loveliest maidens.
Volga himself went looking for the tsar
In his stone chambers;
The iron doors were locked,
There were strong bolts in the doors:
Volga Buslayevich spoke:
"Even if you break one leg, it has to be opened!"
He kicked the iron doors with his foot,
Broke the strong bolts;
Volga took the fine Turkish tsar
By his white hands.
Volga Buslayevich said:
"Tsars are not beaten, not executed."
And slammed the tsar against the brick floor,
And smashed him to bits.
Then Volga rewarded his brave retinue equally,
He gave each man a thousand horses,
And a barrel of beautiful gold,
And one maiden for each brave lad.

THE FOURTH RUSSIAN BOOK FOR READING

The Tsar and the Shirt (A Story)

The tsar was ill and he said: "I will bestow half my kingdom on anyone who can cure me." Then all the wise men gathered and began to debate how best to cure the tsar. No one knew how. Only one wise man said that it was possible to cure him. He said, if one finds a happy man, takes his shirt off him, and puts it on the tsar—he will be cured. So the tsar ordered that his entire kingdom be searched to find a happy person; but envoys of the tsar spent a long time searching throughout the kingdom and were unable to find even one happy person. There wasn't a single one who was satisfied with everything. He who was rich, was in bad health; he who was healthy, was poor; he who was both healthy and rich, had a bad wife, and some had bad children. Everyone was complaining about something. Once, late at night the tsar's son was walking past a little hut and heard someone saying: "Praise be to God. I did my work well, ate my fill, and now I'm going to bed. What else do I need?" The tsar's son was glad to hear this. He ordered that this man's shirt be taken off him, he should be paid as much as he wants, and that shirt should be carried to the tsar. The messengers went in to this happy man and wanted to take off his shirt; but the happy man was so poor that he was wearing no shirt at all.

The Reeds and the Olive Tree (A Fable)

An olive tree and some reeds were starting to argue about who was stronger and sturdier. The olive tree laughed at the reeds because they bent in every wind. The reeds kept silent. A storm came: the reeds swayed, tossed, bent to the ground—and remained unharmed. The olive tree strained its branches against the wind—and broke.

The Wolf and the Peasant (A Story)

Some hunters were pursuing a wolf. And the wolf ran into a peasant. The peasant was coming from the barn, carrying a flail and a sack.

The wolf said: "Peasant, hide me—the hunters are chasing me." The peasant felt sorry for the wolf, hid him in the sack, and threw the sack over his shoulder. The hunters came riding up and asked the peasant if he'd seen a wolf.

"No, I haven't."

The hunters rode off. The wolf jumped out of the sack and threw himself at the peasant, wanting to eat him. So the peasant said:

"Oh, wolf, don't you have a conscience? I saved you, but now you plan to eat me." And the wolf replied:

"Previous good deeds get forgotten."[1]

"No: previous good deeds are remembered, no matter whom you ask. Ask anyone, they'll tell you." But the wolf said:

"Let's walk along the road together. We'll ask the first creature we meet whether good deeds are forgotten or remembered. If they say they're remembered, I'll let you go, but if they say they're forgotten, I'll eat you."

So they went along the road and met an old blind mare. The peasant asked: "Tell us, mare, whether good deeds are remembered or forgotten."

The mare replied:

"Here's how it is: I've lived with my master for twelve years, given birth to twelve foals, all the while plowing and carrying; last year I went blind but kept working on the shelling machine; then, just recently, I no longer had the strength to circle around, and I fell upon the wheel. They kept beating me, pulled me by the tail, and threw me down a steep slope. I barely managed to climb out; but I don't know where I'm going." The wolf said:

"Peasant, do you see? Good deeds are not remembered."

---

1   Literally, "bread and salt," symbols of hospitality.

The peasant said:

"Wait, let's ask a few more creatures."

They went on further. They met an old dog. He was crawling along, dragging his bottom.

The peasant said:

"Tell us, dog, whether good deeds are remembered or forgotten."

"Here's how it is: I lived with my master for fifteen years, guarding his house, barking, and threatening to bite intruders; then I grew old, lost my teeth—they drove me away from the courtyard, and in addition, they struck my hind end with a shaft. Now I'm dragging along and I myself don't know where I'm heading, just further away from my old owner."

The wolf said:

"Do you hear what he's saying?

But the peasant said:

"Wait until the third meeting."

Then they ran into a fox. The peasant said: "Tell us, fox, whether good deeds are remembered or forgotten."

The fox replied:

"Why do you want to know?"

The peasant said:

"This wolf was running away from some hunters and he began begging me for help; I hid him in my sack but now he plans to eat me."

The fox replied:

"Is it really possible that such a large wolf can fit into such a small sack? If I could see that for myself, I could render a decision."

The peasant said:

"He fits completely; ask him yourself."

And the wolf said, "It's true."

Then the fox said:

"I won't believe it, until I can see it. Show me how you crawled in."

Then the wolf shoved his head into the sack and said, "Like this."

The fox said:

"Crawl in completely, because I can't see."

The wolf then crawled completely into the sack. The fox said to the peasant, "Now tie it up." The peasant tied up the sack. The fox said:

"Now show me, peasant, how you grind grain on the threshing floor." The peasant rejoiced and began beating the wolf with his flail.

And then he said: "Look, fox, how grain is milled on the threshing floor," and he struck the fox on the head and killed it. Then he said: "Good deeds are not remembered."

Two Comrades (A Fable)

Two boys were walking through the forest, when a bear jumped out in front of them. One of the boys ran off, climbed a tree, and hid there, while the other boy stayed where he was on the road. There was nothing he could do but drop to the ground and pretend to be dead.

The bear went up to him and started sniffing around: the boy was too frightened even to breathe.

The bear sniffed at his face and, deciding he was dead, went away.

When the bear had gone, the other boy climbed down from the tree and said, laughing, "Well, what did the bear whisper in your ear?"

"He said that people who abandon their comrades in danger are the very worst kind."

The Leap (A True Story)

A ship had sailed around the world and was returning home. The weather was calm and everyone was on deck. A large monkey was frolicking about among the crowd, amusing everybody. It danced, made faces, and imitated various people. Clearly it knew that it was being funny and therefore he carried on even more.

It jumped over to a twelve-year-old boy, the son of the ship's captain, and snatched his hat from his head, put it on its own head, and quickly scampered up the mast. Everyone laughed, but the boy didn't know whether to laugh or cry.

The monkey perched on the bottom crossbeam of the mast, took off the boy's hat, and began tearing it with its teeth and paws. He seemed to be doing it to tease the boy. He pointed at him and made funny faces. The boy shouted and threatened the monkey, but it kept tearing his hat, doing it even more fiercely. The sailors laughed louder, the boy blushed, took off his jacket, and went after the monkey on the mast. In an instant he'd climbed the rope ladder to the first crossbeam. But the monkey was more agile and faster than he was, and at that very moment, just as the boy was about to grab his hat, the monkey quickly climbed even higher.

"You won't get away from me," cried the boy, and started climbing higher. The monkey lured him on, climbing still higher; but the boy, now filled with fury, didn't stop. Thus, in just one minute, the monkey and the boy reached the top of the mast. Up there, holding fast with just one hind paw to a rope, the monkey stretched out its body, extending its long arm,[2] and hung the torn cap on the end

---

2 Monkeys have four arms. (Tolstoy's note)

of the highest crossbeam. Then it made its way to the very tip of the mast and sat there making faces, baring its teeth, and enjoying itself. There was a distance of about two arshins between the boy and the end of the crossbeam where his hat was now hanging. To reach it, he would have to let go of both the rope and the mast.

But by now the boy was very agitated. He let go of the mast and stepped onto the highest crossbeam. All the people on deck had been watching and laughing at the monkey's and the boy's antics. But when they saw the boy let go of the rope and try to balance on the crossbeam, they all froze with terror. If he were to lose his balance and fall, he'd be smashed to bits on the deck. Even if he somehow didn't misstep, reached the end of the crossbeam, and got his hat, it would be hard for him to turn around and get back to the mast. Everyone was looking at him in silence, waiting to see what would happen, when suddenly, someone in the crowd cried out in panic. The boy heard the cry, seemed to return to reality, looked down, and began to teeter.

Just then the captain of the ship, the boy's father, came out of his cabin. He was holding a rifle for shooting seagulls.[3] When he saw his son teetering on the uppermost crossbeam he immediately aimed the gun at him, shouting, "Jump! Jump into the water! Or I'll shoot you!" The boy hesitated, not understanding. "Jump or I'll shoot! One, two. . ." As soon as his father cried "three," the boy tucked his head in and leapt.

His body hit the water like a cannonball, but before the waves could cover him, twenty brave seamen had jumped into the water from the deck. Within forty seconds—it seemed like a long time to everyone—the body of the boy rose to the surface. The seamen grabbed him and brought him back on board. After a few long minutes, water began to pour out of his mouth and nose, and he began to breathe again.

When the captain saw this, he uttered a cry as if something was choking him, and hurried away to his cabin, so no one could see him weep.

The Oak and the Hazel Bush (A Fable)

An old oak dropped an acorn under a hazel bush. The hazel bush said to the oak: "Don't you have enough space under your own branches? You should drop your acorns in an open space. Here I myself am crowded by my shoots, and I don't drop my own nuts on the ground, but give them away to people."

---

3 Seabirds. (Tolstoy's note)

"I've lived two hundred years," said the oak, "and the little oak, which will sprout from that acorn, will live just as long. "Then the hazel bush flew into a rage and said: "If so, I will choke your little oak, and it won't live even for three days." The oak made no reply, but told his little son to sprout out of that acorn.

The acorn got soaked, burst open, clung to the ground with his crooked rootlet, and sent up a shoot.

The hazel bush tried to choke it and shade it from the sun. But the little oak kept stretching upwards and grew stronger in the shade of the hazel bush. A hundred years passed. The hazel bush had long since dried up, but the oak from that acorn rose to the sky and spread its canopy in all directions.

Harmful Air (A True Story)

In the village of Nikolskoe, people went to church on a holiday. In the manor yard were left the following: a herdswoman, the elder, and a groom. The herdswoman went to the well for water. The well was in the yard itself. She pulled out the bucket, but couldn't hold it. The bucket pulled away from her, struck the side of the well, and broke the rope. The herdswoman returned to the hut and said to the elder:

"Aleksandr! Climb down into the well—I've dropped the bucket into it."

Aleksandr said:

"You dropped it, so you get it yourself." The herdswoman said that she would fetch it, if he would let her down into the well.

The elder laughed at her, and said:

"Well, let's go! You have an empty stomach now, so I'll be able to hold you up; after dinner I couldn't do it."

The elder tied a stick to a rope, and the woman sat astride it, took hold of the rope, and began to climb down into the well, while the elder turned the wheel to lower her. In the well there was only one arshin of water. The elder let her down slowly, and kept asking: "A little further?" And the herdswoman cried from below: "Just a little!"

Suddenly the elder felt the rope grow weak: he called the herdswoman, but she didn't answer. The elder looked down into the well, and saw the woman lying with her head in the water, and her feet in the air. The elder called for help, but there was nobody nearby; only the groom came. The elder told him to hold the wheel, and he himself pulled out the rope, sat down on the stick, and began climbing down into the well.

The moment the groom let the elder down to the water, the same thing happened to him. He let go of the rope and fell headfirst on the woman. The groom began to shout, and ran to the church to summon help. Mass was over, and people were coming out of the church. All the men and women ran to the well. They all crowded around it, and everyone hollered, but nobody knew what to do. The young carpenter Ivan made his way through the crowd, took hold of the rope, sat down on the stick, and told them to lower him down into the well. Ivan merely tied himself to the rope with his belt. Two men were lowering him, and the rest looked down into the well, to see what would become of Ivan. Just as he was getting near the water, he dropped his hands from the rope, and would have fallen headfirst, if the belt had not held him. All shouted, "Pull him out!" and Ivan was pulled out.

He hung like dead from the belt; his head was also drooping and beating against the sides of the well. His face was discolored. They pulled him out, took him off the rope, and put him down on the ground. They thought he was dead; but suddenly he drew a deep breath, began to cough, and soon he revived.

Others wanted to climb down into the well, but an old peasant said that they shouldn't go down because there was bad air there, and that bad air had killed people. Then the peasants ran for hooks and began to pull out the elder and the woman. The elder's mother and wife were weeping at the well, and others tried to soothe them; in the meantime the peasants put down their hooks and tried to get out the dead bodies. Twice they got the elder halfway up by his clothes; but he was heavy: his clothes tore and he fell in again. Finally they stuck two hooks into him and pulled him out. Then they also pulled out the herdswoman. Both were already dead and did not revive.

Then, when they started examining the well, they found that indeed there was bad air in it.

Bad Air (A Discussion)

Bad air can sometimes be so heavy that neither man nor any beast can live in it.

There are some places underground where that air gathers, and if a person ends up in one of those places, he dies at once. For this reason they place lamps in mines; before a man goes down into such a place, they lower the lamp. If it goes out, no man is allowed to go there; they keep letting in fresh air until such time as the lamp will burn.

There's one such cave near the city of Naples. There is always about one arshin of bad air in it, but above that, the air is fresh. A man can walk through the cave, and nothing will happen to him, but a dog will die the moment it enters.

Where does this bad air come from? It's made of the same good air we breathe. If you gather a lot of people together in one place, and close all the doors and windows, so that no fresh air can get in, you'll get the same kind of bad air as in the well, and people will die.

One hundred years ago, during a war, the Indians captured 146 Englishmen and locked them up in a cave underground, where fresh air couldn't enter.

After the captured Englishmen had been there a few hours they began to die, and toward the end of the night, 123 had died, and the rest came out more dead than alive, and very sick. At first the air in the cave had been good; but after the captives had inhaled all the good air, and no more fresh air entered, it became bad, and just as in the well, they died. Why does good air become bad when many people gather together? Because, when people breathe, they take in good air and breathe out bad air.

The Wolf and the Lamb (A Fable)

A wolf saw a lamb drinking at a river. The wolf wanted to eat the lamb, and so he began to pester him. He said: "You are muddying my water and won't let me drink."

The lamb said: "Oh, wolf, how could I be muddying your water? I'm standing downstream from you; besides, I drink with the ends of my lips."

And the wolf said: "Well, why did you offend my father last summer?" The lamb said: "But, wolf, I wasn't even born last summer." The wolf got angry and said: "It's impossible to outtalk you. Besides, my stomach is empty, so I'll just eat you."

Specific Gravity (History)

The Greek tsar Hiero of Syracuse[4] ordered his master of goldworks to make a gold crown for the idol of Jupiter and gave him 12 pounds of gold. Dmitry made the crown, and when the tsar weighed it, he found that it weighed exactly 12 pounds. But the tsar heard that Dmitry had stolen much of the gold and replaced it in the crown with silver. The tsar wanted to find out if there was a great deal of silver mixed in the crown, and he ordered that the crown be melted down in order to see the middle of it. There was a clever and learned man who

---

4 Hiero II (c. 308–215 BCE) was the Greek tyrant of Syracuse, from 275–215 BC, and the illegitimate son of a Syracusan noble.

was a relation of the tsar's named Archimedes.[5] He said to the tsar: "Don't have the crown destroyed and waste all that work; I can tell how much silver and how much gold is in it without destroying it." The tsar agreed, and Archimedes did as follows:

He took a pound of gold and a pound of silver and weighed them on a scale; then he weighed them in water. The pound of gold in water sank one small measure less than before, and the pound of silver sank two measures less.

Then Archimedes weighed the whole crown in water, called the tsar, and said: "If you weigh a pound of pure gold in water, one measure remains; but if you weigh silver in water, two measures are left over from the pound; hence, if the crown were made of pure gold and there are 12 pounds in it, then there should be twelve measures left over. Look here." He put eleven pounds on the scale and began to weigh the crown in water. The crown didn't sink. They removed one more measure, and Archimedes said: "Here's the extra measure we removed, and that's the amount Dmitry stole from you." Thus Archimedes found out for certain how much silver had been mixed into the golden crown.

The Lion, the Wolf, and the Fox (A Fable)

An old, sick lion was lying in his den. All the animals came to call on the king, but the fox didn't visit him. So the wolf was glad of the chance, and began to slander the fox in front of the lion.

"The fox doesn't respect you in the least," the wolf said. "It hasn't come even once to call on the king."

The Fox happened to run by as the wolf was saying these words. It heard what the wolf had said, and thought: "Just you wait, wolf, I'll get my revenge on you."

So when the lion began to roar at the fox, the fox said: "Don't have me killed, but let me say a word! I didn't come to see you because I had no free time. I had no free time because I was running all over to ask doctors for a remedy to cure you. I've just found one, so I've come to see you."

The lion said:

"What's the remedy?"

"It's this: if you flay a live wolf, and put on his warm hide. . . ."

When the lion killed the wolf and laid out his hide, the fox laughed, and said:

"That's it, my friend: masters ought to be led to do good, not evil."

---

5 Archimedes (c. 287–c. 212 BC) was an Ancient Greek mathematician, physicist, engineer, astronomer, and inventor from the ancient city of Syracuse in Sicily.

The Tsar's New Clothes (A Story)

A certain tsar was a lover of fine clothes. He thought of nothing else—only how to dress more elegantly. One day two tailors came to see him and said: "We can make you such splendid clothes that no one's ever seen before. Only if someone is stupid and unsuited for his position, he might not even see our clothes. He who's clever, will see them, while he who's stupid will be standing right next to him, but won't see our work." The tsar was very pleased to meet the tailors and ordered them to make a new suit of clothes for him. The tailors were led to a chamber of the palace and given velvet, silk, and gold—everything that was needed to fashion new clothes.

After a week had passed, the tsar sent his minister to find out if the new clothes were ready; the tailors said that all was ready and showed the minister an empty place. The minister knew that a foolish person, who was not suited for his position, wouldn't be able to see the new clothes, so he pretended that he saw the clothes and sang their praises. The tsar ordered that the new clothes be brought to him. They brought them to him and showed him an empty place. He, too, pretended that he saw the new clothes. He took off his old clothes and ordered that they dress him in his new ones. When the tsar went for a walk through town in his new clothes—everyone saw that he had no clothes on at all, but they were all afraid to say that they didn't see anything. They'd heard that only a fool would be unable to see the new clothes. And each person thought that only he didn't see the clothes, and thought that everyone else could see them. So the tsar was strolling through town, and everyone was praising his new clothes. All of a sudden one little fool saw the tsar and cried out; "Look: the tsar's walking through the streets naked!" And the tsar was ashamed that he was undressed, and people could see that he had absolutely nothing on."

The Fox's Tail (A Fable)

A man caught a fox, and asked it: "Who taught you foxes to deceive dogs with your tails?" The fox asked: "What do you mean, deceive? We don't deceive dogs, but simply run away from them as fast as we can." The man said: "No, you deceive them with your tails. When dogs catch up with you and are just about to grab you, you turn your tails to one side; the dogs turn sharply after your tail, but then you run in the opposite direction." The fox laughed and said: "We don't do that to deceive the dogs, but to turn around; when a dog's after us, and we see that we can't get away straight ahead, so we turn to one side; but to do that suddenly, we have to swing our tail in the other direction, just as you do with your arms, when you have to turn while running. That's not our invention; God himself invented it when He created us, so that dogs wouldn't be able to catch all the foxes."

The Silkworm (A Story)

I had some old mulberry trees in my garden. My grandfather had planted them a long time ago. In the fall I was given a zolotnik of silkworm eggs,[6] and was advised to hatch them and raise silkworms. These eggs are dark gray and so small that in that amount I counted 5,835 of them. They are smaller than the tiniest pinhead. They seem quite dead; only when you crush them do they crack.

The eggs had been lying around on my table, and I had almost forgotten about them.

One day, in the spring, I went into the orchard and noticed the buds swelling on the mulberry trees; where the sun was beating down, the leaves were already out. I thought about the silkworm eggs, took them apart at home, and gave them more space. The majority of the eggs were no longer dark gray, as before; some were light gray, while others were lighter still, a milky shade.

The next morning, I looked at the little eggs, and saw that some of the worms had hatched, while other eggs were quite swollen. Evidently they felt even in their shells that their food was ripening.

The worms were black, shaggy, and so small that it was hard to see them. I looked at them through a magnifying glass, and saw that the worms in the eggs lay curled up in rings, and when they hatched they straightened out. I went to the garden for some mulberry leaves; I got about three handfuls, which I put on my table, and began to fix a place for the worms, as I'd been taught to do.

While I was fixing the paper, the worms smelled their food and started to move toward it. I pushed it away, and began to entice the worms onto a leaf, and they headed for it, as dogs do for a piece of meat; they followed the leaf over the tablecloth and across pencils, scissors, and papers. Then I cut some paper into pieces, made holes through them with a penknife, placed leaves on top of them, and with the leaves, put the piece of paper on top of the worms. The worms crawled through the holes, climbed onto the leaf, and started to eat.

---

6   An old Russian measure of weight, equivalent to 1/96th of a Russian pound.

When the other worms hatched, I put a piece of paper with leaves on them, too, and they all crawled through the holes, and began eating. The worms gathered on each leaf and nibbled it from the edges. When they had eaten everything, they crawled across the paper and looked for more food. Then I put new sheets of perforated paper with mulberry leaves on them, and they crawled over to the new food.

They were lying on my shelf; when there was no leaf, they crawled around the shelf, all the way to the very edge, but they never fell off, even though they're blind. As soon as a worm comes to an edge, it lets a web out of its mouth before descending, and then it attaches itself to the edge and lets itself down; it hangs in the air for a while, looks around and, if it wants to go farther down, it does so; if not, it pulls itself up by its web.

For days at a time the worms did nothing but eat. I had to give them more and more leaves. When a new leaf was brought, they moved over to it and made a noise that sounded like rain falling on leaves; that was when they began to eat a fresh leaf.

Thus the older worms lived for five days. They had grown very large and had begun to eat ten times as much as before. On the fifth day, I knew, they would fall asleep and I waited for that to happen. Toward evening, on the fifth day, one of the older worms stuck to the paper and stopped eating and moving.

The whole next day I watched it for a long time. I knew that worms molted several times, because as they grew larger, and found it confining in their old skins, they grew a new one.

My friend and I took turns watching it. In the evening my friend called out: "It's begun to undress: come and see!" I went up to him, and saw that the worm had stuck to the paper with its old skin, had torn a hole at its mouth, thrust forth its head, and was writhing and trying to get out, but the old shirt wouldn't let him. I watched it for a long time as it writhed and couldn't get out: I wanted to help it. I barely touched it with my nail, but right away I saw that I had done something foolish. Under my nail there was some liquid, and the worm died. At first I thought it was blood, but later I learned that the worm has a liquid mass under its skin, so that the skin can slide off more easily. With my nail I'd no doubt disturbed the new skin; though the worm had crawled out, it soon died.

I didn't touch the other worms. All of them made their way out of their skins in the same manner; only a few died; nearly all came out safely, though they struggled for a long time.

After shedding their skins, the worms began to eat more voraciously, and devoured more leaves. Four days later they fell asleep again, and then started crawling out of their skins again. They consumed an even larger quantity of leaves, and were now a quarter-inch in length. Six days later they fell asleep once more, and again came out in new skins, and now became very large and fat; we barely had time to get more leaves ready for them.

On the ninth day the oldest worms quit eating entirely and climbed up the shelves and rods. I gathered them and gave them fresh leaves, but they turned their heads away, and continued crawling away. Then I remembered that when the worms get ready to roll up into larvae, they stop eating and climb upward.

I left them alone and began to watch what they would do.

The oldest worms climbed to the ceiling, scattered about, crawled away, and began to draw out single threads in various directions. I watched one of them. It went into a corner, put out about six threads, each two inches long, hung down from them, bent over in the shape of a horseshoe, and began to turn its head and let out a silk web, which began to cover it all over. By evening it was completely covered as though in a mist; the worm could scarcely be seen. On the following morning the worm could no longer be seen; it was all wrapped in silk, and was continuing to spin.

Three days later they finished spinning, and quieted down.

Later I learned how much thread it spins in those three days. If the whole web were to be unraveled, it would be more than half a mile in length, rarely less. And if we figure out how many times the worm had to toss its head in these three days in order to let out all the web, it would appear that in those three days the worm tosses its head 300,000 times. Consequently, it makes one turn a second, without stopping. But after this work, when we took down a few cocoons and broke them open, we found the worms inside all dried up and white, looking like pieces of wax.

I knew that butterflies would come from these larvae with their white, waxen bodies; but as I looked at them, I couldn't believe it. Nonetheless, I went to look at them on the twentieth day, to see what had become of them.

That day I knew there was to be a change. Nothing could be seen, and I was beginning to think that something was wrong, when suddenly I noticed that the end of one of the cocoons grew dark and moist. I thought that it had probably spoiled, and wanted to throw it away. But then I thought that perhaps it began that way, and so I watched to see what would happen. And, indeed, something began to move at the wet end. For a long time I couldn't make out what it was. Later there appeared something like a head with whiskers. The whiskers moved. Then I noticed a leg sticking out through the hole, then another, and the legs scrambled to get out of the cocoon. It emerged more and more, and I saw a wet butterfly. When all six legs had scrambled out, the back jumped out, too, and the butterfly crawled out and paused. When it dried it was white; it straightened its wings, flew around a bit, circled around, and alighted on the window.

Two days later the butterfly on the windowsill laid its eggs in a row, and stuck them onto it firmly. The eggs were yellow. Twenty-five butterflies laid eggs. I collected five thousand eggs.

The following year I raised more worms and had more silk spun.

The Tsar and the Elephants (A Fable)

An Indian tsar ordered all the blind people be gathered; when they came, he ordered that all his elephants should be shown to them. The blind men went to the stable and began to feel the elephants. One felt a leg, another a tail, a third the stump of a tail,[7] a fourth a belly, a fifth a back, a sixth the ears, a seventh the tusks, and an eighth a trunk. Then the tsar summoned the blind men, and asked them: "What are my elephants like?" One blind man said: "Your elephants are like posts." He had felt the legs. Another blind man said: "They are like brooms." He had felt the end of the tail. A third said: "They are like branches." He had felt the tail stump. The one who had touched the belly said: "The elephants are like a clod of earth." The one who had touched the sides said: "They are like a wall." The one who had touched a back said: "They are like a hill." The one who had touched the ears said: "They are like kerchiefs." The one who had touched the tusks said: "They are like horns." The one who had touched the trunk said that they were like a stout rope.

And all the blind men began to argue and to quarrel among themselves.

Longing Is Worse than Bondage (A Hunter's Story)

We were out hunting bears. My companion had a chance to shoot one: he wounded him, but only in a soft spot. A little blood was left on the snow, but the bear got away.

We met up together in the forest and began to discuss what to do: whether to go and find that bear, or to wait two or three days until the bear would lie down again.

We started asking the peasant bear hunters whether it was possible to get the bear now. An old bear hunter said: "No, one must give the bear a chance to calm down. In about five days it will be possible to get him, but if one goes after him, he will only be frightened and won't lie down."

---

7   That part of the tail where there is flesh. (Tolstoy's note)

But a young bear hunter argued with the old man, and said that we could get him now. "Over this snow," he said, "the bear can't get far; he's fat. He'll lie down again today. And if he doesn't, I'll catch up with him on snowshoes."

My companion, too, didn't want to get the bear now, and advised waiting.

So I said: "What's the use of arguing? Do what you want; I'm going with Demyan, following his track. If we get him, so much the better; if not, there's nothing to do today anyway, and it's still not too late."

And so we did.

My companions went to their sleigh, and then back to the village, but Demyan and I took some bread with us and remained in the forest.

When everyone had left us, Demyan and I examined our guns, tucked our fur coats over our belts, and followed the bear's track.

It was fine weather, chilly and calm. But walking on snowshoes was difficult: the snow was deep and powdery. It hadn't settled in the forest, and besides, fresh snow had fallen the night before, so that our snowshoes sank a few inches in the snow, and in some places even more.

The bear track could be seen from a distance. We could see the way the bear had walked, that in some places he'd sunk in the snow up to his belly and had swept the snow aside. At first we walked in full view of the track, through a forest of large trees; then, when the track entered a small pinewood, Demyan stopped. "Now we must give up the track," he said. "No doubt, he'll lie down here. He's been sitting on his haunches; you can see that by the snow. Let's move away from the track and circle around him. But we must walk quietly and make no noise, not even cough, or we'll scare him."

We went away from the track, to the left. We walked about five hundred steps and then once again we saw the bear's track before us. We followed the track once more, and it led us to the road. We stopped there and began to look around, to see in which direction the bear had gone. Here and there on the road we could see its footprints with all its toes pressed into the snow, while in other prints, it looked as though a peasant was walking in bast shoes. He had, evidently, gone to the village.

We walked along the road. Demyan said to me: "Now we needn't watch the road; if he turns off, either to the right or the left, we'll see in the snow. He'll turn off somewhere; after all, he won't go to the village."

We walked thus about a mile along the road; suddenly we saw the track turn off. We looked at it, and what a wonder! It was a bear's track, but it led not from the road into the woods, but from the woods to the road: the toes were pointing to the road. I said: "This is a different bear." Demyan looked at it, and thought for a while. "No," he said, "it's the same bear, only he's begun to trick us. He left the road backwards." We followed the track, and so it was. The bear had evidently walked about ten steps backwards from the road, until he got beyond a fir tree, and then he'd turned around and gone straight ahead. Demyan stopped, and said: "Now we'll certainly catch up with him. He has no place to lie down but in this swamp. Let us go the roundabout way."

We started out, going through the dense pine forest. I was getting exhausted, and now it was much harder to travel. One minute I would strike against a juniper bush and get caught in it; or else, a small pine tree would get under my feet; or my snowshoes would twist, since I wasn't used to them; or I would strike a stump or a block under the snow. I was beginning to get worn out. I took off my fur coat; sweat was just pouring from me. But Demyan sailed along as if in a boat. It looked as though the snowshoes under him were walking of their own accord. He neither got caught in anything, nor did his shoes twist on him. And he even threw my fur coat over his shoulders, and kept urging me on.

We covered about three versts in a circle, and walked around the swamp. I already started lagging behind—my skis were crossing and my feet were getting tangled. Demyan suddenly stopped in front of me, and waved his arm. I walked over to him. He bent down, pointed, and whispered to me: "Do you see, a magpie chattering on the crowbar: the bird senses the bear from a distance. That's him."

We walked to one side, covered another verst, and came upon the old trail again. Thus we had made a circle around the bear, and he was inside of it. We stopped. I took off my hat and unbuttoned my coat: I felt as hot as in a steam bath, and was as wet as a mouse. Demyan, too, was flushed, and he wiped his face with his sleeve. "Well," he said, "we've done our work, sir; now we can take a rest."

The evening glow could be seen through the forest. We sat down on our snowshoes to rest. We took the bread and salt out of our bags; first I ate a little snow, and then some bread. The bread tasted better than any I had eaten in my entire life. We sat for a while; it began to grow dark. I asked Demyan how far it was to the village. "About twelve versts. We'll reach it at night; but now we must rest. Put on your fur coat, sir, or you'll catch a chill."

Demyan broke off some pine branches, knocked down the snow, made a bed, and we lay down beside each other, with our arms under our heads. I don't remember how I fell asleep. I awoke about two hours later. Something crashed.

I had been sleeping so soundly that I forgot where I was. I looked around me. What on earth was that? Where was I? Above me were some white halls and white columns, white sparkles glistened on everything. I looked up: there was a white, checked cloth, and between the checks was a black vault in which lights of all colors burned. I looked around and recalled that we were in the forest, and that the snow-covered trees had appeared to me as halls, and that the lights were nothing but stars flickering among the branches.

During the night a hoarfrost had fallen, and there was frost on the branches, on my fur coat, and even Demyan was covered with hoarfrost; it was coming down from above. I woke Demyan. We got on our snowshoes and started walking. The forest was quiet. All that could be heard was the sound we made as we slid over the soft snow, or when a tree would crackle from the frost, and a hollow sound would echo through the woods. Only once did something living stir close to us and run away again. I thought it was the bear. We walked over to the place where the noise had come from, and we saw hare tracks. The young aspens had been nibbled down. The hares had been feeding on them.

We came out to the road, tied the snowshoes behind us, and continued on our way. It was easier to walk. The snowshoes rattled and rumbled over the beaten road; the snow creaked under our boots; the cold hoarfrost stuck to our faces like down. The stars seemed to run toward us along the branches: they would flash, and go out again, just as though the sky were rushing around.

My companion was asleep; I woke him up. I told him how we'd made a circle around the bear, and told the landlord to summon the beaters for the morning. We ate our supper and lay down to sleep.

I was so tired that I could have slept until dinner, but my companion roused me. I jumped up and saw that he was all dressed and busy with his gun.

"Where's Demyan?"

"He's been in the forest for quite a while. He checked the circle, and has been back to lead the beaters out." I washed, dressed, and loaded my guns. We climbed into the sleigh and set off.

There was a hard frost, the air was calm, and the sun wasn't visible yet: there was a mist above, and the hoarfrost was still settling.

We traveled about three versts by the road and reached the forest. We saw blue smoke in a hollow; and some peasants, men and women, were standing around with clubs.

We climbed out of the sleigh and went up to the people. Some peasants were sitting there, roasting potatoes, joking with the women.

Demyan was with them. The people got up, and Demyan made them stand in a circle, which we had made during our trip last night. The men and women lined up in single file: there were thirty of them and they could be seen only from their belts up, and they went into the woods; then my companion and I followed their tracks.

Though they had made a path, which was hard to follow; still, we couldn't fall, because it was like walking between two walls.

Thus we walked for about a verst. I looked up, and there was Demyan running toward us from the other side on snowshoes, waving his arm for us to come to him.

We went up to him and he showed us where to stand. I took up my position and looked around.

To the left of me was a tall pine forest. I could see far through it, and beyond the trees I saw the black shape of a peasant hunter. Opposite me was a young pine grove, as tall as a man. In this grove the branches were hanging down and sticking together from the snow. The path through the middle of the grove was covered with snow. This path was leading straight towards me. To the right was a dense pine forest, and beyond the grove there was a meadow. And in this clearing I saw Demyan place my companion.

I examined my two guns, cocked them, and began thinking about where to take up my stand. Behind me, about three steps away, there was a big pine tree. "I'll stand by that pine, and will lean the other gun against it." I made my way to that pine, walking through knee-deep snow. I tramped down a space of about four feet each way, and there took my stand. One gun I took into my hands, and the other, with hammer raised, I placed against the tree. I unsheathed my dagger and put it back in its scabbard, to be sure that in case of need it would come out easily.

I had hardly prepared myself, when I heard Demyan shouting from the woods: "Start now, start!" And as Demyan shouted, peasants in the circle cried, each one in a different tone of voice: "Let's go now! Oo-oo-oo!" and the women cried, in their high voices: "Ay! Eekh!"

The bear was inside the circle. Demyan was driving him. The people all around shouted; only my companion and I stood still, didn't speak or move, and waited for the bear. I stood, looked, and listened: my heart was pounding. I was clutching my gun and trembling. Now, now—he'll jump out, I thought, and I'll aim and shoot, and he'll fall. Suddenly to the left I heard something tumbling through the snow, but it was still far away. I looked into the tall pine forest: about fifty steps from me, behind the trees, stood something large and black. I aimed and waited. I thought it might come closer. I saw it move its ears and turn around. Now I could see the whole of him from the side. It was an enormous beast. I aimed hastily. Bang! I heard the bullet strike the tree. Through the smoke I saw the bear head back for cover and disappear into the forest. "Well," I thought, "my business is ruined: he won't run up to me again; either my companion will have a chance to shoot at him, or he'll go through between the peasants, but never again toward me." I reloaded the gun, stood, and listened. The peasants were shouting from all directions, but on the right, not far from my companion, I heard a woman yell, "Here he is! Here he is! Here he is! This way! This way! Oy, oy, oy! Ay, ay, ay!"

Apparently there was the bear, in full sight. I was no longer expecting it to come toward me, and I looked to the right toward my companion. I saw Demyan running without his snowshoes along the path, a stick in his hand, going up to my companion, sitting down next to him, and pointing at something with the stick, as though he were aiming. I saw my companion raise his gun and aim in the direction where Demyan was pointing. Bang! He fired it off. "Well," I thought, "he's killed him." But then I saw that my companion was not running after the bear. "Evidently, he missed, or didn't hit him right. He'll get away," I thought, "but he won't come toward me. What was that?" Suddenly I heard something in front of me: somebody was flying like a whirlwind, scattering snow nearby, and panting. I looked ahead of me, but he was rushing headlong toward me along the path through the dense pine growth. I could see that the bear was beside himself with fear. When he was within five steps of me I could see the whole of him: his chest was black, his reddish-colored head was enormous. He was racing straight toward me, scattering snow in all directions. I could see by the bear's eyes that he didn't see me and in his fright he was rushing headlong. He was rushing straight for the pine where I was standing. I raised my gun, and fired, but he kept coming still nearer. I saw that I hadn't hit him: the bullet flew past. He heard nothing, plunged onward, but he didn't see me. I lowered the gun, almost leaned it against his head. Bang! This time I hit him, but still didn't kill him.

He raised his head, dropped his ears, bared his teeth, and headed straight toward me. I grasped the other gun; but before I had it in my hand, he was already on me, knocked me down, and had flown over me. "Well," I thought, "that's good, he won't touch me." I was just getting up, when I felt something pressing against me and holding me down. In his rush he ran past me, but he turned around and brushed against me with his whole breast. I felt something heavy upon me, something warm over my face, and I felt him taking my face into his jaws. My nose was already in his mouth, and I felt hot, and smelled his blood. He pressed my shoulders with his paws, and I couldn't budge. All I could do was pull my head out of his jaws and press it against my breast, and I turned my nose and eyes away. But he was trying to get at my eyes and nose. I felt him dig the teeth of his upper jaw into my forehead, right below the hairline, and the lower jaw into my cheekbones, and he began to crush me. It was as though my head was being cut with knives. I jerked and pulled my head out, but he chewed and chewed, snapping at me like a dog. I would turn my head away, but he would catch it again. "Well," I thought, "my end has come." Suddenly I felt lighter. I looked up, and he was gone: he had jumped off me and now he ran away.

When my companion and Demyan saw that the bear had knocked me into the snow, they dashed toward me. My companion wanted to get there as fast as possible, but lost his way; instead of running along the trodden path, he ran straight ahead, and fell down. While he was trying to get up out of the snow, the bear was gnawing at me. Demyan ran up to me along the path, without a gun, just with the stick he had in his hands, and he kept shouting, "He's devouring the gentleman! He's devouring the gentleman!" And he kept running and shouting at the bear, "Oh, you wretched beast! What are you doing? Stop! Stop!"

The bear listened to him, stopped, and ran away. When I got up, there was a great deal of blood on the snow, just as though a sheep had been killed; the flesh over my eyes was hanging in rags. Because of all the excitement, I felt no pain.

My companion ran up to me, while the peasants gathered around me. They looked at my wounds, and washed them with snow. I had entirely forgotten about my wounds and only asked, "Where's the bear? Where has he gone?" Suddenly we heard, "Here he is! Here he is!" We saw the bear running toward us once again. We grasped our guns, but no one managed to shoot: he ran past us. The bear was enraged: he wanted to chew on me again, but when he saw so many people he became frightened. We saw by the track that the bear was bleeding from the head. We wanted to follow him, but now my head began hurt, and so we drove into town to see a doctor.

The doctor sewed up my wounds with silk stitches, and they soon began to heal.

A month later we went out again to hunt that bear; but I didn't get the chance to kill him. The bear wouldn't leave its cover; it kept walking around and around, roaring terribly. Demyan finished him off. My shot had crushed his lower jaw and knocked out a tooth.

This bear was very large and had beautiful black fur. I had the skin stuffed, and it's now adorning my room. The wounds on my head have healed: one can scarcely see where they were.

The Hen and the Chicks (A Fable)

A brooding hen hatched some chicks, but didn't know how to keep them safe from harm. So she said to them: "Climb back into your shells! When you're inside, I will sit on you as before, and will keep you from any harm." The chicks did as they were told and tried to crawl back into their shells, but they were unable to do so, and only crushed their wings. Then one of the little chicks said to his mother:

"If we're to stay in our shells all the time, you should never have hatched us."

Gases (A Discussion)

I

Air is diverse, although it's always light and invisible.

Water evaporates in air, and becomes airborne; and when there is a great deal of water in the air, it becomes humid; when there's little water—it's arid. When people breathe in an enclosed space, the air becomes bad, unhealthy; but in open areas or in the forest—the air is healthy, good. This occurs because in the enclosed room, bad air was added to the ordinary air—bad air is exhaled by people and all other animals.

That's because there are various parts to the air, and the eye cannot tell them apart: they all resemble ordinary air. These various substances, are various gases mixed in the air like water with vinegar or with wine. If you pour vodka into water, the water and vodka combine in such a way that you can't tell with your eyes whether there's vodka in it or not, and whether there's a lot or a little. But if you sniff—you can tell; similarly in air, there is a different mixture, but the eyes can't tell anything, you can feel it only when you breathe it for a long time. It is pleasant and healthy to breathe in good air; in bad air it is difficult and sometimes injurious.

For breathing, there is one gas that is more important than any other: it's called *oxygen*. If you collect this gas separately, and stick a burning splinter into it, it will burst into flame at once. Therefore, wood and every other material burns more strongly in its presence. But if there's no oxygen in the air and you place a burning splinter in it, it will be extinguished.

That's why air is needed for combustion, because it contains oxygen. In order to make something burn, people blow on it or wave at it; whereas if you want to extinguish something that's started burning, make it so there is no air left around it: cover it, confine it on all sides, and it will go out.

The other part of air is *nitrogen*. It's not possible to breathe in it and things cannot burn.

The third part of air is *carbon dioxide*. It's also unsuitable for breathing or for combustion. There is not much of this gas in air, but there's always some present. However, when a lot of it gathers, it sinks and collects below, because it is heavier than the other gases.

The fourth part of air is water vapor, airborne water.

When we breathe, oxygen passes into our body, and in the air, which we exhale, there is less oxygen than in ordinary air, but there is more carbon dioxide. That's why air becomes bad from breathing.

Trees, grasses, and all plants also breathe, except they don't inhale air as we do with our chest, but absorb it through all their leaves and young bark. It's also impossible to see the exhalation of air from all the leaves; and this air is also not ordinary: it contains less carbon dioxide and more oxygen. Therefore plants need carbon dioxide, which is unnecessary and harmful to animals. That's why in the forest the air is so healthy: there's less carbon dioxide and more oxygen.

II

If, into a bucket of water, you toss some stones, corks, straw, dry and damp wood, sprinkle some sand, clay, salt, and also pour in some oil, and vodka, and shake and mix it all together, then look what happens: you will see that the stones, clay, and sand sink to the bottom, the dry wood, straw, corks, and oil float on the surface, the salt and the vodka dissolve and disperse so that they become invisible. At first it will all swirl around, move, and bump into each other, but then it will all find its own place and stop moving: whatever is heavier will sink to the bottom, and whatever is lighter will rise to the top.

It's the same way in the air above the earth: all the gases find their places. Those that are heavier than air sink down; those that are lighter, rise above; those that can dissolve, disperse throughout the air.

If there were no new gases formed, and if they didn't combine with others, and if they didn't change, then the air would remain above the earth and not move at all, like water in the bucket, when it settles; but on earth new gases are constantly being formed, and those which are there already, combine with others.

Every person, every animal, when he breathes, selects oxygen from the air, combines it with substances in his body, and exhales it in the form of a different gas. Every plant—grass, or a tree—absorbs carbon dioxide and exhales oxygen. Water in one place is changed from a liquid into an airborne gas, water vapor, and invisible steam; and in another place airborne water becomes a liquid. As a result different gases always circulate in the air: the lighter ones move to the top, the heavier ones, sink down; the gases are moving all the time, just as materials do in a bucket of water. But most of all, the air keeps moving and this happens because as soon as the air warms, it rises up, and when it cools, it sinks down. When on a sunny day the sun shines from one side into the window, in the rays of the sun, the dust becomes visible, swirling and jumping up and down. That's the warm and cool air circulating and carrying around particles of dust.

The Lion, the Ass, and the Fox (A Fable)

A lion, an ass, and a fox went out to hunt. They caught a large number of animals, and the lion told the ass to divide them up. The ass divided them into three equal parts and said: "Now, take them!"

The lion grew angry, ate the ass, and told the fox to divide them up anew. The fox gathered them all into one heap, and left a very small part for himself. The lion looked and said: "What a clever fox! Who taught you to divide so well?"

She said: "Well, I saw what happened to the ass!"

The Old Poplar Tree (A Story)

For five years our garden was neglected. I hired workers with axes and shovels, and began working with them in the garden myself. We cut out and chopped down all the dry branches, wild shoots, and the unnecessary trees and bushes. The poplars and bird cherries spread more than the rest and choked out the other trees. A poplar grows out from its roots, and it can't be dug out; the roots have to be chopped underground. Beyond the pond stood an enormous poplar, its trunk was the size of two men embracing. There was a clearing around it, overgrown with poplar shoots. I ordered them to be cut: I wanted the spot to look more cheerful, but above all, I wanted to make it easier for the old poplar, because I thought that all those young trees came from its roots, and were draining it of its sap. When we were cutting out these young poplars, I felt sorry as I saw them chop the sap-filled roots underground, and even though all four of us pulled at the poplar that had been cut down, we couldn't pull it out. It held on with all its might, and didn't wish to die. I thought that, apparently, they had to live, since they clung to life so tenaciously. But it was necessary to cut them down, and so I did. Only later, I learned that they shouldn't have been destroyed.

I thought that the shoots were draining the sap away from the old poplar, but it turned out to be the other way around. When I was cutting them down, the old poplar was already dying. When the leaves came out, I saw (it grew from two boughs) that one was bare and that same summer it dried up completely. The tree had been dying for quite some time, and the tree knew it, so it had tried to pass its life along to its shoots.

That was why they grew so fast. I had wanted to make it easier for the old tree—and killed all its children.

The Bird Cherry Tree (A Story)

A bird cherry grew out on a path of hazel bushes and was choking the bushes. I thought for a long time about whether to cut down the bird cherry or not. It made me sad to cut it down. This bird cherry grew not like a bush, but like a tree, about six inches in diameter and thirty feet high, full of branches and very bushy, all sprinkled with bright, white, fragrant blossoms. You could smell it from a distance. I probably wouldn't have cut it down, but one of the workers (whom I had told before to cut down all the bird cherry trees) had begun to chop it down without me. When I came, he'd already cut in about three inches, and the sap splashed under the axe whenever it struck the same spot. "It can't be helped—apparently such was its fate," I thought, and I picked up an axe myself and began to chop it along with the peasant.

It's a pleasure to do any work, and a pleasure to chop. It's a pleasure to let the axe enter deeply at a slant, then to chop out the chip by a straight cut, and to chop farther and farther into the tree.

I had forgotten all about the bird cherry, and was thinking only of chopping it down as quickly as possible. When I got out of breath, I put down my axe and together with the peasant pushed against the tree and tried to make it topple. We rocked it a little: the tree trembled with its leaves and the dew showered down on us, and the white, fragrant petals of the blossoms came sprinkling down.

At the same time something seemed to cry out—the middle of the tree creaked; we pressed against it, and it was as though something wept; there was a crash in the middle and the tree fell down. It broke at the notch and, swaying, fell into the grass with all its branches and blossoms. The twigs and blossoms trembled for a little while after the fall, and then they stopped moving.

"It was a fine tree!" said the peasant. "I really feel sorry for it!" I myself felt so sorry for it that I hurried away to the other workers.

How Trees Walk (A Story)

One day we were clearing an overgrown path on a hillock near the pond. We cut down a lot of brier bushes, willows, and poplars—then came the turn of a bird cherry tree. It was growing on the path, and it was so old and stout that it couldn't be less than ten years old. And yet I knew that five years ago the garden had been cleared. I couldn't understand how such an old bird cherry tree could have grown up there. We cut it down and went along farther. Farther away, in another grove, there grew a similar bird cherry, even fatter than the first. I looked at its root, and saw that it was growing under an old linden tree. The linden was choking it with its branches, and the bird cherry had stretched about twelve feet in a straight line, and only then emerged into the light, raised its head, and began to blossom.

I cut it down at the root and was surprised to find it so fresh, while the root was rotten. After we had cut it down, the peasants and I tried to pull it away; but no matter how hard we pulled, we were unable to move it: it was as though it was stuck fast. I said: "See if it's caught somewhere." A worker crawled under it, and called out: "It has another root; it's on the path!" I walked over to him, and saw that it was true.

So as not to be choked by the linden, the bird cherry had moved away from underneath the linden out onto the path, about eight feet from its former location. The root, which I had cut down, was rotten and dry, but the new one was fresh. The bird cherry had evidently felt that it couldn't exist under the linden, so it had stretched out, dropped a branch to the ground, made a root of that branch, and left the other root. Only then did I understand how the first bird cherry had grown out on the road. It had evidently done the same thing—but it had enough time to abandon the old root, and so I couldn't find it.

The Corncrake and His Mate (A Fable)

A corncrake had made his nest in the meadow late in the year, and at mowing time his mate was still sitting on her eggs. Early in the morning the peasants came to the meadow, took off their coats, sharpened their scythes, and started, one after another, mowing down the grass and arranging it in rows. The corncrake flew up to see what the mowers were doing. When he saw a peasant swing his scythe and cut a snake in two, he rejoiced, flew back to his mate, and said: "Don't fear the peasants! They've come to cut the snakes to pieces; the snakes have given us no rest for quite some time." But his mate said: "The peasants are cutting the grass, and with the grass, they're cutting everything in their way—snakes, the corncrake's nest, and the corncrake's head. My heart anticipates nothing good: but I can't carry the eggs away, or fly from the nest for fear of cooling them."

When the mowers came to the nest of the corncrake, one of the peasants swung his scythe and cut off the head of the corncrake's mate, put the eggs in his bosom, and gave them to the children to play with.

How Balloons Are Made (A Discussion)

If you put a blown-up air bladder under water and let go of it, it will jump up to the surface of the water and will float on it. Exactly the same way, when water is boiled in a pot, it becomes airborne at the bottom, over the fire—and is turned into a gas. After a little of that watery gas is collected, it rises as a bubble. First one bubble comes up, then another, and when all of the water is heated, the bubbles keep rising without stopping. Then the water is boiling.

Just as the bubbles leap to the surface, full of airborne water because they're lighter than water, so will an air bladder filled with hydrogen, or with hot air, rise, because hot air is lighter than cold, and hydrogen is lighter than all other gases.

Balloons are made with hydrogen or with hot air. With hydrogen they're made as follows: they take a large air bladder, attach it to posts by ropes, and fill it with hydrogen. The moment the ropes are untied, the balloon rises up in the air, and keeps rising until it gets beyond the heavy air, which is heavier than hydrogen. When it gets up into the lighter air, it begins to swim in it like a bladder on the surface of water. Hot air balloons are constructed like this: they make a large empty ball, with a neck below, like an upturned pitcher, and attach a handful of cotton to its mouth; then that cotton is soaked with spirits and ignited. The fire heats the air in the balloon, and makes it lighter than the cold air, and the balloon is drawn upward, like the air bladder in the water. And the balloon will rise until it comes to air, which is lighter than the hot air in the balloon.

Nearly one hundred years ago two Frenchmen, the brothers Montgolfier,[8] invented the hot air balloons. They made a balloon of canvas and paper and filled it with hot air—the balloon flew. Then they made another, a larger balloon, and tied to it a sheep, a rooster, and a duck, and let it go. The balloon rose and came down safely. Then they attached a little basket under the balloon, and a man seated himself in it. The balloon flew so high that it disappeared from view; it flew away, and came down safely. Then they thought of filling a balloon with hydrogen, and they began to fly even higher and faster.

In order to fly with a balloon, they attach a basket under it, and two, three, or even eight people are seated in this basket, and they take food and drink with them.

In order to rise and descend as one pleases, there's a valve in the balloon, and the man who is flying it, can pull a rope to open or close the valve. If the balloon rises too high, and the man who is flying it wants to come down, he opens the valve—the gas escapes, the balloon is compressed, and begins to descend. There are always bags of sand in the balloon. When a bag of sand is thrown out, the balloon gets lighter, and it ascends. If the one who is flying the balloon wants to descend, but sees that it is not a good place to land—either a river or a forest— he pours the sand out of the bags, and the balloon grows lighter and rises again.

---

8 The Montgolfier brothers—Joseph-Michel Montgolfier and Jacques-Étienne Montgolfier— were aviation pioneers and balloonists, who lived in the second half of the eighteenth century.

The Tale of the Aeronaut

People gathered to see how I would fly. The balloon was ready. It was trembling, pulling upward on four ropes, creasing one moment, and swelling the next. I said farewell to my friends, got in the basket, looked around to make sure all my supplies were in place, and cried: "Let go!" The ropes were cut, and the balloon rose upwards, slowly at first—like a stallion, which breaks loose and looks around—and suddenly it was yanked upward and took off so fast that the basket shuddered and rocked. Below people started applauding, shouting, and waving their kerchiefs and hats. I waved my hat and before I'd managed to put it back on my head, I was already so high in the air that I could scarcely make out the people below. At first I was terrified and a chill ran through my veins; but then I felt cheerful and forgot to be frightened. I could barely hear the noise from the town. The people below sounded like bees buzzing. Streets, houses, the river, and the gardens in town were visible beneath me as if in a painting. It seemed to me that I was tsar over the whole town and all the people—it was that enjoyable up there. I was quickly rising, only the ropes in the basket were lightly trembling; twice a wind turned me around; but then I couldn't tell whether I was flying or standing in one place. I could only tell that I was climbing because the picture of the town kept getting smaller and smaller, and one could see further and further away. The earth seemed to grow beneath me, becoming broader and broader, and all of a sudden I noticed that the earth beneath me resembled a cup. The edges were curved—and on the bottom of the cup was the town. I was feeling more and more cheerful. It was easy and cheerful to breathe and I felt like singing. I started singing, but my voice was so weak, that I was surprised and frightened by it.

The sun was still high, but there was a cloud on the horizon—suddenly it covered the sun. I was frightened again, and, to have something to do, I got out my barometer and looked at it, and thanks to it I found out that I had already ascended four versts. When I was putting it put it back in its place, something fluttered near me, and I saw a dove. I remembered that I had brought along a dove to release it with a note to carry down. I wrote on a piece of paper that I was alive and well at a distance of four versts, and tied the note to the dove's neck. The dove sat on the edge of the basket and looked at me with its reddish eyes. It seemed to me that he was asking me not to push him off. Since it had become overcast, nothing was visible below. But nothing could be done; I needed to send the dove down. It was shuddering with all its feathers when I took it in hand. Then I stretched out my arm and tossed him out of the basket. Frequently flapping its wings, it flew sideways, dropping down like a stone. I looked at the barometer again and I saw that I was already at a height of five versts above the earth and felt that I had insufficient air and was breathing more often. I pulled on the rope to release some gas and descend, but whether I was feeling weak or something had broken, the valve didn't open. My heart stood still. I couldn't tell if I was still rising; nothing was moving but it was getting harder and harder for me to breathe. "If I can't stop the balloon," I thought, "it will burst and I will perish." To find out whether I was still ascending or staying in one place, I tossed some paper out of the basket. The papers, like stones, flew down. That meant that I was still ascending, like an arrow. With all my strength I grabbed the rope and yanked. Thank God, the valve opened, and something began whistling. I tossed out more paper; it fluttered near me and rose up. That meant I was descending. Below nothing was still visible; it looked like a sea of mist was spreading beneath me. I descended into fog: it was clouds. Then the wind started blowing, carrying me along, and soon the sun came out, and once again I saw the cup of the earth beneath me. But there was no sign of our town, only some forests and two blue stripes—rivers. Once more I felt joyful and I didn't want to descend; but suddenly something made a noise near me and I saw an eagle.

He regarded me with astonished eyes and paused on his wings. I was flying down past him like a stone. I began to toss out the ballast to slow down.

Soon I could see fields, the forest, a village near the forest, and a herd that was heading to the village. I heard the voices of people and the sounds of the herd. My balloon was descending slowly. They saw me. I shouted and tossed them the ropes. People came running. I saw that a young lad was the first to catch the rope. Other people grabbed hold, tied the balloon to a tree, and I got out. I had flown only three hours. This village was 250 versts from my town.

The Cow and the Billy Goat (A Story)

An old woman had a cow and a billy goat. The two animals were in the same herd. At milking time the cow was restless. The old woman brought out some bread and salt, gave it to the cow, and kept saying: "Stand still, mother cow; take it, take it! I will bring you some more, but stand still."

The next evening the billy goat came home from the field before the cow, and spread its legs, and stood in front of the old woman. The old woman waved a towel at it, but the billy goat stood still and didn't move. He remembered that the woman had promised the cow some bread if she would stand still. When the woman saw that the goat wouldn't budge, she picked up a stick, and beat him.

When the billy goat walked away, the woman once again began to feed the cow with bread and to talk to her.

"There's no honesty in people," thought the goat. "I stood still better than the cow, but I was beaten."

He stepped aside, came at full speed, knocked against the pail, spilled the milk, and injured the old woman.

The Raven and Its Young (A Fable)

A raven built his nest on an island and after its young had hatched, it began moving them from the island to the mainland. At first it picked up one of its young in its claws and flew with it across the sea. When the old raven reached the middle of the sea, it grew tired and began flapping its wings less often and thought: I'm strong now and he's weak, and I shall carry him across the sea; but when he becomes big and strong, and I become weak due to old age, will he remember my efforts and carry me from place to place? And the old raven asked the young one: "When I grow weak, and you'll be strong, will you carry me from place to place? Tell me the truth!" The young raven was afraid that his father might drop him into the sea, and he said, "I will." But the old raven didn't believe his son and let go of him from his claws. The young raven dropped like a lump and fell into the sea, and there he drowned. The old raven flew alone back to his island. Then the old raven picked up another of his young and also carried him across the sea. Once again he became exhausted in the middle of his flight and asked his son if he would carry him from place to place when he was old. The son was frightened that his father would drop him, and he said, "I will."

The father didn't believe this son either and dropped him into the sea. When the old raven got back to his nest, he had only one young raven left. He picked up his last son and flew across the sea with him. When he reached the middle and became tired, he asked: "When I'm old, will you feed me and carry me from place to place?" The young raven said: "No, I won't." "Why not?" asked his father. "When you're old and I'm big, I'll have my own nest and my own young and will feed and carry my own children." Then the old raven thought: "He's told the truth; for that I will exert myself and carry him across the sea." And the old raven didn't drop the young raven; with his last strength, he flapped his wings and carried him to the mainland, so that he could build his own nest and raise his own young.

The Sun—Heat (A Discussion)

In the winter on a calm, frosty day go out into a field, or into the woods, and look around and listen: you're surrounded by snow, rivers are frozen, dry blades of grass stick out, and trees are bare—nothing is moving.

Look in the summer: rivers are running and rippling, frogs are croaking and plunging into every puddle; birds fly from place to place, whistle, and sing; flies and gnats whirl around and buzz; trees and grass grow and wave to and fro.

Freeze a pot of water, and it will become as hard as a rock. Put the frozen pot on the fire: the ice will begin to break up, melt, and move; the water will begin to stir, and bubbles will rise; then, when it begins to boil, the water whirls about and makes some noise. The same thing happens in the world from heat. Without heat everything is dead; with heat, everything moves and lives. If there's little heat, there's little motion; with more heat, there's more motion; with lots of heat, there's lots of motion; with a great deal of heat, there's also a great deal of motion.

Where does heat in the world come from? The heat comes from the sun.

In winter the sun moves low in the sky, to one side, and its beams don't fall straight on the earth, and nothing moves. Once the sun begins to move higher above our heads, to shine straight down on the earth, everything in the world warms up and begins to stir.

When the snow settles down, ice begins to melt in rivers; water flows down from the mountains; vapor rises from the water to the clouds, and rain begins to fall. What causes it all? The sun. Seeds swell and put out rootlets; the rootlets take hold of the ground; old roots send up new shoots, and trees and the grass begin to grow. Who has caused all that? The sun.

Bears and moles get up; flies and bees awaken; mosquitoes are hatched, and, when it's warm, fish emerge from their eggs. Who's done it all? The sun.

The air gets warmed in one place and rises; in its place comes colder air, and there's a breeze. Who's done that? The sun.

The clouds rise and begin to gather and scatter—lightning flashes. Who has made that fire? The sun.

Grass, grain, fruits, and trees grow; animals find their food, people eat their fill and gather food and fuel for the winter; they build themselves houses, railways, cities. Who has prepared it all? The sun.

A man has built himself a house. What it's made of? Timbers. The timbers were cut from trees, but the trees were made to grow by the sun.

The stove is heated with wood. Who's made the wood grow? The sun.

Man eats bread and potatoes. Who's made them grow? The sun. Man eats meat. Who's fed the animals and birds? The grass. But the grass is made to grow by the sun.

A man builds himself a house from brick and lime. Bricks and lime are baked by firewood. The wood's been prepared by the sun.

Everything that people need that's useful, all that is prepared in advance by the sun; much of the sun's heat is spent on it. That's why everyone needs bread because the sun has made it grow, and because there's much of the sun's heat in it. Bread warms the one who eats it.

The reason that wood and logs are needed is because they contain much heat. He who buys wood for the winter, is buying the sun's heat; and in the winter he burns the wood whenever he wants it, and lets the sun's heat come into his room.

When there's heat, there's motion. No matter what motion it may be, it all comes from heat, either directly from the sun, or from the heat, which the sun has stored in coal, firewood, bread, and grass.

Horses and oxen pull, men work, what *moves* them? Heat. From where do they get heat? From food. And the food's been prepared by the sun.

Watermills and windmills turn around and grind. Who moves them? Wind and water. And what drives the wind? Heat. And what drives the water? Again, it's heat. Heat raises the water in the shape of vapor, and without this, the water would never fall as rain. A machine works: it's moved by steam. And who makes steam? Wood. And the sun's heat is stored in the firewood.

Heat makes motion, and motion makes heat. Both heat and motion come from the sun.

Why Is There Evil in the World? (A Fable)

A hermit was living in the forest, where the animals were not afraid of him. He and the animals talked together and understood each other.

Once the hermit lay down under a tree, and a raven, a dove, a stag, and a snake gathered in the same place, to pass the night. The animals began to discuss why there was evil in the world.

The raven said: "All the evil in the world comes from hunger. When I eat my fill, I sit down on a branch and croak a little, and all is cheerful and good, and everything gives me pleasure; but just let me go hungry for a day or two, and everything becomes so repugnant, that even I don't feel like looking at God's world. But something draws me on, and I fly from place to place, and get no peace. When I catch a glimpse of some meat, it only makes me feel sicker than ever, and I rush to it without much thinking. At times people throw sticks and stones at me, and wolves and dogs grab me, but I don't give in. Oh, how many of my brothers are perishing from hunger! All evil comes from hunger."

The dove said: "In my opinion, evil comes not from hunger, but from love. If we lived alone, we would have little trouble. One head is not poor, and if it is, it's only one. But we always live in pairs. And you come to love your mate so much that you get no rest: you keep thinking of her all the time, wondering whether she's had enough to eat, and whether she's feeling warm. And when your mate flies away from you, you feel entirely lost, and you keep thinking that a hawk may carry her off, or people may catch her; so you set out to find her and fly to your own ruin—either into a hawk's claws, or into a snare. And when your mate is lost, nothing affords you any joy. You don't eat or drink, and spend all the time searching and weeping. Oh, so many of us perish this way! All the evil comes not from hunger, but from love."

The snake said: "No, the evil comes neither from hunger, nor from love, but from rage. If we lived peacefully, without getting into a rage, everything would be fine. But, as it is, whenever things don't go exactly right, we get mad, and then nothing pleases us. All we think about is how to take revenge on someone. Then we forget ourselves, and merely hiss, creep, and try to find someone to bite. And we don't feel sorry for anyone. And we rage until we destroy ourselves. All the evil in the world comes from rage."

The stag said: "No, all the evil in the world comes not from rage, nor from love, nor from hunger, but from fear. If it were possible not to be afraid, everything would be well. We have swift feet and great strength: we can defend ourselves with our horns against a small animal, and we can flee from a larger one. But how can I help being frightened? Let a branch crackle in the forest, or a leaf rustle, and I tremble with fear; my heart flutters as though it wanted to jump out, and I fly away as fast as I can. Sometimes a hare runs by, or a bird flaps its wings, or a dry twig breaks, and you think it's a beast, and run straight toward him. Or you run away from a dog and run into the hands of a man. Frequently you get frightened and run, not knowing where, and rush down a steep hill at full speed, and you get killed. You sleep, closing only one eye; you keep listening and being afraid. We get no rest. All the evil comes from fear."

Then the hermit said:

"Not from hunger, nor love, nor rage, nor from fear come all our sufferings, but all the evil in the world comes from our own body. From it come hunger, love, rage, and fear."

Galvanism (A Discussion)

Once there was a learned Italian named Galvani.[9] He had an electric machine and showed his students what electricity was. He rubbed the glass hard with silk smeared in grease, and then he brought a brass knob near it, which was attached to the glass, and a spark would fly from the glass to the brass knob. He explained to them that the same kind of a spark came from sealing wax and amber. He showed them that feathers and bits of paper were sometimes attracted, and sometimes repelled, by electricity, and explained the reason for it. He did all kinds of experiments with electricity, and he showed all this to his students.

Once his wife grew ill. He called the doctor and asked what to do to treat her. The doctor told him to prepare a soup for her made from frogs. Galvani gave an order to have edible frogs caught. They caught the frogs, killed them, and left them on his table.

Before the cook came for the frogs, Galvani kept on showing the electric machine to his students, and sending sparks through it.

Suddenly he saw the dead frogs jerk their legs on the table. He watched, and saw that every time he sent a spark through the machine, the frogs' legs jerked. Galvani collected more frogs and began to do experiments with them. Every time he sent a spark through the machine, the dead frogs moved their legs as though they were still alive.

It occurred to Galvani that live frogs moved their legs because electricity passed through them. Galvani knew that there was also electricity in the air, that it was more noticeable in amber and glass, but that it was also in the air, and that thunder and lightning came from electricity in the air.

So he tried to discover whether the dead frogs would also move their legs from the electricity in the air. For this purpose he took the frogs, skinned them, chopped off their heads and front legs, and hung them on brass hooks on the roof, beneath an iron gutter. He thought that as soon as there was a storm, and

---

9 Luigi Galvani (1737–1798) was an Italian physician, physicist, biologist, and philosopher, who studied animal electricity. In 1780, he discovered that the muscles of dead frogs' legs would twitch when struck by an electrical spark.

the air filled with electricity, it would pass from the brass rod into the frogs, and they would begin to move.

But storms passed by several times, and the frogs didn't move. Galvani was in the process of taking them down and, as he was doing so, he touched an iron gutter with a frog's leg, and the leg jerked. Galvani took down the frogs and tried the following experiment: he tied an iron wire to the brass hook, and kept touching the leg with the wire, and it kept jerking.

Thus Galvani concluded that all animals were alive only because they contained electricity; that the electricity jumped from the brain to the flesh, and that made the animals move. At that time nobody had experimented with this matter, and they didn't know any better, so they all believed Galvani. But then another learned man, Volta,[10] experimented in his own way, and proved to everybody that Galvani was mistaken. He tried touching the frog in a different way, not with a copper hook and an iron wire, but either with a copper hook and a copper wire, or with an iron hook and an iron wire—and the frogs didn't move. Only when Volta touched them with an iron wire that was connected to a copper wire did the frogs move.

That made Volta think that the electricity was not in the dead frog but in the iron and copper. He began with some experiments and found it to be the case: whenever he brought the iron and the copper together, there was electricity; and this electricity made the dead frogs jerk their legs. Volta started trying to produce electricity in a different manner than before. Previously people would generate electricity by rubbing glass or sealing wax. But Volta got electricity by combining iron and copper. He tried to connect iron and copper and other metals, and by the mere combination of other metals (silver, platinum, zinc, lead, iron), he produced electric sparks.

After Volta other people tried to increase electricity by pouring all kinds of liquids—water and acids—between the metals. These liquids made the electricity more powerful, so that it was no longer necessary, as before, to rub to produce it; it was enough to put the pieces of several metals in a bowl and fill the bowl with a liquid, and there would be electricity in that bowl, and the sparks would come from the wires.

When this kind of electricity was discovered, people began to apply it: they invented a way of gold and silver plating by means of electricity, and discovered electric light, and a way to transmit signals from place to place over a long distance by means of electricity.

---

10 Alessandro Volta (1745–1827) was an Italian physicist and chemist who was a pioneer of electricity and power and is credited as the inventor of the electric battery.

For this purpose pieces of different metals are placed in jars, and liquids are poured over them. Electricity is collected in these jars and transferred by means of wires to the place where it's needed, and from there, the wire is put into the ground. The electricity runs through the ground back to the jars, and rises from the earth by means of the other wire; thus the electricity keeps going around and around, as in a ring—from the wire into the ground, and along the ground, and up into the wire, and again through the earth. Electricity can travel in either direction, just as one desires: first, it can go along the wire and return through the earth, or else go through the earth, and then return through the wire.

The telegraph is made as follows: electricity is sent through a wire, and this wire is wound around an iron column. And above the column a small metal hammer is attached. And when electricity flows through the wire, the iron column wrapped in wire, attracts the hammer. If on the other end, even if it's a hundred versts away, they separate the ends of the wire, electricity stops circulating and the needle stops acting as a magnet, and the hammer falls away from it. When they connect the ends again, the little hammer is attracted. Thus it's possible from one station to tap the hammer at another station. And by means of these taps conventional signs can be transmitted.

The Peasant and the Water Sprite (A Fable)

A peasant dropped his ax in the river; he sat down on the bank in grief, and began to weep.

A water sprite heard the peasant and took pity on him. He pulled a gold ax out of the river, and said: "Is this your ax?"

The peasant said: "No, it's not mine."

The water sprite brought out another, a silver ax.

Again the peasant said: "It's not my ax."

Then the water sprite brought out the real ax.

The peasant said: "Now, that's my ax."

The water sprite made the peasant a present of all three axes, for having told the truth.

At home the peasant showed the axes to his friends, and told them what had happened.

So one of the peasants made up his mind to do the same thing: he went to the river, deliberately threw his ax into the water, sat down on the bank, and began to weep.

The water sprite brought out a gold ax, and asked: "Is this your ax?"

The peasant was glad, and called out: "It's mine, mine!"

The water sprite didn't give him the gold ax, nor did he give him back his own ax, because he'd told a lie.

The Raven and the Fox (A Fable)

A raven got himself a piece of meat, and sat down on a tree. A fox wanted to get the meat from him. It went up to him, and said:

"Oh, raven, as I look at you—because of your size and beauty—you really ought to be a tsar! And you certainly would be one, if you had a good voice."

The raven opened his mouth wide and began to croak with all his might. The meat fell out. The fox grabbed it and said:

"Oh, raven! If you also had any good sense, you'd certainly be a tsar."

A Prisoner of the Caucasus (A True Story)

I

A certain gentleman named Zhilin was serving as an army officer in the Caucasus.

One day he received a letter from home. It was from his aging mother, who wrote: "I'm getting old, and would like to see my dear son once more before I die. Come and bid me farewell and bury me; then, if God pleases, return to your service again with my blessing. And I have found a girl for you, who is smart and good, and who owns some property. If you come to love her, you might marry her and remain at home for good."

Zhilin thought it over: "It is quite true, the old lady is failing fast and I might not have another chance to see her alive. I'd better go, and, if the girl is nice, why not marry her?"

So he went to his colonel, obtained a leave of absence, said good-bye to his comrades, treated the soldiers to four buckets of vodka as a farewell gesture, and got ready to leave.

It was a time of war in the Caucasus. The roads were safe neither by day nor night. If ever a Russian ventured to walk or ride any distance from his fort, the Tatars would either kill him or take him off to the hills. So it had been arranged that twice every week a body of soldiers would march from one fortress to the next to convey travelers from point to point. Ahead and behind came soldiers; people kept in the middle.

It was summer. At daybreak the baggage train got ready under the shelter of the fortress; the soldiers marched out, and everyone started along the road. Zhilin was on horseback, and a cart with his things went with the baggage train. They had twenty-five versts to go. The baggage train moved slowly; sometimes the soldiers stopped, or a wheel might come off one of the carts, or a horse would refuse to go on, and then everybody had to wait.

When by the sun it was already past noon, they had only gone halfway. It was dusty and hot; the sun was scorching and there was nowhere to take shelter. It was bare steppe all round—not a tree or a bush along the road.

Zhilin rode ahead; he stopped and waited for the baggage to catch up with him. Then he heard a signal horn sound behind him: the company had stopped again. So he began to think: "Wouldn't it be better to go on without the soldiers? My horse is sound: if I run into Tatars, I can gallop away. Or, is it wiser not to go?"

As he sat considering, Kostilin, an officer carrying a gun, rode up to him and said:

"Come along, Zhilin, let's go on by ourselves. It's unbearable; I'm famished, and the heat's terrible. My shirt's wringing wet."

Kostilin was a stout, heavy man, and perspiration was running down his red face. Zhilin thought a while, and then asked:

"Is your gun loaded?"

"Yes it is."

"Well, then, let's go, but on the condition that we stay together."

So they rode forward along the road across the plain, talking, but keeping a look out on both sides. They could see far all round.

But after crossing the plain, the road ran through a valley between two hills. Zhilin said: "We had better climb that hill and have a look around, for the enemy may be on us before we even know it."

But Kostilin answered: "What's the use? Let's go on."

Zhilin, however, wouldn't agree.

"No," he said; "you can wait down here if you like; I'll go and have a look around."

And he turned his horse to the left, and proceeded up the hill. Zhilin's horse was a hunting horse, and carried him up the hillside as if it had wings. (He had bought it out of a herd as a colt for a hundred rubles, and had broken it in himself.) Hardly had he reached the top of the hill, when he saw some thirty Tatars not much more than a hundred yards ahead of him. As soon as he caught sight of them, he began to turn around, but the Tatars had also seen him, and came after him at full gallop, getting their guns out as they rode. Down galloped Zhilin as fast as his horse's legs could carry him, shouting to Kostilin:

"Get your gun ready!" And, in his thoughts, he said to his horse: "Get me out of this, my pet; don't stumble; if you do, it's all over. Once I reach my gun, they won't get me."

But, instead of waiting, as soon as he caught sight of the Tatars, Kostilin turned back toward the fortress at full speed, whipping his horse first on one side, then on the other; its swishing tail was all that could be seen in the dust.

Zhilin realized the situation was bad; his gun was gone, and what could he do with nothing but his sword? He let his horse go toward the soldiers, hoping to escape, but there were six Tatars galloping to cut him off. The horse under him was a good one, but theirs were even better; and besides, they were galloping across his path. He tried to rein in his horse and turn back, but his horse was going so fast, it couldn't stop, and dashed on straight towards the Tatars. He saw a red-bearded Tatar on a gray horse, his gun raised, coming at him, yelling and baring his teeth.

"Well," thought Zhilin, "I know you, devils that you are. If you take me alive, you'll put me in a pit and flog me. I won't be taken alive!"

Zhilin, though not a big fellow, was brave. He drew his sword and dashed straight at the red-bearded Tatar, thinking: "Either I'll catch him with my horse, or cut him down with my sword.'

He was still a horse's length away, when he was fired at from behind, and his horse was hit. It fell to the ground with all its weight, pinning down Zhilin's leg.

He tried to stand up, but two stinking Tatars were already sitting on him and tying his hands behind his back. He made an effort and flung them off, but three others jumped down from their horses and began beating his head with the butts of their rifles. His eyes grew dim, and he began to stumble. The Tatars seized him, and, taking spare girths from their saddles, twisted his hands behind him, tied them with a Tatar knot, and dragged him to the saddle. They knocked his cap off, pulled off his boots, searched him all over, tore his clothes, and took his money and his watch. Zhilin looked back at his horse. It lay there on its side, poor thing, just as it had fallen; struggling, its legs in the air, unable to reach the ground. There was a hole in its head, and black blood was pouring out, turning the dust to mud for a couple of arshins around.

One of the Tatars went up to the horse and began removing its saddle; it was still kicking, so he took out a dagger and cut its windpipe. A whistling sound came from its throat, the horse gave one last lurch, and it was all over.

The Tatars took the saddle and trappings. The red-bearded Tatar mounted his own horse, and the others lifted Zhilin into the saddle behind him. To prevent him from falling off, they strapped him to the Tatar's girdle; and then they all rode away to the hills.

So Zhilin sat behind the Tatar, swaying from side to side, his head striking against the Tatar's stinking back. He could see nothing but that muscular back and sinewy neck, with its closely shaven, bluish nape. Zhilin's head was wounded: blood had dried above his eyes. He could neither shift his position in the saddle nor wipe the blood off. His arms were bound so tightly that his collarbones ached.

They rode up and down hills for a long time. Then they reached a river, which they forded, and came to a hard road leading across a valley.

Zhilin tried to see where they were heading, but his eyelids were stuck together with blood, and he couldn't turn his head.

Twilight began to fall; they crossed another little river, and rode up a stony hillside. There was a smell of smoke, and dogs were barking. They had reached an aul.[11] The Tatars got off their horses; Tatar children came and stood round Zhilin, shrieking with pleasure; they began throwing stones at him.

A Tatar drove the children away, took Zhilin off the horse, and called a worker. A Nogai with high cheekbones,[12] wearing nothing but a shirt (and that, so torn that his breast was completely bare), answered the call. The Tatar gave him an order. He went and fetched some shackles: two blocks of oak with iron rings attached, and a clasp and a lock fixed to one of the rings.

They untied Zhilin's arms, fastened the shackles to his leg, and dragged him to a barn, where they pushed him in and locked the door. Zhilin fell on a pile of manure. He lay still a while, then groped about to find a softer place, and lay down.

II

All that night Zhilin hardly slept. It was the time of year when the nights were short, and daylight soon showed itself through a crack in the wall. He rose, scratched to make the crack bigger, and began to look out.

Through the hole he saw a road leading downhill; to the right was a Tatar hut with two trees near it. A black dog lay on the threshold, and a goat and kids were moving about wagging their tails. Then he saw a young Tatar woman in a long, loose, brightly colored gown, with trousers and high boots visible under it. She had a caftan over her head, on which she carried a large metal jug filled with water. She was leading by the hand a small, closely shaven Tatar boy, who

---

11 A Tatar village. (Tolstoy's note)
12 A Turkic ethnic group that lives in the North Caucasus region.

wore nothing but a shirt; and as she went along balancing herself, the muscles of her back quivered. This woman carried the water into the hut, and, soon after, the red-bearded Tatar of yesterday came out dressed in a silk tunic, with a silver-hilted dagger hanging by his side, shoes on his bare feet, and a tall black sheepskin cap set far back on his head. He came out, stretched, and stroked his red beard. He stood awhile, gave an order to his servant, and set off somewhere.

Then two lads rode past to water their horses. The horses' snouts were wet. Some other closely shaven boys ran out, without any trousers, wearing nothing but their shirts. They crowded together, came to the barn, picked up a twig, and began pushing it in at the crack. Zhilin gave a shout, and the boys shrieked and scampered off, their bare little legs gleaming as they ran.

Zhilin was very thirsty: his throat was parched, and he thought: "If only they would come to check on me!" Then he heard someone unlocking the barn door. The red-bearded Tatar entered, and with him was another, smaller man, dark-skinned, with shining black eyes, red cheeks, and a short beard. He had a merry face, and was constantly laughing. This man was even more richly dressed than the first. He wore a blue silk tunic trimmed with gold, a large silver dagger in his belt, red morocco slippers adorned with silver, and over these a pair of thick shoes, and he had a white sheepskin cap on his head.

The red-bearded Tatar entered, muttered something as if he were annoyed, and stood leaning against the doorpost, playing with his dagger, and glaring askance at Zhilin, like a wolf. The dark one, quick and lively, moving as if on springs, came straight up to Zhilin, squatted down in front of him, grinned, slapped him on the shoulder, and began babbling very fast in his own language. His teeth showed, and he kept winking, clicking his tongue, and repeating, "Well, Russ, well, Russ."

Zhilin couldn't understand a word, but said, "Drink! Give me some water to drink!"

The dark man only laughed. "Well, Russ," he said again, and continued muttering in his own tongue.

Zhilin made signs with lips and hands that he wanted something to drink.

The dark man understood, and laughed. Then he looked out of the door, and called to someone: "Dina!"

A little girl came running in: she was about thirteen, slight, thin, and resembling the dark Tatar. Evidently she was his daughter. She, too, had clear black eyes, and her face was pretty. She had on a long blue gown with wide sleeves, and no belt. The hem of her gown, the front, and the sleeves, were all trimmed with red. She wore trousers and slippers, and over the slippers other shoes with high heels. Around her neck she had a necklace made of Russian silver coins.

She was bareheaded, and her black hair was woven in a braid with a ribbon and ornamented with medals and a silver ruble.

Her father gave an order, and she ran away and returned with a little metal jug. She handed the water to Zhilin and sat down, crouching so that her knees were as high as her head; and there she sat with eyes wide-open, watching Zhilin drink, as though he were some wild animal.

When Zhilin handed the empty jug back to her, she gave such a sudden jump back, like a wild goat, that it made even her father laugh. He sent her away to fetch something else. She took the jug, ran out, and brought back some unleavened bread on a round board; once more she sat down, crouching, and staring at him.

Then the Tatars went away and locked the door again.

After a while the Nogai came and said: "*Ai-da*, master, *Ai-da!*"

He, too, knew no Russian. All Zhilin could make out was that he was told to go somewhere.

Zhilin followed the Nogai, but limped, for the shackles pulled his feet to one side so that he could hardly walk at all. On getting out of the barn he saw a Tatar village of about ten houses, and a Tatar church with a small tower. Three horses stood saddled before one of the houses; boys were holding them by the reins. The dark Tatar emerged from this house, and beckoned with his hand for Zhilin to follow him. He was laughing, kept saying something in his own language, and returned into the house. Zhilin entered. The room was nice: the walls were smoothly plastered with clay. Near the front wall lay a pile of bright-colored featherbeds; the side walls were covered with rich carpets used as hangings, and on these were fastened guns, pistols, and swords, all inlaid with silver. Close to one of the walls was a small stove on a level with the earthen floor. The floor itself was as clean as a threshing-floor. A large space in one corner was spread over with felt, on which lay rugs, and on these rugs were cushions stuffed with down. And on these cushions sat five Tatars, the dark one, the red-haired one, and three guests. They were all wearing indoor slippers, and each had a cushion behind his back. Before them were standing millet *lepeshki* on a round board,[13] melted butter in a bowl, and a jug of *buza*, or Tatar beer. They ate the *lepeshki* and their hands were all covered in butter.

The dark man jumped up and ordered that Zhilin to be placed on one side, not on the carpet but on the bare ground; then he sat down on the carpet again, and offered *lepeshki* and *bouza* to his guests.[14] The servant made Zhilin sit down,

---

13 Caucasian flatbread.
14 A malt drink made by fermenting various grains: wheat or millet in the Caucasus, Albania, Bulgaria, Romania, North Macedonia, Serbia, and Bosnia and Herzegovina.

after which he took off his own overshoes, put them by the door where the other shoes were standing, and sat down nearer to his masters on the felt. He was drooling as he watched them eat.

The Tatars had some *bliny*, and a Tatar woman dressed in the same way as the girl—in a long gown and trousers, with a kerchief on her head—came and took away what was left, and brought in a handsome basin, and a jug with a narrow spout. The Tatars washed their hands, folded them, went down on their knees, blew to the four quarters, and said their prayers. After they had talked for a while, one of the guests turned to Zhilin and began speaking in Russian.

"You were captured by Kazi-Mohammed," he said, pointing at the red-bearded Tatar. "And Kazi-Mohammed has given you to Abdul Murat," pointing at the dark one. "Abdul Murat is now your master."

Zhilin was silent. Then Abdul Murat began to talk, laughing, pointing to Zhilin, and repeating, "Soldier Russ, well, Russ."

The interpreter said, "He orders you to write home and ask them to send a ransom payment; as soon as the money comes, he will set you free."

Zhilin thought for a moment, and said, "How much ransom does he want?"

The Tatars talked a while, and then the interpreter said, "Three thousand rubles."

"No," said Zhilin, "I can't pay that much."

Abdul jumped up and, waving his arms, talked to Zhilin, thinking, as before, that he would understand. The interpreter translated: "How much will you pay?"

Zhilin thought for a while, and then said, "Five hundred rubles." At this the Tatars began speaking very quickly, all together. Abdul began to shout at the red-bearded one, and jabbered so fast that spit spurted from his mouth. The red-bearded one only screwed up his eyes and clicked his tongue.

They quieted down after a while, and the interpreter said, "Five hundred rubles is not enough for the master. He himself paid two hundred for you. Kazi-Mohammed was in debt to him, and he took you in payment. Three thousand rubles! Less than that won't do. If you refuse to write, you'll be put into a pit and flogged with a whip!"

"Eh", thought Zhilin, "the more one fears them, the worse it will be."

So he sprang to his feet, and said, "You tell that dog that if he tries to frighten me, I won't write at all, and he'll get nothing. I was never afraid of you dogs, and I will never be!"

The interpreter translated, and once again they all began talking at once.

They jabbered for a long time in their language, and then the dark man jumped up, came up to Zhilin, and said: "*Dzhigit* Russ, *dzhigit* Russ!"

Dzhigit in their language means "Fine fellow." He laughed and then said something to the interpreter, who translated: "One thousand rubles will satisfy him."

Zhilin stuck to his own offer: "I will not pay more than five hundred. And if you kill me, you'll get nothing at all."

The Tatars talked a while, then they sent the servant somewhere, and kept looking, one minute at Zhilin, the next at the door. The servant returned, followed by a stout, bare-footed, tattered man, who also had his leg shackled.

Zhilin gasped with surprise: he recognized Kostilin. He, too, had been caught. They were put side by side, and began to tell each other what had occurred. While they talked, the Tatars looked on in silence. Zhilin related what had happened to him; and Kostilin told how his horse had stopped, his gun misfired, and this same Abdul had overtaken and captured him.

Abdul jumped up, pointed to Kostilin, and said something.

The interpreter translated that now they both belonged to the same master; the one who paid the ransom first, would be set free first.

"There now," he said to Zhilin, "you get angry, but your comrade here is calm; he's written home, and they'll send five thousand rubles. So he'll be well fed and well treated."

Zhilin replied: "My comrade can do as he likes; maybe he's rich, but I'm not. It must be as I said. Kill me, if you like—you'll gain nothing by it; but I won't ask for more than five hundred rubles."

For a while they were silent. Suddenly up sprang Abdul, brought a little box, took out a pen, ink, and a bit of paper, gave them to Zhilin, slapped him on the shoulder, and made a sign that he should write. He'd agreed to take five hundred rubles.

"Wait a while!" said Zhilin to the interpreter; "tell him that first he must feed us properly, give us proper clothes and boots, and let us stay together. It will be more cheerful for us. And we must have these shackles taken off our feet," and Zhilin looked at his master and laughed. The master also laughed, heard out the interpreter, and said:

"I will give them the best clothes: a cloak and boots fit to be married in. I will feed them like princes; and if they like, they can live together in the barn. But I won't take off the shackles, or they'll run away. They'll be taken off, however, at night." And he jumped up and slapped Zhilin on the shoulder, exclaiming: "You good, Me good!"

Zhilin wrote the letter, but addressed it incorrectly, so that it wouldn't ever reach its destination, thinking to himself: "I'll run away!"

Zhilin and Kostlin were taken back to the barn and given some maize straw, a jug of water, some bread, two old cloaks, and some worn-out military boots— evidently taken from the bodies of Russian soldiers. At night their shackles were taken off, and the prisoners were locked in the barn.

III

Zhilin and his comrade lived like this for a whole month. The master kept laughing and said: "You, Ivan, good! Me, Abdul, good!" But he fed them badly, giving them nothing but unleavened bread of millet flour baked into *lepeshki*, or sometimes only unbaked dough.

Kostilin wrote home a second time: he kept moping and waiting for the money to arrive. He would sit in the barn sleeping, or counting the days until a letter could come; but he didn't write another one. Whereas Zhilin knew his letter would reach no one, and he didn't write another either. He thought:

"Where could my mother find enough money to ransom me? As it is, she's been living chiefly on what I used to send her. If she had to raise five hundred rubles, she'd be completely ruined. With God's help I'll manage to escape!"

So he kept on the lookout, trying to figure out a way out. He would walk about the aul whistling; or he'd sit working, modeling dolls of clay, or weaving baskets out of twigs: Zhilin was a master with his hands.

Once he modeled a doll with a nose, hands, and feet wearing a Tatar dress, and put it up on the roof.

Once when the Tatar women went to fetch water, the master's daughter, Dina, saw the doll and called the other women, who put down their jugs and stood looking and laughing. Zhilin took down the doll and held it out to them. They laughed, but dared not take it. He put down the doll and went into the barn, waiting to see what would happen.

Dina ran up to the doll, looked round, grabbed it, and ran away.

In the morning, at daybreak, he looked out. Dina came out of the house and sat down on the threshold with the doll, which she'd dressed up in bits of red rags, and she rocked it like a baby, singing a Tatar lullaby. An old woman came out and scolded her, snatched the doll away, broke it to bits, and sent Dina about her tasks.

But Zhilin made another doll, better than the first, and gave it to Dina. Once Dina brought a little jug, put it on the ground, sat down gazing at him, laughing, and pointing to the jug.

"What makes her so happy?" wondered Zhilin. He took the jug thinking it was water, but it turned out to be milk. He drank the milk and said: "That's good! How pleased Dina was!" "Good, Ivan, good!" she said; she jumped up and clapped her hands. Then, seizing the empty jug, she ran away.

After that, she secretly brought him some milk every day. The Tatars make a kind of *lepeshki* with goat's milk, which they dry on the rooftops of their houses; sometimes, on the sly, she would bring him some. And once, when Abdul had killed a sheep, she brought him a bit of mutton in her sleeve. She would just throw the things down and run away.

One day there was a heavy storm, and the rain poured down in torrents for a full hour. All the streams became muddy. The water at the ford rose till it was three arshins high, and the current was so strong that it tossed stones around. Rivulets flowed everywhere, and the rumbling in the hills never ceased. When the storm was over, the water ran in streams down the village street. Zhilin asked his master to lend him a knife; with it he shaped a small cylinder and, cutting some little boards, he made a wheel to which he fixed two dolls, one on each side.

The little girls brought him some bits of cloth, and he dressed the dolls, one as a male peasant, the other as a female. Then he fastened them in their places, and set the wheel so that the stream would move it. The wheel began to turn and the two dolls jumped.

The whole village gathered around. Little boys, little girls, Tatar men, and women, all came and clicked their tongues.

"Ay, Russ! Ay, Ivan!"

Abdul had a Russian clock, which was broken. He called Zhilin and showed it to him, clicking his tongue.

"Give it to me, I'll fix it for you," said Zhilin.

He took it apart with a little knife, sorted the pieces, and put them together again, and gave it back. The clock started working again.

The master was delighted, and made him a present of one of his old quilted coats, which was full of holes. There was nothing to be done about it: Zhilin had to accept it. At any rate, he could use it as a cover at night.

From that time Zhilin's fame spread; and Tatars came from distant villages, bringing him the lock of a gun, a pistol, or a clock to mend. His master gave him some tools—pincers, gimlets, and a file.

One day a Tatar fell ill, and they came to Zhilin saying, "Come and treat him!" Zhilin knew nothing about doctoring, but he went to look, and thought to himself, "Perhaps he'll get well on his own anyway." He went back to the barn, mixed some water with sand, and then in the presence of the Tatar, whispered a few words over it and gave it to the sick man to drink. Luckily for him, the Tatar recovered. Zhilin began to pick up a little of their language, and some of the Tatars grew accustomed to him. When they wanted him, they would call: "Ivan! Ivan!" Others, however, still looked at him askance, as if he were a wild beast.

The red-bearded Tatar disliked Zhilin. Whenever he saw him he frowned and turned away, or swore at him. There was also an old man there who did not live in the aul, but used to come up from the foot of the hill. Zhilin saw him only when he passed on his way to the mosque. He was short and had a white cloth wound round his hat. His beard and mustache were clipped and white as snow; and his face was wrinkled and red as a brick. His nose was hooked like a hawk's, his gray eyes looked cruel, and he had no teeth except for two canines. He would pass, wearing a turban on his head, leaning on his staff, glaring around him like a wolf. If he saw Zhilin he would snort with anger and turn away.

Once Zhilin went down the hill to see where the old man lived. He went down along the pathway and came to a little garden surrounded by a stone wall; behind the wall he saw cherry and apricot trees, and a hut with a flat roof. He came closer, and saw hives made of woven straw, as well as bees flying around humming. The old man was kneeling, busy doing something with a hive. Zhilin stretched to look, and his shackles rattled. The old man turned around, and, giving a yell, snatched a pistol from his belt and fired at Zhilin, who just managed to hide himself behind the stonewall.

The old man went to Zhilin's master to complain. The master called Zhilin, and said with a laugh, "Why did you go to the old man's house?"

"I did him no harm," replied Zhilin. "I only wanted to see how he lived."

The master repeated what Zhilin said. But the old man was furious; he hissed and jabbered, showing his canine teeth, and shaking his fists at Zhilin.

Zhilin could not understand all, but gathered that the old man was telling Abdul he ought to kill the Russians, and not keep them in the aul. The old man went away.

Zhilin began asking the master who this old man was. What sort of fellow was he? The master said:

"He's a great man! He was the bravest of our horsemen; he killed many Russians, and at one time he was very rich. He had three wives and eight sons, and they all lived in one village. Then the Russians came, destroyed the village, and killed seven of his sons. Only one was left, and he gave himself up to the Russians. The old man also went and gave himself up, and lived among Russians for three months. At the end of that time he found his son, killed him with his own hands, and then escaped. After that he gave up fighting, and went to Mecca to pray to God; that is why he wears a turban. One who has been to Mecca is called 'Hajji,' and wears a turban. He doesn't like you folks. He tells me to kill you. But I can't do it. I've paid money for you and, besides, I've grown fond of you, Ivan. Far from killing you, I wouldn't even let you go if I hadn't promised." Then he laughed, saying in Russian, "You, Ivan, good; Me, Abdul, good!"

IV

Zhilin lived like this for a month. During the day he strolled around the aul or busied himself with some handicraft, but at night, when all was silent, he dug at the floor of the barn. It was no easy task digging, because of the stones; but he worked away at them with his file, and at last had made a hole under the wall large enough to get through. "If only I could get to know the lay of the land," he thought, "and which way to go! But none of the Tatars will tell me."

So he chose a time when the master was away from home, and set off after dinner to climb the hill beyond the village and have a look around. But before leaving home the master always gave orders to his son to watch Zhilin, and not to lose sight of him. So the lad ran after Zhilin, shouting:

"Don't go! Father doesn't allow it. I'll call the neighbors if you won't come back."

Zhilin tried to convince him, and said: "I'm not going far; I only want to climb that hill. I want to find a herb—to cure sick people. You can come with me if you like. How can I run away with these shackles on? Tomorrow I'll make a bow and arrows for you."

So he persuaded the lad, and off they went to have a look at the hill. It didn't seem far to the top; but it was hard walking with shackles on his legs. Zhilin went on and on, and he finally made it to the top. There he sat down and noted the lay of the land. To the south, beyond the hill, was a valley in which a herd of horses was pasturing and at the bottom of the valley one could see another aul. Beyond that there was a steeper hill, and another beyond that. Between the hills, in the blue distance, were forests; still further off were mountains, rising higher and higher. The highest ones were covered with snow, white as sugar; and one snowy peak towered above all the rest. To the east and to the west were other hills; here and there smoke rose from auls in the ravines. "Ah," he thought, "all that is Tatar country." And he turned towards the Russian side. At his feet he saw a river, and the aul he lived in, surrounded by little gardens. He could see women, like tiny dolls, sitting by the river rinsing out clothes. Beyond the aul was a hill, lower than the one to the south, and beyond it, two more hills well wooded; and between these, a smooth bluish plain, and far, far across the plain something that looked like a cloud of smoke. Zhilin tried to remember where the sun used to rise and set when he was living in the fort, and he saw that there was no mistake: the Russian fort must be on that plain. When he escaped, he would have to make his way between those two hills.

The sun was beginning to set. The white, snowy mountains turned red, and the dark hills turned darker; mists rose from the ravine, and the valley, where he supposed the Russian fort to be, seemed on fire with the glow of the sunset. Zhilin looked carefully. Something seemed to be quivering in the valley like smoke from a chimney, and he felt sure the Russian fortress was over there.

It had grown late. The mullah's cry could be heard. The herds were being driven home, the cows were lowing, and the lad kept saying, "Let's go home!" But Zhilin didn't feel like it.

At last, however, they went back. "Well," thought Zhilin, "now that I know the way, it is time to escape." He thought about running away that night. The nights were dark—the moon had waned. But as ill luck would have it, the Tatars returned home that evening. They generally came back from driving cattle in good spirits. But this time they had no cattle. All they brought home was the body of a Tatar—the red-headed one's brother—who'd been killed. They came back looking sullen, and they all gathered together for the burial. Zhilin also came out to see it. They wrapped the body in a piece of linen, without any coffin, and carried it out of the village, and laid it on the grass under some plane trees. The mullah and the old men came. They wound clothes round their caps, took off their shoes, and squatted on their heels, side by side, near the body.

The mullah was in front: behind him in a row were three old men wearing turbans, and behind them, the other Tatars. All cast their eyes down and sat in silence. This continued a long time, until the mullah raised his head and said: "Allah!" (which means God). He said that one word, and they all cast their eyes down again, and were silent again for a long time. They sat quite still, without moving. Again the mullah lifted his head and said, "Allah!" and they all repeated: "Allah! Allah!" and fell silent again. The body lay motionless on the grass, and they sat still as though they too were dead. Not one of them moved. There was no sound but that of the leaves of the plane trees stirring in the breeze. Then the mullah said a prayer, and they all rose. They lifted the body and carried it in their arms to a hole in the ground. It was not an ordinary hole, but was hollowed out under the ground like a vault. They took the body under its arms and by its legs, bent it, and let it down gently, pushing it under the earth in a sitting posture, with its hands folded in front.

The Nogai brought some green reeds, which they stuffed into the hole, and, quickly covering it with soil, they smoothed the ground, and set an upright stone at the head of the grave. Then they trod on the earth, and sat down again in a row before the grave, keeping silent for a long time.

"Allah! Allah! Allah!" they said, sighed, and stood up.

The red-bearded Tatar gave money to the old men; then he too rose, took a whip, struck himself with it three times on the forehead, and went home.

The next morning Zhilin saw the red-haired Tatar, followed by three others, leading a mare out of the village. When they were beyond the village, the red-bearded Tatar took off his quilted coat and turned up his sleeves, showing his stout arms. Then he drew a dagger and sharpened it on a whetstone. The other Tatars raised the mare's head, and he cut her throat, threw her down, and began skinning her, loosening the hide with his big hands. Women and girls came and began to wash the entrails and innards. The mare was cut up, the pieces taken into the hut, and the whole village collected at the red-haired Tatar's hut for a funeral feast.

For three days they went on eating the flesh of the mare, drinking bouza, and praying for the dead man. All the Tatars were at home. On the fourth day at dinnertime, Zhilin saw them preparing to leave. Horses were brought out, they got ready, and some ten of them (the red-headed one among them) rode away; but Abdul stayed home. It was a new moon, and the nights were still dark.

"Well!" thought Zhilin, "tonight's the time to escape. And he told Kostilin; but Kostilin felt too timid.

"How can we escape?" he said. "We don't even know the way."

"I know the way," said Zhilin.

"But we can't reach the fort in one night.'

"If we can't," said Zhilin, "we'll spend the night in the forest. See here, I've saved some flat *lepeshki*. What's the good of sitting around here? If they send your ransom—well and good; but suppose they don't manage to get it? The Tatars are angry now, because the Russians have killed one of their men. They're talking about killing us."

Kostilin thought it over and over.

"Well, let's go," he said.

V

Zhilin crept into the hole, widened it so that Kostilin could also get through, and then they both sat waiting until all would be quiet in the aul.

As soon as it was, Zhilin crept under the wall, got out, and whispered to Kostilin, "Come on!" Kostilin crept out, but in so doing he caught a stone with his foot and made a noise. The master had a very vicious watchdog, a spotted one called Ulyashin. Zhilin had been careful to feed him for some time before. Ulyashin heard the noise and began to bark and jump, and the other dogs did the same. Zhilin gave a slight whistle, and threw him a bit of cheese. Ulyashin knew Zhilin, wagged his tail, and stopped barking.

But the master had heard the dog, and shouted to him from his hut, "Quiet! Quiet!" Ulyashin!'

Zhilin scratched Ulyashin behind the ears, and the dog quieted down and rubbed against his legs, wagging his tail.

They sat hidden behind a corner for a while. All became quiet again, only a sheep coughed inside the shed, and the water rippled over the stones in the hollow. It was dark, the stars were high overhead, and the new moon showed red as it set, horns upward, behind the hill. In the valleys the fog was white as milk.

Zhilin rose and said to his companion, "Well, friend, let's go!"

They started out, but had gone only a few steps when they heard the mullah crying from the roof, "Allah, *Besmilla! Ilrakhman!*" That meant that people would be going to the mosque. So they sat down again, hiding behind a wall, and waited a long time until all the people had passed. At last everything became quiet again.

"Now then! May God be with us!" They crossed themselves, and started once more. They passed through the yard and went down the hillside to the river, crossed the river, and went along the valley. The mist was thick, but only near the ground; overhead the stars were shining quite brightly. Zhilin directed their course by the stars. It was cool in the mist, and easy walking; only their boots were uncomfortable, being worn out and trodden down. Zhilin took his boots off, threw them away, and went barefoot, jumping from stone to stone, and guiding his course by the stars. Kostilin began to lag behind.

"Slow down," he said, "these blasted boots have made my feet sore."

"Take them off!" said Zhilin. "It will be easier walking without them."

Kostilin started walking barefoot, but that was even worse. The stones cut his feet, and he kept lagging behind. Zhilin said: "If your feet get cut, they'll heal again; but if the Tatars catch up with us, they'll kill us, and that will be worse!"

Kostilin made no reply, but went on, groaning all the time. They walked through the valley for a long time. Then, to the right, they heard dogs barking. Zhilin stopped, looked around, and began climbing the hill, feeling his way with his hands.

"Hey!" he said, "we've gone wrong; we went too far to the right. Here's another aul, one that I saw from the hill. We must turn back and go up that hill to the left. There must be a wood there.'

But Kostilin said:

"Wait at least a bit! Let me catch my breath. My feet are all cut and bleeding."

"Never mind, friend! They'll heal. You should jump more lightly. Like this!"

And Zhilin ran back and turned to the left up the hill towards the wood.

Kostilin kept lagging behind and groaning. Zhilin only hushed him and went on.

They climbed the hill and found a wood. They entered it and forced their way through the brambles, which tore their clothes. At last they came to a path and followed it.

"Stop!" They heard the tramp of hoofs on the path, and they waited, listening. It sounded like the tramping of a horse's feet, but then ceased. They moved on, and again they heard the tramping. When they paused, it also stopped. Zhilin crept nearer to it, and saw something standing on the path where it was not quite so dark. It looked like a horse, but not quite like one, and on it was something strange, not like a man. He heard it snorting. "What on earth can it be?" Zhilin gave a low whistle, and it dashed away from the path into the thicket; the woods were filled with the noise of crackling, as if a hurricane were sweeping through, breaking the branches.

Kostilin was so frightened that he sank to the ground. But Zhilin laughed and said: "It's only a deer. Don't you hear him breaking the branches with his antlers? We are afraid of him, and he's afraid of us.'

They went on. The constellation of the Great Bear was already setting. It was near morning, and they didn't know whether they were going the right way or not. Zhilin thought it was the way he'd been brought by the Tatars, and that they were still some ten versts from the Russian fort; but he had nothing certain to go on, and at night one can easily lose the way. After a time they came to a clearing. Kostilin sat down and said: "Do as you like, I won't make it! My feet won't carry me."

Zhilin tried to convince him.

"No, I'll never get there; I can't go on!"

Zhilin grew angry, spat, and cursed him.

"Well, then, I'll go on alone. Farewell!'

Kostilin jumped up and followed. They went on about four more versts. The mist in the wood had settled down even more thickly; they couldn't see anything in front of them, and the stars had grown dim.

Suddenly they heard the sound of a horse's hoofs in front. They heard its shoes strike the stones. Zhilin lay down flat, and listened with his ear to the ground.

"Yes, so it is! A horseman is coming towards us."

They ran off the path, crouched among the bushes, and waited. Zhilin crept to the road, looked, and saw a Tatar on horseback driving a cow, humming to himself. The Tatar rode past. Zhilin returned to Kostilin.

"God has led him past us. Get up; let's go on!"

Kostilin tried to stand, but he fell back again.

"I can't, so help me God, I can't! I have no strength left."

He was a heavy, stout man, and had been sweating. Chilled by the mist, his feet bleeding, he'd grown quite wilted.

Zhilin tried to lift him up, when suddenly Kostilin screamed out:

"Ow, that hurts!"

Zhilin's heart sank.

"Why are you yelling? The Tatar is still close; he'll hear you!" And he thought to himself, "He's really done for. What should I do with him? It's not right to desert a comrade."

"Well, then, get up, and climb up on my back. I'll carry you, if you really can't walk."

He helped Kostilin up, and put his arms under his thighs. Then he went out onto the path, carrying him on his back.

"Only, for Christ's sake," said Zhilin, "don't choke me with your hands! Hold on to my shoulders."

Zhilin found his load heavy; his feet were bleeding, too, and he was exhausted. Now and then he stooped to balance Kostilin better, jerking him so that he should sit higher up, and then he went on again.

The Tatar must have heard Kostilin scream. Zhilin suddenly heard someone galloping behind and shouting in the Tatar tongue. He darted in among the bushes. The Tatar seized his gun and fired, but didn't hit them; he shouted in his own language, and then galloped off along the road.

"Well, now we're done for, friend!" said Zhilin. "That cur will gather the Tatars together to hunt us down. Unless we can get a couple of versts away from here, we're lost!' And he thought to himself, 'Why the devil did I saddle myself with this lump? I would have gotten away long ago if I'd been alone."

Kostilin said, "Go on alone. Why should you perish because of me?"

"No I won't go. It isn't right to desert a comrade."

Once again he took Kostilin onto his shoulders and staggered on. They went on in that way for another verst or so. They were still in the forest, and couldn't see the end of it. But the mist was already dispersing, and clouds seemed to be gathering; the stars were no longer visible. Zhilin was quite exhausted. They came to a spring walled in by stones alongside the path. Zhilin stopped and set Kostilin down.

"Let me have a rest and get a drink," he said, "and let's eat some of the *lepeshki*. It can't be much farther now."

But hardly had he lain down to drink, when he heard the sound of horses' hooves behind him. Again they darted to the right among the bushes, and lay down under a steep slope.

They heard Tatar voices. The Tatars stopped at the very spot where they had turned off the path. The Tatars talked a while, and then set the dogs on the scent. There was a sound of crackling twigs, and someone's dog appeared from behind the bushes. It stopped, and began barking.

Then the Tatars, also strangers, climbed down, seized Zhilin and Kostilin, bound them, put them on horses, and rode away with them.

When they had ridden about three versts, they met Abdul, their owner, with two other Tatars following him. After talking with the strangers, he put Zhilin and Kostilin on two of his own horses and took them back to the aul.

Abdul wasn't laughing now, and he didn't say a word to them.

They were back at the aul by daybreak, and were set down on the street. The children came crowding round, throwing stones, shrieking, and beating them with whips.

The Tatars gathered in a circle, and the old man from the foot of the hill was also there. They began discussing; Zhilin heard them considering what to do with him and Kostilin. Some said they ought to be sent farther into the mountains; but the old man said: "They should be killed!" Abdul argued with him, saying: "I paid money for them, and I must get some ransom for them." But the old man said: "They won't pay you anything, but will only bring misfortune. It's a sin to feed Russians. Kill them, and be done with it!"

They dispersed. After they'd gone, the master came up to Zhilin and said: "If the money for your ransom isn't sent to me within two weeks, I will flog you to death; and if you try to run away again, I'll kill you like a dog! Write a letter, and write it properly!"

Paper was brought to them, and they wrote the letters. Shackles were put on their legs, and they were taken behind the mosque to a deep pit about five arshins, into which they were lowered.

VI

Life was now very hard for them. Their shackles were never removed, and they weren't allowed out into the fresh air. Unbaked dough was thrown to them as if they were dogs, and water was lowered down in a can. It was damp and stuffy in the pit, and there was a terrible stench. Kostilin grew quite ill, his body became swollen, he ached all over, and moaned or slept all the time. Zhilin, too, grew downcast; he saw that things looked bad and he couldn't think of any way to escape.

He tried to dig a tunnel, but there was nowhere to put the soil. His master noticed it, and threatened to kill him.

One day he was squatting on the floor of the pit, thinking about freedom, feeling very downhearted, when suddenly a cake fell into his lap, then another, and then a shower of cherries. He looked up, and there was Dina. She looked at him, laughed, and ran away. And Zhilin thought: "Maybe Dina would help me?"

He cleared out a little place in the pit, scraped up some clay, and began modeling toys. He made men, horses, and dogs, thinking, "When Dina comes I'll toss them up to her."

But Dina didn't come the next day. Zhilin heard the tramp of horses; some men rode past, and the Tatars gathered near the mosque. They shouted and argued; the word "Russians" was repeated several times. He could hear the voice of the old man. Though he couldn't distinguish what was being said, he guessed that Russian troops were somewhere nearby, and that the Tatars, afraid they might raid the aul, didn't know what to do with their prisoners.

After talking awhile, they left. Suddenly he heard a rustling overhead, and saw Dina crouching at the edge of the pit, her knees higher than her head, and bending over so that the coins of her plait were dangling above the pit. Her eyes gleamed like stars. She drew two *lepeshki* out of her sleeve and threw them to him. Zhilin took them and said, "Why didn't you come before? I've made some toys for you. Here, catch!" And he began tossing the toys up to her, one by one.

But she shook her head and wouldn't look at them.

"Don't," she said. She sat silent for a while, and then she said, "Ivan, they want to kill you! And she pointed to her own throat.

"Who wants to kill me?"

"Father—the old men are ordering him to do it. But I feel sorry for you!"

Zhilin answered:

"Well, if you feel sorry for me, bring me a long pole."

She shook her head, as if to say, "I can't!"

He clasped his hands and implored her: "Dina, please! Dear Dinushka,[15] I beg you!"

"I can't!" she said, shaking her head. "They'd see me. They're all at home." And she went away.

So when evening came, Zhilin sat and wondered what would happen next. The stars were visible, but the moon had not yet risen. The mullah's voice was heard; then all was silent. Zhilin was beginning to doze, thinking: "The girl will be afraid to do it!"

Suddenly he felt clay falling on his head. He looked up, and saw a long pole poking into the opposite wall of the pit. It kept poking around for a time, and then it came down, sliding into the pit. Zhilin was very glad. He took hold of it and lowered it. It was a strong pole, one that he'd seen before on the roof of his master's hut.

He looked up. The stars were shining high in the sky, and just above the pit, Dina's eyes gleamed in the dark like a cat's eyes. She stooped with her face close to the edge of the pit, and whispered, "Ivan! Ivan!" waving her hand in front of her face to show that he should speak very softly.

"What?" asked Zhilin.

"All but two of them have left."

Then Zhilin said:

---

15 An affectionate diminutive form of Dina.

"Well, Kostilin, come on; let's have one last try; I'll help you up."

But Kostilin wouldn't hear of it.

"No," said he. "It's clear I can't get away from here. How can I go, when I have hardly strength to turn round?"

"Well then, farewell! Don't think ill of me!" They exchanged kisses. Zhilin seized the pole, told Dina to hold onto it, and began to climb. He slipped once or twice; the shackles hindered him. Kostilin helped him, and he managed to get to the top. Dina, with her little hands, pulled with all her might at his shirt, laughing.

Zhilin drew out the pole and said:

"Put it back in its place, Dina, or they'll notice, and you'll be beaten."

She dragged the pole away, and Zhilin went down the hill. When he'd gone down the steep incline, he took a sharp stone and tried to wrench the lock off the shackles. But it was a strong lock and he couldn't manage to break it; besides, it was difficult to reach. Then he heard someone running down the hill, springing lightly. He thought: "Surely, that's Dina again." Dina came running, took a stone, and said, "Let me try."

She knelt down and tried to break the lock, but her little hands were as slender as thin twigs, and she lacked the strength. She threw the stone away and began to cry. Then Zhilin set to work again on the lock, and Dina squatted beside him with her hand on his shoulder. Zhilin looked round and saw a red light to the left behind the hill. The moon was just rising. "Ah!" he thought, "before the moon has risen I must pass the valley and be in the forest." So he rose and threw away the stone. Shackles or not, he must go on.

"Farewell, Dinushka dear!" he said. "I will never forget you!"

Dina seized hold of him and felt around with her hands for a place to put some *lepeshki* she'd brought. He took them from her.

"Thank you, you clever girl. Who will make dolls for you when I'm gone?" And he stroked her head.

Dina burst into tears, hiding her face in her hands. Then she ran up the hill like a young goat. Only the coins in her plait clinked against her back in the darkness.

Zhilin crossed himself, took the lock of his shackles in his hand to prevent its clattering, and went along the road, dragging his shackled leg, and looking towards the place where the moon was about to rise. Now he knew the way. If he went straight ahead he'd have to walk nearly eight versts. If he could only reach the woods before the moon had quite risen! He crossed the river; the light behind the hill was growing whiter. Still looking at it, he went along the valley. The moon was not yet visible. The light became brighter, and one side of the valley was growing lighter and lighter; shadows were drawing in towards the foot of the hill, creeping nearer and nearer to him.

Zhilin went on, keeping in the shade. He was hurrying, but the moon was moving still faster; the tops of the hills on the right were already lit up. As he was approaching woods, the white moon appeared from behind the hills, and it became as light as day. One could see all the leaves on the trees. It was light on the hill, but silent, as if nothing were alive; no sound could be heard but the bubbling of the little river below.

Zhilin reached the woods without meeting anyone, chose a little dark spot, and sat down to rest.

He rested, and ate one of the *lepeshki*. Then he found a stone and set to work again knocking off the shackles. He knocked until his hands grew sore, but couldn't break the lock. He stood up and went along the road. After walking about one verst he was quite exhausted, and his feet were aching. He had to stop every ten steps. "There is nothing else to do," he thought. "I must drag on as long as I have any strength left. If I sit down, I won't be able to get up again. I can't reach the fortress; but as soon as day breaks, I'll lie down in the forest, remain there all day, and continue on again at night."

He walked all night. Two Tatars on horseback passed him; but he heard them a long way off, and hid behind a tree.

The moon began to grow paler, the dew, to fall. It was getting near dawn, and Zhilin hadn't reached the end of the forest. "Well," he thought, "I'll walk another thirty steps, and then turn into the forest and sit down." He walked another thirty steps, and saw that he was at the end of the forest. He went to the edge; it was now quite light, and straight before him was the plain and the Russian fortress. To the left, quite close at the foot of the slope, a fire was dying down, and the smoke from it was spreading all around. There were men gathered around the fire.

He looked intently, and saw guns glistening. They were soldiers—Cossacks!

Zhilin was filled with joy. He gathered his remaining strength and set off down the hill, saying to himself: "God forbid that any mounted Tatar should see me now, in the open field! Near as I am, I couldn't get away in time."

Hardly had he had this thought, a couple of hundred yards off, on a hillock to the left, he saw three Tatars at a distance of two desyatines. They spotted him, too, and made a rush for him. His heart sank. He waved his arms, and shouted with all his might, "Brothers, brothers! Help!"

The Cossacks heard him, and a party of them on horseback darted forward to cut across the Tatars' path.

The Cossacks were far away and the Tatars were close by; but Zhilin, too, made a last effort. Lifting the shackles with his hand, he ran towards the Cossacks, hardly knowing what he was doing, crossing himself and shouting, "Brothers! Brothers! Brothers!"

There were about fifteen Cossacks.

The Tatars got frightened, and stopped before they reached him. Zhilin ran up to the Cossacks.

They surrounded him and began questioning him. "Who are you? What are you? Where are you from?" But Zhilin was quite beside himself, and could only weep and keep repeating, "Brothers! Brothers!"

Then the soldiers came running up and crowded round Zhilin—one gave him some bread, another buckwheat, a third vodka: one wrapped a cloak round him, another broke off his shackles.

The officers recognized him, and took him to the fortress. The soldiers were glad to see him back, and his comrades all gathered round him.

Zhilin told them all that had happened to him, and he said:

"That's the way I made a trip home and got married!" he said. "No. It seems clear that fate was against it!"

So he stayed on serving in the Caucasus. A month passed before Kostilin was released, after paying five thousand rubles in ransom. He was almost dead when they brought him back.

Mikulushka Selyaninovich (A Story in Verse)

Once Volga the bright rode out with his retinue
Through villages and towns to collect taxes,
To collect tribute from the peasants:
The master rode out into the broad field—
And he heard the plowman in the broad field:
He could hear the plowman plow and whistle,
He could hear from a distance the wooden plow squeaking,
The plow bumping up against stones,
But the plowman was nowhere to be seen in the field,
And Volga headed up to that plowman,
Riding from morning until evening,
But Volga couldn't reach the plowman.
He rode from morning 'til evening,
But he couldn't find him.
He could hear the peasant plowing and whistling,
From a distance, he could hear the wooden plow squeaking,
The plow bumping up against stones,
But the plowman was nowhere to be seen in the field,
On the third day Volga rode until lunchtime—

And Volga rode up to that plowman
A peasant is plowing, and urging the horse,
He plows furrows from one end to the other,
Turning up stones and roots with his plow,
As he gets to the end of a row,
He can't be seen from the other.
And the plowman has a plow made of maple wood,
The blades in that wooden plow are made of steel,
The silken tugs are fastened,
The filly pulling the plow is light bay.
Volga says to that plowman:
"Greetings, peasant plowman! God help you.
May God help you plow and till the soil,
And loosen up a broad furrow,
And dig up roots and stones!"
The peasant speaks these words:
"Thank you, Volga—we are grateful;
God's help, is probably necessary to us,
God's help to plow and till the soil.
Are you going far with your retinue?
Is God taking you far—where are you heading?"
Volga says the following words:
"I'm going, oh, peasant, with my retinue,
Through villages and towns for payments,
To collect contributions from the peasants:
Ay, come with me as a comrade!"
The peasant drove the plow into the furrow,
He took the silken harness and undid it,
He took the filly and released her from the plow,
He jumped on the filly and plopped down on it,
He went with Volga as his comrade.
And the peasant said the following words:
"It's not right, Volga, that
I left my plow in the furrow,
It should be pulled out;
The dirt should be shaken off the plow,
And the plow should be tossed into the bushes . . ."
Volga then sent ten young brave men,
Ordered them to pull the plow out of the furrow,

Ordered them to shake the dirt off the plow,
Then toss the plow into the bushes.
The young men rode up to the plow,
Jumped down from their fine horses into the furrow,
Together grabbed the maple wood plow.
It was impossible to raise this plow from the ground.
They kept turning the plow by the shaft,
But can't yank it from the ground,
And can't shake off the soil from the plow,
And toss it into the bushes.
So Volga sends for his whole retinue,
Orders them to pull the plow out of the soil,
Orders them to shake the soil off the plow,
And toss it into the bushes.
So the whole retinue took hold of the plow,
All together took hold of the maple wood plow,
They only turned the plow on its shaft,
But can't pull it out of the ground,
But can't shake the soil off the plow,
And toss it into the bushes.
At this moment a peasant bumpkin came riding up,
He dismounted from his light-bay horse,
Walked over to his maple wood plow,
With his one hand he grabbed it, kept shaking it,
And pulled the plow out of the ground,
And shook the dirt off it,
He scraped off the chunks of dirt with his cudgel,
And tossed the plow into the bushes.
They all mounted their fine horses and away they rode.
They rode out onto the road—
The peasant's filly was walking,
While Volga's horse was already galloping
The peasant's horse started going at a trot,
Volga's steed began to lag behind.
The peasant calmly rode in front, not shaking,
Volga was going at full speed following him.
Volga began to call to the peasant,
And began to wave his cap at him.
"You, peasant-plowman, stop and wait a bit,

One can't keep up with you."
The peasant looked back at Volga,
He began to hold back his filly,
And they slowed to a walk along the road,
And Volga said the following words:
"You have, oh, peasant, a fine horse—
If your horse were a steed,
I'd pay a price of 500 rubles for it,"
And the peasant said the following:
"But you're so stupid, Volga, you're talking nonsense.
I took this filly from its mother.
I paid 500 rubles for the foal
And if it were a steed—it would be priceless."
And Volga said the following words:
"And what's your name, peasant,
And how am I to call you by your patronymic?
And the peasant said the following:
"And I will harvest some rye, arrange it in stacks,
Will take it home, there I will grind it.
And brew some beer, invite the peasants,
And the peasants will start to shout,
"Hey Mikula Bright, you Mikulushka,
Mikulushka Bright, Selyaninovich!"